International Technical Su

MW00973324

Designing an IBM Storage Area Network

May 2000

Take Note!

Before using this information and the product it supports, be sure to read the general information in Appendix A, "Special notices" on page 253.

First Edition (May 2000)

This edition applies to components, programs, architecture, and connections between multiple platforms and storage systems and a diverse range of software and hardware.

Comments may be addressed to:
IBM Corporation, International Technical Support Organization
Dept. 471F Building 80-E2
650 Harry Road
San Jose, California 95120-6099

When you send information to IBM, you grant IBM a non-exclusive right to use or distribute the information in any way it believes appropriate without incurring any obligation to you.

Contents

Figures

Tables

Preface

As we now appear to have safely navigated the sea that was the transition from one century to the next, the focus today is not on preventing or avoiding a potential disaster, but exploiting current technology. There is a storm on the storage horizon. Some may call it a SAN-storm that is approaching.

Storage Area Networks have lit up the storage world like nothing before it. SANs offer the ability to move data at astonishingly high speeds in a dedicated information management network. It is this dedicated network that provides the promise to alleviate the burden placed on the corporate network in this e-world.

Traditional networks, like LANs and WANs, which have long been the workhorses of information movement are becoming tired with the amount of load that is placed upon them, and usually slow down just when you want them to go faster. SANs offer the thoroughbred solution. More importantly, an IBM SAN solution offers the pedigree and bloodlines which have been proven in the most competitive of arenas.

Whichever way you look at the SAN-scape, IBM has a solution, product, architecture, or service, that will provide a comprehensive, enterprise-wide, SAN-itized environment.

This redbook is written for those professionals tasked with designing a SAN to provide solutions to business problems that exist today. We propose and detail a number of solutions that are available today, rather than speculating on what tomorrow may bring.

In this IBM Redbook we have two objectives. The first is to show why a SAN is a much-sought-after beast, and the benefits that this brings to the business world. We show the positioning of a SAN, the industry-wide standardization drives to support a SAN, introduce Fibre Channel basics, describe the technical topology of a SAN, detail Fibre Channel products, and IBM SAN initiatives. All of these combine to lay the foundations of what we will cover with our second objective. This is to weed out the hype that is associated with SANs. We show practical decisions to be considered when planning a SAN, how a SAN can be created in a clustering environment, how a SAN can be created to consolidate storage, how to extend distances using a SAN, and how to provide a safe environment that will failover if necessary.

To support our objectives, we have divided this book into two parts: the first part shows why you would want to implement a SAN, as well as the products, concepts, and technology which support a SAN; in the second part, we show the design approach and considerations of a SAN, and how this can be further expanded and exploited.

The team that wrote this redbook

This redbook was produced by a team of specialists from around the world working at the International Technical Support Organization San Jose Center.

Jon Tate is a project leader for Storage Solutions at the International Technical Support Organization, San Jose Center. Before joining the ITSO in 1999, he worked in the IBM Technical Support Center, providing level 2 support for IBM storage products. Jon has 14 years of experience in storage software and management, services and support. Jon can be reached at tatej@us.ibm.com

Geoff Cole is a Senior Consultant and Sales Support Manager in IBM's Europe, Middle East and Africa (EMEA) SAN and Storage Solutions Center team. Geoff is a British national based in London. He joined IBM more than 29 years ago in the days of System/360, and is now enjoying the frenetic world of SAN. He has 15 years experience in IBM's storage business. He held a number of sales and marketing roles in the United Kingdom, United States and Germany. Until recently he was based in the EMEA SSD Customer Executive Briefing Center in Mainz, Germany. Geoff holds a Master of Arts degree in Politics, Philosophy and Economics from Oxford University. He is a regular speaker on SAN and storage related topics at IBM customer groups and external conferences in Europe. Geoff can be reached at cole@de.ibm.com

Ivo Gomilsek is an IT Specialist for PC Hardware in IBM Slovenia. He is an IBM Certified Professional Server Specialist, Red Hat Certified Engineer, OS/2 Warp Certified Engineer and Certified Vinca Co-StandbyServer for Windows NT Engineer. Ivo was a member of the team that wrote the redbook *Implementing Vinca Solutions on IBM Netfinity Servers* and *Netfinity and Linux Integration Guide*. His areas of expertise include IBM Netfinity servers, network operating systems (OS/2, Linux, Windows NT), Lotus Domino Servers and Storage Area Networks (SAN). He works in Product Support Services (PSS) as level-2 support for IBM Netfinity servers, and high availability solutions for IBM Netfinity servers and Linux. He is also heavily involved in SAN projects in his region. Ivo has been employed at IBM for 4 years. Ivo can be reached at ivo.gomilsek@si.ibm.com

Jaap van der Pijll is a Senior IT specialist in IBM Global Services, ISP Financial Services in the Netherlands. He has worked in a variety of areas which include OS/2, Windows 9x/NT/2000 system integration, software distribution, storage management, networking and communications. Recently Jaap worked as a team leader advisor for hardware and software missions. Jaap joined IBM more than 25 years ago in the serene days of System/360, and is now enjoying the world of SAN. Jaap can be reached at

`vdpijll@nl.ibm.com`

Figure 1. Authors, left to right — Ivo, Jaap, Jon and Geoff

Thanks to the following people for their invaluable contributions to this project:

Lisa Haut-Mikkelsen
IBM SSD

Mark Blunden
International Technical Support Organization, San Jose Center

Barry Mellish
International Technical Support Organization, San Jose Center

Kjell Nystrom
International Technical Support Organization, San Jose Center

Sandy Albu
IBM Netfinity Systems

Ruth Azevedo
IBM SSD

Mark Bruni
IBM SSD

Steve Cartwright (and his team)
McData Corporation

Bettyann Cernese
Tivoli Systems

Jerry Coale
IBM SSD

Jonathan Crutchfield
Tivoli Systems

Scott Drummond
IBM SSD

Jack Flynn
IBM SSD

Michael F. Hogan
IBM Global Services

Scott Jensen
Brocade Communications Systems, Inc.

Patrick Johnston
Brocade Communications Systems, Inc.

Richard Lyford
McData Corporation

Sean Meagher
McData Corporation

Anthony Pinto
IBM Global Services

Jay Rafati
Brocade Communications Systems, Inc.

Mark Sausville
Brocade Communications Systems, Inc.

Omy Shani
Brocade Communications Systems, Inc.

Ronald Soriano
IBM Global Services

Peter Thurston
IBM SSD

Leigh Wolfinger
McData Corporation

Comments welcome

Your comments are important to us!

We want our Redbooks to be as helpful as possible. Please send us your comments about this or other Redbooks in one of the following ways:

- Fax the evaluation form found in "IBM Redbooks review" on **page 283 to** the fax number shown on the form.
- Use the online evaluation form found at `http://www.redbooks.ibm.com/`
- Send your comments in an Internet note to `redbook@us.ibm.com`

Part 1. SAN basic training

Many businesses turned a blind eye to the e-business revolution. It was not something that could ever affect them and as they had always done business this way, why should they change? Just another fad. It would be easy to look at a SAN as just another fad. But, before you do that, just take a look over your shoulder and look at the products, the initiatives, the requirements that are thrust on a business, the stock price of SAN providers and see if this looks likely to go away. It won't. Data is a commodity — always has been, always will be. If you choose to treat this commodity with disdain, don't be surprised at the end result. There are plenty of companies that will treat this commodity with respect and care for it attentively. Like those that adopted e-business when it was in its infancy.

In Part 1, we introduce the concepts, products, initiatives, and technology that underpins a SAN. We give an overview of the terminology and products that are associated with the SAN world.

By the way, does anyone know what happened to those companies that did not adopt e-business?

Chapter 1. Introduction to Storage Area Networks

Everyone working in the Information Technology industry is familiar with the continuous developments in technology, which constantly deliver improvements in performance, capacity, size, functionality and so on. A few of these developments have far reaching implications because they enable applications or functions which allow us fundamentally to rethink the way we do things and go about our everyday business. The advent of Storage Area Networks (SANs) is one such development. SANs can lead to a proverbial "paradigm shift" in the way we organize and use the IT infrastructure of an enterprise.

In the chapter that follows, we show the market forces that have driven the need for a new storage infrastructure, coupled with the benefits that a SAN brings to the enterprise.

1.1 The need for a new storage infrastructure

The 1990's witnessed a major shift away from the traditional mainframe, host-centric model of computing to the client/server model. Today, many organizations have hundreds, even thousands, of distributed servers and client systems installed throughout the enterprise. Many of these systems are powerful computers, with more processing capability than many mainframe computers had only a few years ago.

Storage, for the most part, is directly connected by a dedicated channel to the server it supports. Frequently the servers are interconnected using local area networks (LAN) and wide area networks (WAN), to communicate and exchange data. This is illustrated in Figure 2. The amount of disk storage capacity attached to such systems has grown exponentially in recent years. It is commonplace for a desktop Personal Computer today to have 5 or 10 Gigabytes, and single disk drives with up to 75 GB are available. There has been a move to disk arrays, comprising a number of disk drives. The arrays may be "just a bunch of disks" (JBOD), or various implementations of redundant arrays of independent disks (RAID). The capacity of such arrays may be measured in tens or hundreds of GBs, but I/O bandwidth has not kept pace with the rapid growth in processor speeds and disk capacities.

Distributed clients and servers are frequently chosen to meet specific application needs. They may, therefore, run different operating systems (such as Windows NT, UNIX of differing flavors, Novell Netware, VMS and so on), and different database software (for example, DB2, Oracle, Informix, SQL

Server). Consequently, they have different file systems and different data formats.

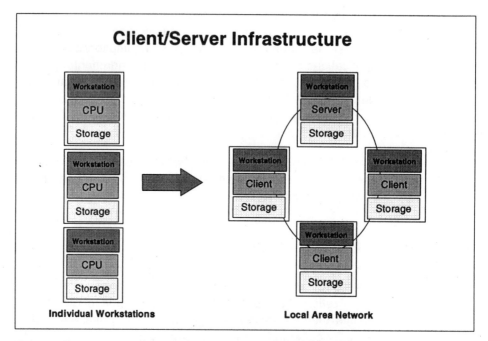

Figure 2. Typical distributed systems or client server infrastructure

Managing this multi-platform, multi-vendor, networked environment has become increasingly complex and costly. Multiple vendor's software tools, and appropriately-skilled human resources must be maintained to handle data and storage resource management on the many differing systems in the enterprise. Surveys published by industry analysts consistently show that management costs associated with distributed storage are much greater, up to 10 times more, than the cost of managing consolidated or centralized storage. This includes costs of backup, recovery, space management, performance management and disaster recovery planning.

Disk storage is often purchased from the processor vendor as an integral feature, and it is difficult to establish if the price you pay per gigabyte (GB) is competitive, compared to the market price of disk storage. Disks and tape drives, directly attached to one client or server, cannot be used by other systems, leading to inefficient use of hardware resources. Organizations often find that they have to purchase more storage capacity, even though free capacity is available, but is attached to other platforms. This is illustrated in Figure 3.

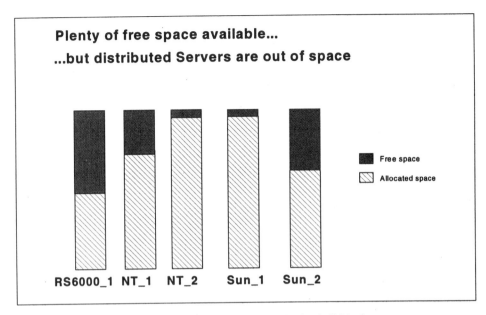

Figure 3. Inefficient use of available disk capacity attached to individual servers

Additionally, it is difficult to scale capacity and performance to meet rapidly changing requirements, such as the explosive growth in e-business applications.

Data stored on one system cannot readily be made available to other users, except by creating duplicate copies, and moving the copy to storage that is attached to another server. Movement of large files of data may result in significant degradation of performance of the LAN/WAN, causing conflicts with mission critical applications. Multiple copies of the same data may lead to inconsistencies between one copy and another. Data spread on multiple small systems is difficult to coordinate and share for enterprise-wide applications, such as e-business, Enterprise Resource Planning (ERP), Data Warehouse, and Business Intelligence (BI).

Backup and recovery operations across a LAN may also cause serious disruption to normal application traffic. Even using fast Gigabit Ethernet transport, sustained throughput from a single server to tape is about 25 GB per hour. It would take approximately 12 hours to fully backup a relatively moderate departmental database of 300 GBs. This may exceed the available window of time in which this must be completed, and it may not be a practical solution if business operations span multiple time zones. It is increasingly evident to IT managers that these characteristics of client/server computing are too costly, and too inefficient. The islands of information resulting from the distributed model of computing do not match the needs of the e-business enterprise.

We show this in Figure 4.

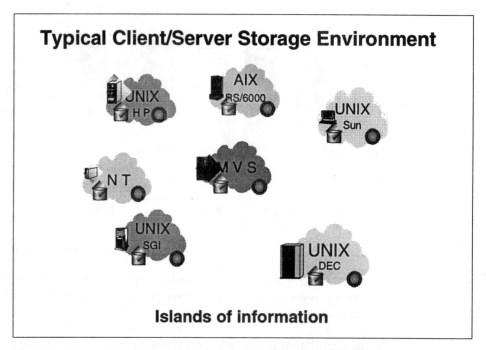

Figure 4. Distributed computing model tends to create islands of information

New ways must be found to control costs, to improve efficiency, and to properly align the storage infrastructure to meet the requirements of the business. One of the first steps to improved control of computing resources throughout the enterprise is improved connectivity.

In the topics that follow, we look at the advantages and disadvantages of the standard storage infrastructure of today.

1.2 The Small Computer Systems Interface legacy

The Small Computer Systems Interface (SCSI) is the conventional, server centric method of connecting peripheral devices (disks, tapes and printers) in the open client/server environment. As its name indicates, it was designed for the PC and small computer environment. It is a bus architecture, with dedicated, parallel cabling between the host and storage devices, such as disk arrays. This is similar in implementation to the Original Equipment

Manufacturer's Information (OEMI) bus and tag interface commonly used by mainframe computers until the early 1990's. SCSI shares a practical aspect with bus and tag, in that cables and connectors are bulky, relatively expensive, and are prone to failure.

The amount of data available to the server is determined by the number of devices which can attach to the bus, and by the number of buses attached to the server. Up to 15 devices can be attached to a server on a single SCSI bus. In practice, because of performance limitations due to arbitration, it is common for no more than four or five devices to be attached in this way, thus limiting capacity scalability.

Access to data is lost in the event of a failure of any of the SCSI connections to the disks. This also applies in the event of reconfiguration or servicing of a disk device attached to the SCSI bus, because all the devices in the string must be taken offline. In today's environment, when many applications need to be available continuously, this downtime is unacceptable.

The data rate of the SCSI bus is determined by the number of bits transferred, and the bus cycle time (measured in megaherz (MHz)). Decreasing the cycle time increases the transfer rate, but, due to limitations inherent in the bus architecture, it may also reduce the distance over which the data can be successfully transferred. The physical transport was originally a parallel cable comprising eight data lines, to transmit eight bits in parallel, plus control lines. Later implementations widened the parallel data transfers to 16 bit paths (SCSI Wide), to achieve higher bandwidths.

Propagation delays in sending data in parallel along multiple lines lead to a well known phenomenon known as skew, meaning that all bits may not arrive at the target device at the same time. This is shown in Figure 5.

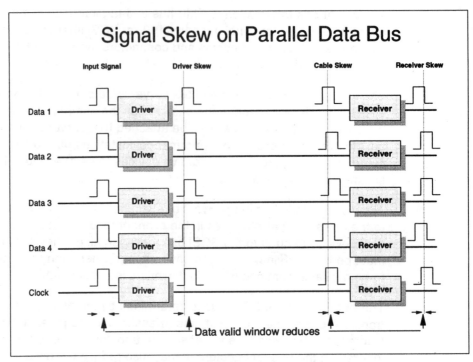

Figure 5. SCSI Propagation delay results in skew

Arrival occurs during a small window of time, depending on the transmission speed, and the physical length of the SCSI bus. The need to minimize the skew limits the distance that devices can be positioned away from the initiating server to between 2 to 25 meters, depending on the cycle time. Faster speed means shorter distance. The distances refer to the maximum length of the SCSI bus, including all attached devices. The SCSI distance limitations are shown in Figure 6. These distance limitations may severely restrict the total GB capacity of the disk storage which can be attached to an individual server.

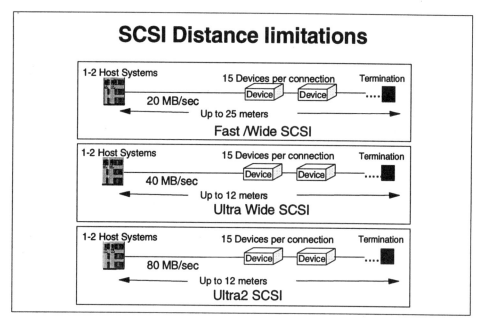

Figure 6. SCSI bus distance limitations

Many applications require the system to access several devices, or for several systems to share a single device. SCSI can enable this by attaching multiple servers or devices to the same bus. This is known as a multi-drop configuration. A multi-drop configuration is shown in Figure 7.

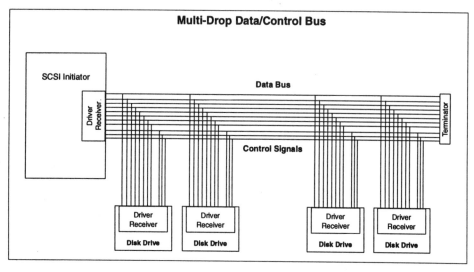

Figure 7. Multi-drop bus structure

To avoid signal interference, and therefore possible data corruption, all unused ports on a parallel SCSI bus must be properly terminated. Incorrect termination can result in transaction errors or failures.

Normally, only a single server can access data on a specific disk by means of a SCSI bus. In a shared bus environment, it is clear that all devices cannot transfer data at the same time. SCSI uses an arbitration protocol to determine which device can gain access to the bus. Arbitration occurs before and after every data transfer on the bus. While arbitration takes place, no data movement can occur. This represents an additional overhead which reduces bandwidth utilization, substantially reducing the effective data rate achievable on the bus. Actual rates are typically less than 50% of the rated speed of the SCSI bus.

In addition to being a physical transport, SCSI is also a protocol, which specifies commands and controls for sending blocks of data between the host and the attached devices. SCSI commands are issued by the host operating system, in response to user requests for data. Some operating systems, for example, Windows NT, treat all attached peripherals as SCSI devices, and issue SCSI commands to deal with all read and write operations.

It is clear that the physical parallel SCSI bus architecture has a number of significant speed, distance, and availability limitations, which make it increasingly less suitable for many applications in today's networked IT infrastructure. However, since the SCSI protocol is deeply embedded in the way that commonly encountered operating systems handle user requests for data, it would be a major inhibitor to progress if we were obliged to move to new protocols.

1.3 Storage network solutions

Today's enterprise IT planners need to link many users of multi-vendor, heterogeneous systems to multi-vendor shared storage resources, and they need to allow those users to access common data, wherever it is located in the enterprise. These requirements imply a network solution, and two types of network storage solutions are now available:

- Network attached storage (NAS)
- Storage Area Network (SAN)

1.3.1 What network attached storage is

NAS solutions utilize the LAN in front of the server, and transmit data over the LAN using messaging protocols, such as TCP/IP and Net BIOS. We illustrate this in Figure 8.

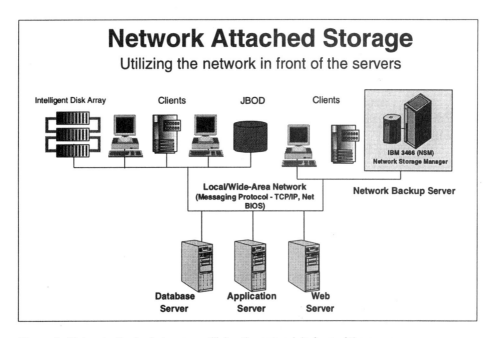

Figure 8. Network attached storage - utilizing the network in front of the servers

By making storage devices LAN addressable, the storage is freed from its direct attachment to a specific server. In principle, any user running any operating system can address the storage device by means of a common access protocol, for example, Network File System (NFS). In addition, a task, such as back-up to tape, can be performed across the LAN, enabling sharing of expensive hardware resources between multiple servers. Most storage devices cannot just attach to a LAN. NAS solutions are specialized file servers which are designed for this type of attachment.

NAS, therefore, offers a number of benefits, which address some of the limitations of parallel SCSI. However, by moving storage transactions, such as disk accesses, and tasks, such as backup and recovery of files, to the LAN, conflicts can occur with end user traffic on the network. LANs are tuned to favor short burst transmissions for rapid response to messaging requests, rather than large continuous data transmissions. Significant overhead can be imposed to move large blocks of data over the LAN, due to the small packet size used by messaging protocols. For instance, the maximum packet size for Ethernet is about 1500 bytes. A 10 MB file has to be segmented into more than 7000 individual packets, (each sent separately by the LAN access method), if it is to be read from a NAS device. Therefore, a NAS solution is best suited to handle cross platform direct access applications, not to deal with applications requiring high bandwidth.

NAS solutions are relatively low cost, and straightforward to implement as they fit in to the existing LAN environment, which is a mature technology. However, the LAN must have plenty of spare capacity to justify NAS implementations. A number of vendors, including IBM, offer a variety of NAS solutions. These fall into two categories:

- File servers
- Backup/archive servers

However, it is not the purpose of this redbook to discuss these. NAS can be used separately or together with a SAN, as the technologies are complementary. In general terms, NAS offers lower cost solutions, but with more limited benefits, lower performance and less scalability, than Fibre Channel SANs.

1.3.2 What a Storage Area Network is

A SAN is a specialized, high speed network attaching servers and storage devices. It is sometimes called "the network behind the servers". A SAN allows "any to any" connection across the network, using interconnect elements such as routers, gateways, hubs and switches. It eliminates the traditional dedicated connection between a server and storage, and the concept that the server effectively "owns and manages" the storage devices. It also eliminates any restriction to the amount of data that a server can access, currently limited by the number of storage devices, which can be attached to the individual server. Instead, a SAN introduces the flexibility of networking to enable one server or many heterogeneous servers to share a common storage "utility", which may comprise many storage devices, including disk, tape, and optical storage. And, the storage utility may be located far from the servers which use it. We show what the network behind the servers may look like, in Figure 9.

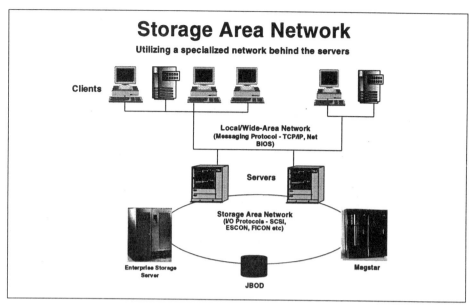

Figure 9. Storage Area Network - the network behind the servers

A SAN differs from traditional networks, because it is constructed from storage interfaces. SAN solutions utilize a dedicated network behind the servers, based primarily (though, not necessarily) on Fibre Channel architecture. Fibre Channel provides a highly scalable bandwidth over long distances, and with the ability to provide full redundancy, including switched, parallel data paths to deliver high availability and high performance.

Therefore, a SAN can bypass traditional network bottlenecks. It supports direct, high speed transfers between servers and storage devices in the following ways:

- **Server to storage.** This is the traditional method of interaction with storage devices. The SAN advantage is that the same storage device may be accessed serially or concurrently by multiple servers.

- **Server to server.** This is high speed, high volume communications between servers.

- **Storage to storage.** For example, a disk array could backup its data direct to tape across the SAN, without processor intervention. Or, a device could be mirrored remotely across the SAN.

A SAN changes the server centric model of the typical open systems IT infrastructure, replacing it with a data centric infrastructure.

1.3.3 What about ESCON and FICON?

Sceptics might already be saying that the concept of SAN is not new. Indeed, for System 390 (S/390) users, the implementation of shared storage on a dedicated network has been common since the introduction of Enterprise System Connection (ESCON) in 1991.

However, for UNIX, Windows NT and other open systems users, the need for such capability is now extremely high. As we have shown, the traditional SCSI parallel bus architecture, most commonly used in these environments, is no longer capable of handling their growing data intensive application requirements. These users are faced with many of the same problems which challenged mainframe users in the late 1980s and early 1990s, and which largely were solved by ESCON.

But the ESCON architecture does not answer the open systems needs of today, due to a number of critical limitations. ESCON is primarily a S/390 solution, which does not support open systems protocols for data movement, and ESCON is limited in performance (nominally 17 MB/second), relative to technologies available today. An enhancement to ESCON is provided by Fibre Connection (FICON). Figure 10 shows how FICON enhances ESCON.

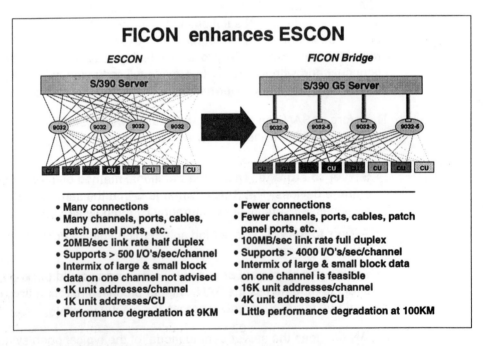

Figure 10. FICON enhances ESCON

The S/390 FICON architecture retains ESCON topology and switch management characteristics. FICON channels can deliver data rates up to 100 MB/second full-duplex, and they extend channel distances up to 100 kilometers. More storage controllers and devices can be supported per FICON link, relieving channel constraints in configuring S/390 processors.

The FICON architecture is fully compatible with existing S/390 channel command words (CCWs) and programs. But, most importantly, FICON uses Fibre Channel for transportation of data, and, therefore, in principle, is capable of participating with other platforms (UNIX, Windows NT, Novell Netware, etc.) in a Fibre Channel enterprise SAN. However, this capability is not yet supported, due to a number of network management requirements imposed by the S/390 architecture.

IBM expects a transition period, during which S/390 FICON SANs will develop separately from Fibre Channel Protocol (FCP) open systems SANs, which use the SCSI protocol. In the longer term, FCP and FICON SANs will merge into a true Enterprise SAN. IBM has published a number of IBM Redbooks on the subject of FICON and an example of this is *Introduction to IBM S/390 FICON*, SG24-5176. Additional redbooks that describe FICON can be found at the IBM Redbooks site by using the search argument *FICON*.

www.redbooks.ibm.com

For this reason, this book will focus exclusively on FCP open systems elements of IBM's Enterprise SAN which are available today.

1.4 What Fibre Channel is

Fibre Channel is an open, technical standard for networking which incorporates the "channel transport" characteristics of an I/O bus, with the flexible connectivity and distance characteristics of a traditional network. Notice the European spelling of Fibre, which is intended to distinguish it from fiber-optics and fiber-optic cabling, which are physical hardware and media used to transmit data at high speed over long distances using light emitting diode (LED) and laser technology.

Because of its channel-like qualities, hosts and applications see storage devices attached to the SAN as if they are locally attached storage. Because of its network characteristics it can support multiple protocols and a broad range of devices, and it can be managed as a network. Fibre Channel can use either optical fiber (for distance) or copper cable links (for short distance at low cost).

Fibre Channel is a multi-layered network, based on a series of American National Standards Institute (ANSI) standards which define characteristics and functions for moving data across the network. These include definitions of physical interfaces, such as cabling, distances and signaling; data encoding and link controls; data delivery in terms of frames, flow control and classes of service; common services; and protocol interfaces.

Like other networks, information is sent in structured packets or frames, and data is serialized before transmission. But, unlike other networks, the Fibre Channel architecture includes a significant amount of hardware processing to deliver high performance. The speed currently achieved is 100 MB per second, (with the potential for 200 MB and 400 MB and higher data rates in the future). In all Fibre Channel topologies a single transmitter sends information to a single receiver. In most multi-user implementations this requires that routing information (source and target) must be provided. Transmission is defined in the Fibre Channel standards across three transport topologies:

- **Point to point** — a bi-directional, dedicated interconnection between two nodes, with full-duplex bandwidth (100 MB/second in each direction concurrently).

- **Arbitrated loop** — a uni-directional ring topology, similar to a token ring, supporting up to 126 interconnected nodes. Each node passes data to the next node in the loop, until the data reaches the target node. All nodes share the 100 MB/second Fibre Channel bandwidth. Devices must arbitrate for access to the loop. Therefore, with 100 active devices on a loop, the effective data rate for each is 1 MB/second, which is further reduced by the overhead of arbitration. A loop may also be connected to a Fibre Channel switch port, therefore, enabling attachment of the loop to a wider switched fabric environment. In this case, the loop may support up to 126 devices.

  Many fewer devices are normally attached in practice, because of arbitration overheads and shared bandwidth constraints. Due to fault isolation issues inherent with arbitrated loops, most FC-AL SANs have been implemented with a maximum of two servers, plus a number of peripheral storage devices. So FC-AL is suitable for small SAN configurations, or SANlets.

- **Switched fabric** — The term Fabric describes an intelligent switching infrastructure which delivers data from any source to any destination.The interconnection of up to 2^{24} nodes is allowed, with each node able to utilize the full 100 MB/second duplex Fibre Channel bandwidth. Each logical connection receives dedicated bandwidth, so the overall bandwidth is multiplied by the number of connections (delivering a maximum of 200

MB/second x *n* nodes). The fabric itself is responsible for controlling the routing of information. It may be simply a single switch, or it may comprise multiple interconnected switches which function as a single logical entity. Complex fabrics must be managed by software which can exploit SAN management functions which are built into the fabric. Switched fabric is the basis for enterprise wide SANs.

A mix of these three topologies can be implemented to meet specific needs. Fibre Channel arbitrated loop (FC-AL) and switched fabric (FC-SW) are the two most commonly used topologies, satisfying differing requirements for scalability, distance, cost and performance. A fourth topology has been developed, known as slotted loop (FC-SL); But, this appears to have limited application, specifically in aerospace, so it is not discussed in this book.

Fibre Channel uses a serial data transport scheme, similar to other computer networks, streaming packets, (frames) of bits one behind the other in a single data line. To achieve the high data rate of 100 MB/second the transmission clock frequency is currently 1 Gigabit, or 1 bit per 0.94 nanoseconds.

Serial transfer, of course, does not suffer from the problem of skew, so speed and distance is not restricted as with parallel data transfers as we show in Figure 11.

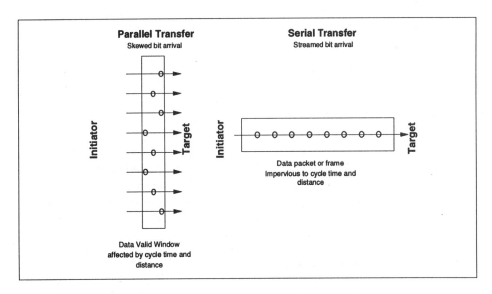

Figure 11. Parallel data transfers versus serial data transfers

Serial transfer enables simpler cabling and connectors, and also routing of information through switched networks. Today, Fibre Channel can operate over distances of up to 10 km, link distances up to 90 km by implementing cascading, and longer with the introduction of repeaters. Just as LANs can be interlinked in WANs by using high speed gateways, so can campus SANs be interlinked to build enterprise wide SANs.

Whatever the topology, information is sent between two nodes, which are the source (transmitter or initiator) and destination (receiver or target). A node is a device, such as a server (personal computer, workstation, or mainframe), or peripheral device, such as disk or tape drive, or video camera. Frames of information are passed between nodes, and the structure of the frame is defined by a protocol. Logically, a source and target node must utilize the same protocol, but each node may support several different protocols or data types.

Therefore, Fibre Channel architecture is extremely flexible in its potential application. Fibre Channel transport layers are protocol independent, enabling the transmission of multiple protocols. It is possible, therefore, to transport storage I/O protocols and commands, such as SCSI-3 Fibre Channel Protocol, (or FCP, the most common implementation today), ESCON, FICON, SSA, and HIPPI. Network packets may also be sent using messaging protocols, for instance, TCP/IP or Net BIOS, over the same physical interface using the same adapters, cables, switches and other infrastructure hardware. Theoretically then, multiple protocols can move concurrently over the same fabric. This capability is not in common use today, and, in any case, currently excludes concurrent FICON transport (refer to 1.3.3, "What about ESCON and FICON?" on page 14). Most Fibre Channel SAN installations today only use a single protocol.

Using a credit based flow control methodology, Fibre Channel is able to deliver data as fast as the destination device buffer is able to receive it. And low transmission overheads enable high sustained utilization rates without loss of data.

Therefore, Fibre Channel combines the best characteristics of traditional I/O channels with those of computer networks:

- High performance for large data transfers by using simple transport protocols and extensive hardware assists

- Serial data transmission

- A physical interface with a low error rate definition

- Reliable transmission of data with the ability to guarantee or confirm error free delivery of the data

- Packaging data in packets (frames in Fibre Channel terminology)

- Flexibility in terms of the types of information which can be transported in frames (such as data, video and audio)

- Use of existing device oriented command sets, such as SCSI and FCP

- A vast expansion in the number of devices which can be addressed when compared to I/O interfaces — a theoretical maximum of more than 16 million ports

It is this high degree of flexibility, availability and scalability; the combination of multiple protocols at high speeds over long distances; and the broad acceptance of the Fibre Channel standards by vendors throughout the IT industry, which makes the Fibre Channel architecture ideal for the development of enterprise SANs.

For more details of the Fibre Channel architecture, refer to Chapter 3, "Fibre Channel basics" on page 45.

1.5 What the business benefits of a Fibre Channel SAN are

Today's business environment creates many challenges for the enterprise IT planner. SANs can provide solutions to many of their operational problems.

1.5.1 Storage consolidation and sharing of resources

By enabling storage capacity to be connected to servers at a greater distance, and by disconnecting storage resource management from individual hosts, a SAN enables disk storage capacity to be consolidated. The results can be lower overall costs through better utilization of the storage, lower management costs, increased flexibility, and increased control.

This can be achieved physically or logically.

1.5.1.1 Physical consolidation
Data from disparate storage subsystems can be combined on to large, enterprise class shared disk arrays, which may be located at some distance from the servers. The capacity of these disk arrays can be shared by multiple servers, and users may also benefit from the advanced functions typically offered with such subsystems. This may include RAID capabilities, remote mirroring, and instantaneous data replication functions, which might not be available with smaller, integrated disks.The array capacity may be

partitioned, so that each server has an appropriate portion of the available GBs. This is shown in Figure 12.

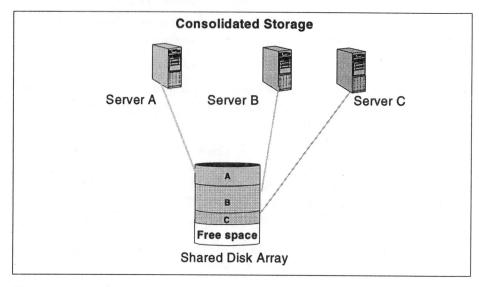

Figure 12. Consolidated storage - efficiently shared capacity

Available capacity can be dynamically allocated to any server requiring additional space. Capacity not required by a server application can be re-allocated to other servers. This avoids the inefficiency associated with free disk capacity attached to one server not being usable by other servers. Extra capacity may be added, in a non-disruptive manner.

1.5.1.2 Logical consolidation

It is possible to achieve shared resource benefits from the SAN, but without moving existing equipment. A SAN relationship can be established between a client and a group of storage devices that are not physically co-located (excluding devices which are internally attached to servers). A logical view of the combined disk resources may allow available capacity to be allocated and re-allocated between different applications running on distributed servers, to achieve better utilization. Consolidation is covered in greater depth in *IBM Storage Solutions for Server Consolidation*, SG24-5355.

Figure 13 shows a logical consolidation of independent arrays.

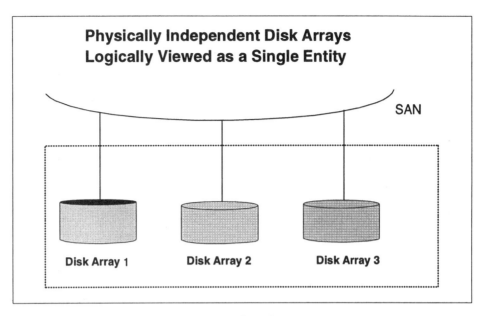

**Physically Independent Disk Arrays
Logically Viewed as a Single Entity**

SAN

Disk Array 1   Disk Array 2   Disk Array 3

Figure 13. Logical consolidation of dispersed disk subsystems

1.5.2 Data sharing

The term "data sharing" is used somewhat loosely by users and some vendors. It is sometimes interpreted to mean the replication of files or databases to enable two or more users, or applications, to concurrently use separate copies of the data. The applications concerned may operate on different host platforms. A SAN may ease the creation of such duplicated copies of data using facilities such as remote mirroring.

Data sharing may also be used to describe multiple users accessing a single copy of a file. This could be called "true data sharing". In a homogeneous server environment, with appropriate application software controls, multiple servers may access a single copy of data stored on a consolidated storage subsystem.

If attached servers are heterogeneous platforms (for example a mix of UNIX and Windows NT), sharing of data between such unlike operating system environments is complex. This is due to differences in file systems, data formats, and encoding structures. IBM, however, uniquely offers a true data sharing capability, with concurrent update, for selected heterogeneous server environments, using the Tivoli SANergy File Sharing solution. Details can be found in Chapter 8, "Tivoli SANergy File Sharing" on page 169, and at:
www.sanergy.com

The SAN advantage in enabling enhanced data sharing may reduce the need to hold multiple copies of the same file or database. This reduces duplication of hardware costs to store such copies. It also enhances the ability to implement cross enterprise applications, such as e-business, which may be inhibited when multiple data copies are stored.

1.5.3 Non-disruptive scalability for growth

There is an explosion in the quantity of data stored by the majority of organizations. This is fueled by the implementation of applications, such as e-business, e-mail, Business Intelligence, Data Warehouse, and Enterprise Resource Planning. Industry analysts, such as IDC and Gartner Group, estimate that electronically stored data is doubling every year. In the case of e-business applications, opening the business to the Internet, there have been reports of data growing by more than 10 times annually. This is a nightmare for planners, as it is increasingly difficult to predict storage requirements.

A finite amount of disk storage can be connected physically to an individual server due to adapter, cabling and distance limitations. With a SAN, new capacity can be added as required, without disrupting ongoing operations. SANs enable disk storage to be scaled independently of servers.

1.5.4 Improved backup and recovery

With data doubling every year, what effect does this have on the backup window? Backup to tape, and recovery, are operations which are problematic in the parallel SCSI or LAN based environments. For disk subsystems attached to specific servers, two options exist for tape backup. Either it must be done to a server attached tape subsystem, or by moving data across the LAN.

1.5.4.1 Tape pooling

Providing tape drives to each server is costly, and also involves the added administrative overhead of scheduling the tasks, and managing the tape media. SANs allow for greater connectivity of tape drives and tape libraries, especially at greater distances. Tape pooling is the ability for more than one server to logically share tape drives within an automated library. This can be achieved by software management, using tools, such as Tivoli Storage Manager; or with tape libraries with outboard management, such as IBM's 3494.

1.5.4.2 LAN-free and server-free data movement

Backup using the LAN moves the administration to centralized tape drives or automated tape libraries. However, at the same time, the LAN experiences very high traffic volume during the backup or recovery operations, and this can be extremely disruptive to normal application access to the network. Although backups can be scheduled during non-peak periods, this may not allow sufficient time. Also, it may not be practical in an enterprise which operates in multiple time zones.

We illustrate loading the IP network in Figure 14.

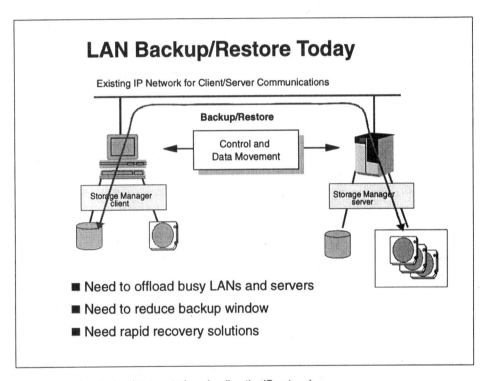

Figure 14. LAN backup/restore today - loading the IP network

SAN provides the solution, by enabling the elimination of backup and recovery data movement across the LAN. Fibre Channel's high bandwidth and multi-path switched fabric capabilities enables multiple servers to stream backup data concurrently to high speed tape drives. This frees the LAN for other application traffic. IBM's Tivoli software solution for LAN-free backup offers the capability for clients to move data directly to tape using the SAN. A future enhancement to be provided by IBM Tivoli will allow data to be read directly from disk to tape (and tape to disk), bypassing the server. This solution is known as server-free backup. LAN-free and server-free backup solutions are illustrated in 7.2.2.2, "Tivoli SAN exploitation" on page 157.

1.5.5 High performance

Applications benefit from the more efficient transport mechanism of Fibre Channel. Currently, Fibre Channel transfers data at 100 MB/second, several times faster than typical SCSI capabilities, and many times faster than standard LAN data transfers. Future implementations of Fibre Channel at 200 and 400 MB/second have been defined, offering the promise of even greater performance benefits in the future. Indeed, prototypes of storage components which meet the 2 Gigabit transport specification are already in existence, and may be in production in 2001.

The elimination of conflicts on LANs, by removing storage data transfers from the LAN to the SAN, may also significantly improve application performance on servers.

1.5.6 High availability server clustering

Reliable and continuous access to information is an essential prerequisite in any business. As applications have shifted from robust mainframes to the less reliable client/file server environment, so have server and software vendors developed high availability solutions to address the exposure. These are based on clusters of servers. A cluster is a group of independent computers managed as a single system for higher availability, easier manageability, and greater scalability. Server system components are interconnected using specialized cluster interconnects, or open clustering technologies, such as Fibre Channel - Virtual Interface mapping.

Complex software is required to manage the failover of any component of the hardware, the network, or the application. SCSI cabling tends to limit clusters to no more than two servers. A Fibre Channel SAN allows clusters to scale to 4, 8, 16, and even to 100 or more servers, as required, to provide very large shared data configurations, including redundant pathing, RAID protection, and so on. Storage can be shared, and can be easily switched from one server to another. Just as storage capacity can be scaled non-disruptively in a SAN, so can the number of servers in a cluster be increased or decreased dynamically, without impacting the storage environment.

1.5.7 Improved disaster tolerance

Advanced disk arrays, such as IBM's Enterprise Storage Server (ESS), provide sophisticated functions, like Peer-to-Peer Remote Copy services, to address the need for secure and rapid recovery of data in the event of a disaster. Failures may be due to natural occurrences, such as fire, flood, or earthquake; or to human error. A SAN implementation allows multiple open servers to benefit from this type of disaster protection, and the servers may even be located some distance (up to 10 km) from the disk array which holds the primary copy of the data. The secondary site, holding the mirror image of the data, may be located up to a further 100 km from the primary site.

IBM has also announced Peer-to-Peer Copy capability for its Virtual Tape Server (VTS). This will allow VTS users to maintain local and remote copies of virtual tape volumes, improving data availability by eliminating all single points of failure.

1.5.8 Allow selection of "best of breed" storage

Internal storage, purchased as a feature of the associated server, is often relatively costly. A SAN implementation enables storage purchase decisions to be made independently of the server. Buyers are free to choose the best of breed solution to meet their performance, function, and cost needs. Large capacity external disk arrays may provide an extensive selection of advanced functions. For instance, the ESS includes cross platform functions, such as high performance RAID 5, Peer-to-Peer Remote Copy, Flash Copy, and functions specific to S/390, such as Parallel Access Volumes (PAV), Multiple Allegiance, and I/O Priority Queuing. This makes it an ideal SAN attached solution to consolidate enterprise data.

Client/server backup solutions often include attachment of low capacity tape drives, or small automated tape subsystems, to individual PCs and departmental servers. This introduces a significant administrative overhead as users, or departmental storage administrators, often have to control the backup and recovery processes manually. A SAN allows the alternative strategy of sharing fewer, highly reliable, powerful tape solutions, such as IBM's Magstar family of drives and automated libraries, between multiple users and departments.

1.5.9 Ease of data migration

Data can be moved non-disruptively from one storage subsystem to another using a SAN, without server intervention. This may greatly ease the migration of data associated with the introduction of new technology, and the retirement of old devices.

1.5.10 Reduced total costs of ownership

Expenditure on storage today is estimated to be in the region of 50% of a typical IT hardware budget. Some industry analysts expect this to grow to as much as 75% by the end of the year 2002. IT managers are becoming increasingly focused on controlling these growing costs.

1.5.10.1 Consistent, centralized management

As we have shown, consolidation of storage can reduce wasteful fragmentation of storage attached to multiple servers. It also enables a single, consistent data and storage resource management solution to be implemented, such as IBM's StorWatch tools, combined with software such as Tivoli Storage Manager and Tivoli SAN Manager, which can reduce costs of software and human resources for storage management.

1.5.10.2 Reduced hardware costs

By moving data to SAN attached storage subsystems, the servers themselves may no longer need to be configured with native storage. In addition, the introduction of LAN-free and server-free data transfers largely eliminate the use of server cycles to manage housekeeping tasks, such as backup and recovery, and archive and recall. The configuration of what might be termed "thin servers" therefore might be possible, and this could result in significant hardware cost savings to offset against costs of installing the SAN fabric.

1.5.11 Storage resources match e-business enterprise needs

By eliminating islands of information, typical of the client/server model of computing, and introducing an integrated storage infrastructure, SAN solutions match the strategic needs of today's e-business.

This is shown in Figure 15.

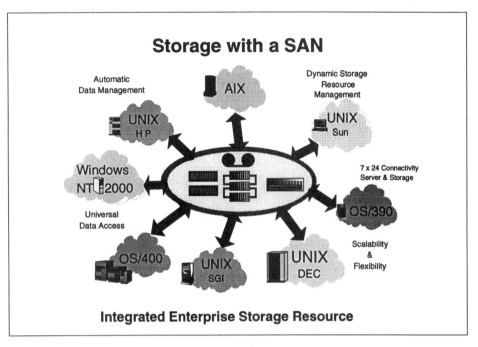

Figure 15. *SAN solutions match e-business strategic needs*

1.6 SAN market trends

In view of SAN's potential to deliver valuable business benefits, we should not be surprised at the substantial interest being shown by users, vendors and analysts alike. While early adopters have been installing limited SAN solutions since 1998, significant awareness among business users began to be generated during 1999. Many vendors announced SAN products and solutions in 1999, and this trend is accelerating in the year 2000. Analysts now estimate that industry revenue for network attached storage (both SAN and NAS), will grow rapidly during the next two years. Indeed, by the year 2003, IDC estimates that SAN attached disk arrays will reach 48% of the revenue for externally attached disk arrays. NAS is expected to reach 23%, while disk arrays attached in the traditional manner directly to servers will account for only 29%. This is a dramatic shift in the IT infrastructure in a very short time frame. We illustrate this in Figure 16.

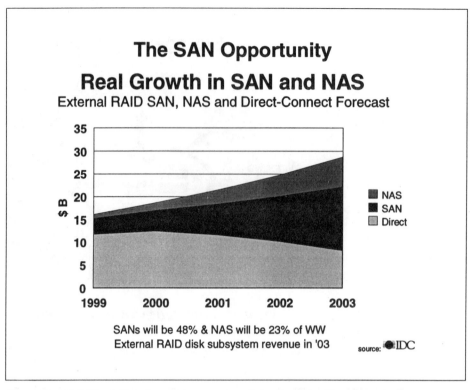

Figure 16. SAN Attach Disk Array $Revenue Growth by Operating Environment

It is also no surprise that the main drivers for SAN solutions are coming from the open systems environment. In 1999, for the first time, industry revenues for open systems disk arrays (UNIX, Windows NT, etc.) are estimated to have overtaken revenues for S/390 attached arrays. By the year 2003, IDC estimates that disk array revenues from the open environment will be approximately six times greater, while S/390 array revenues will remain relatively flat. This is illustrated in Figure 17.

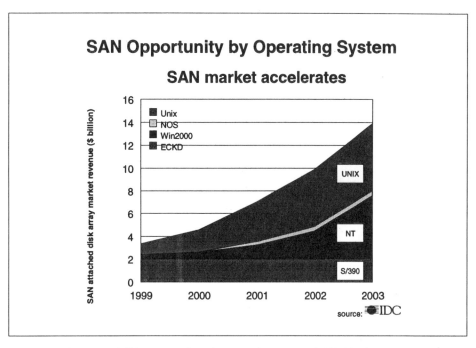

Figure 17. Forecast of $M revenue share by operating system (1999-2003)

IBM's own estimates are, that by the year 2003, some 70% of all medium and large enterprises will install Fibre Channel SAN solutions to address varying business needs.

Stock markets around the world, especially Wall Street, are excited by the opportunities offered by the emerging Fibre Channel technology, and this is reflected in soaring stock prices of specialist manufacturers and developers of fabric components.

As with any new technology, it is up to the user to assess its relevance and value; and to decide if and when to deploy appropriate solutions. But buyers should also beware. It is easy to assume that, because other mature network solutions operate in a particular way (for example, in relation to the interoperability of solution components) so does Fibre Channel. This is not necessarily the case, because Fibre Channel standards for storage networking are still emerging. The purpose of this book is to discuss some of the factors which IT architects and planners should take into consideration, as they begin to investigate, and to design, business oriented SAN solutions for their enterprise.

Chapter 2. The drive for SAN industry standardization

Given the strong drive towards SANs from users and vendors alike, one of the most critical success factors is the ability of systems and software from different vendors to operate together in a seamless way. Standards are the basis for the interoperability of devices and software from different vendors.

A good benchmark is the level of standardization in today's LAN and WAN networks. Standard interfaces for interoperability and management have been developed, and many vendors compete with products based on the implementation of these standards. Customers are free to mix and match components from multiple vendors to form a LAN or WAN solution. They are also free to choose from several different network management software vendors to manage their heterogeneous network.

The major vendors in the SAN industry recognize the need for standards, especially in the areas of interoperability interfaces and application programming interfaces (APIs), as these are the basis for wide acceptance of SANs. Standards will allow customers a greater breadth of choice, and will lead to the deployment of cross-platform, multi-vendor, enterprise-wide SAN solutions.

2.1 SAN industry associations and organizations

A number of industry associations, standards bodies and company groupings are involved in developing, and publishing SAN standards. The major groups linked with SAN standards are shown in Figure 18.

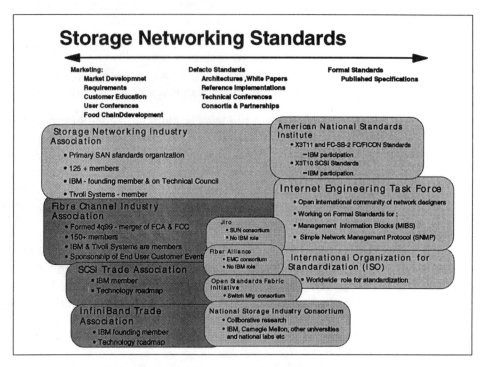

Figure 18. Groups involved in setting Storage Networking Standards

The roles of these associations and bodies fall into three categories:

- *Market development* — These associations are involved in market development, establishing requirements, conducting customer education, user conferences, and so on. The main organizations are the Storage Network Industry Association (SNIA); Fibre Channel Industry Association (merging the former Fibre Channel Association and the Fibre Channel Loop Community); and the SCSI Trade Association (SCSITA). Some of these organizations are also involved in the definition of defacto standards.

- *Defacto standards* — These organizations and bodies tend to be formed from two sources. They include working groups within the market development organizations, such as SNIA and FCIA. Others are partnerships between groups of companies in the industry, such as Jiro, Fibre Alliance, and the Open Standards Fabric Initiative (OSFI), which work as pressure groups towards defacto industry standards. They offer architectural definitions, write white papers, arrange technical conferences, and may reference implementations based on developments by their own partner companies. They may submit these specifications for formal standards acceptance and approval.

The OSFI is a good example, comprising the five manufacturers of Fibre Channel switching products. In July 1999, they announced an initiative to accelerate the definition, finalization, and adoption of specific Fibre Channel standards that address switch interoperability.

- *Formal standards* — These are the formal standards organizations like IETF, ANSI, and ISO, which are in place to review, obtain consensus, approve, and publish standards defined and submitted by the preceding two categories of organizations.

IBM and Tivoli Systems are heavily involved in most of these organizations, holding positions on boards of directors and technical councils and chairing projects in many key areas. We do this because it makes us aware of new work and emerging standards. The hardware and software management solutions we develop, therefore, can provide early and robust support for those standards that do emerge from the industry organizations into pervasive use. Secondly, IBM, as the innovation and technology leader in the storage industry, wants to drive reliability, availability, serviceability, and other functional features into standards. The standards organizations in which we participate are included in the following sections.

2.1.1 Storage Networking Industry Association

Storage Networking Industry Association (SNIA) is an international computer industry forum of developers, integrators, and IT professionals who evolve and promote storage networking technology and solutions. SNIA was formed to ensure that storage networks become efficient, complete, and trusted solutions across the IT community. SNIA is accepted as the primary organization for the development of SAN standards, with over 125 companies as its members, including all the major server, storage, and fabric component vendors. SNIA also has a working group dedicated to the development of NAS standards. SNIA is committed to delivering architectures, education, and services that will propel storage networking solutions into a broader market. IBM is one of the founding members of SNIA, and has senior representatives participating on the board and in technical groups. For additional information on the various activities of SNIA, see its Web site at:

www.snia.org

2.1.2 Fibre Channel Industry Association

The Fibre Channel Industry Association (FCIA) was formed in the autumn of 1999 as a result of a merger between the Fibre Channel Association (FCA) and the Fibre Channel Community (FCC). The FCIA currently has more than 150 members in the United States and through its affiliate organizations in Europe and Japan. The FCIA mission is to nurture and help develop the broadest market for fibre channel products. This is done through market development, education, standards monitoring and fostering interoperability among members' products. IBM is a principal member of the FCIA. For additional information on the various activities of FCIA, see its Web site at:

www.fibrechannel.com

2.1.3 The SCSI Trade Association

The SCSI Trade Association (SCSITA) was formed to promote the use and understanding of small computer system interface (SCSI) parallel interface technology. The SCSITA provides a focal point for communicating SCSI benefits to the market, and influences the evolution of SCSI into the future. IBM is a founding member of the SCSITA. For more information, see its Web site at:

www.scsita.org

2.1.4 InfiniBand (SM) Trade Association

The demands of the Internet and distributed computing are challenging the scalability, reliability, availability, and performance of servers. To meet this demand a balanced system architecture with equally good performance in the memory, processor, and input/output (I/O) subsystems is required. A number of leading companies have joined together to develop a new common I/O specification beyond the current PCI bus architecture, to deliver a channel based, switched fabric technology that the entire industry can adopt. InfiniBand™ Architecture represents a new approach to I/O technology and is based on the collective research, knowledge, and experience of the industry's leaders. IBM is a founding member of InfiniBand (SM) Trade Association. For additional information, see its Web site at:

www.futureio.org

2.1.5 National Storage Industry Consortium

The National Storage Industry Consortium membership consists of over fifty US corporations, universities, and national laboratories with common interests in the field of digital information storage. A number of projects are sponsored by NSIC, including network attached storage devices (NASD), and network attached secure disks. The objective of the NASD project is to develop, explore, validate, and document the technologies required to enable the deployment and adoption of network attached devices, subsystems, and systems. IBM is a founding member of the NSIC. For more information, see its Web site at:

```
www.nsic.org
```

2.1.6 Internet Engineering Task Force

The Internet Engineering Task Force (IETF) is a large, open international community of network designers, operators, vendors, and researchers concerned with the evolution of the Internet architecture, and the smooth operation of the Internet. It is responsible for the formal standards for the Management Information Blocks (MIB) and for Simple Network Management Protocol (SNMP) for SAN management. For additional information on IETF, see its Web site at:

```
www.ietf.org/overview.html
```

2.1.7 American National Standards Institute

American National Standards Institute (ANSI) does not itself develop American national standards. It facilitates development by establishing consensus among qualified groups. IBM participates in numerous committees, including those for Fibre Channel and storage area networks. For more information on ANSI, see its Web site at:

```
www.ansi.org
```

2.2 SAN software management standards

Traditionally, storage management has been the responsibility of the host server to which the storage resources are attached. With storage networks the focus has shifted away from individual server platforms, making storage management independent of the operating system, and offering the potential for greater flexibility by managing shared resources across the enterprise SAN infrastructure. Software is needed to configure, control, and monitor the SAN and all of its components in a consistent manner. Without good software tools, SANs cannot be implemented effectively.

The management challenges faced by SANs are very similar to those previously encountered by LANs and WANs. Single vendor proprietary management solutions will not satisfy customer requirements in a multi-vendor heterogeneous environment. The pressure is on the vendors to establish common methods and techniques. For instance, the need for platform independence for management applications, to enable them to port between a variety of server platforms, has encouraged the use of Java.

The Storage Network Management Working Group (SNMWG) of SNIA is working to define and support open standards needed to address the increased management requirements imposed by SAN topologies. Reliable transport of the data, as well as management of the data and resources (such as file access, backup, and volume management) are key to stable operation. SAN management requires a hierarchy of functions, from management of individual devices and components, to the network fabric, storage resources, data and applications. This is shown in Figure 19.

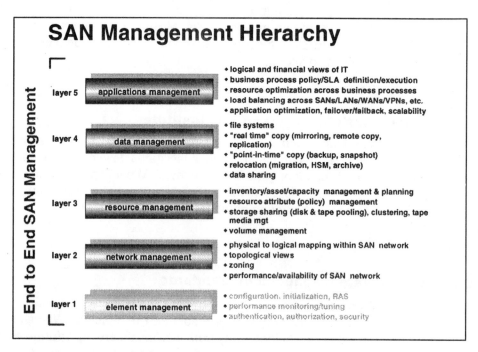

Figure 19. SAN management hierarchy

These can be implemented separately, or potentially as a fully integrated solution to present a single interface to manage all SAN resources.

2.2.1 Application management

Application Management is concerned with the availability, performance, and recoverability of the applications that run your business. Failures in individual components are of little consequence if the application is unaffected. By the same measure, a fully functional infrastructure is of little use if it is configured incorrectly or if the data placement makes the application unusable. Enterprise application and systems management is at the top of the hierarchy and provides a comprehensive, organization-wide view of all network resources (fabric, storage, servers, applications). A flow of information regarding configuration, status, statistics, capacity utilization, performance, and so on, must be directed up the hierarchy from lower levels. A number of industry initiatives are directed at standardizing the storage specific information flow using a Common Information Model (CIM) sponsored by Microsoft, or application programming interfaces (API), such as those proposed by the Jiro initiative, sponsored by Sun Microsystems, and others by SNIA and SNMWG.

Figure 20 illustrates a common interface model for heterogeneous, multi-vendor SAN management.

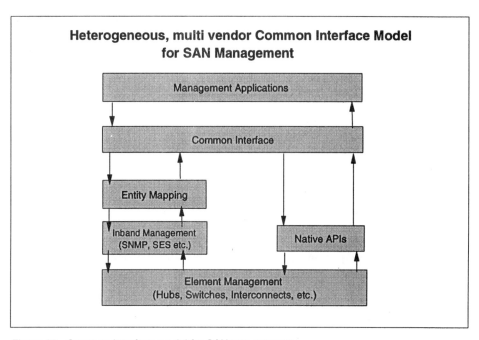

Figure 20. Common interface model for SAN management

2.2.2 Data management

More than at any other time in history, digital data is fueling business. Data Management is concerned with Quality-of-Service (QoS) issues surrounding this data, such as:

- Ensuring data availability and accessibility for applications
- Ensuring proper performance of data for applications
- Ensuring recoverability of data

Data Management is carried out on mobile and remote storage, centralized - host attached storage, network attached storage (NAS) and SAN attached storage (SAS). It incorporates backup and recovery, archive and recall, and disaster protection.

2.2.3 Resource management

Resource Management is concerned with the efficient utilization and consolidated, automated management of existing storage and fabric resources, as well as automating corrective actions where necessary. This requires the ability to manage all distributed storage resources, ideally through a single management console, to provide a single view of enterprise resources. Without such a tool, storage administration is limited to individual servers. Typical enterprises today may have hundreds, or even thousands, of servers and storage subsystems. This makes impractical the manual consolidation of resource administration information, such as enterprise-wide disk utilization, or regarding the location of storage subsystems. SAN resource management addresses tasks, such as:

- Pooling of disk resources
- Space management
- Pooling and sharing of removable media resources
- Implementation of "just-in-time" storage

2.2.4 Network management

Every e-business depends on existing LAN and WAN connections in order to function. Because of their importance, sophisticated network management software has evolved. Now SANs are allowing us to bring the same physical connectivity concepts to storage. And like LANs and WANs, SANs are vital to the operation of an e-business. Failures in the SAN can stop the operation of an enterprise.

SANs can be viewed as both physical and logical entities.

SAN physical view
The physical view identifies the installed SAN components, and allows the physical SAN topology to be understood. A SAN environment typically consists of four major classes of components:

- End-user computers and clients
- Servers
- Storage devices and subsystems
- Interconnect components

End-user platforms and server systems are usually connected to traditional LAN and WAN networks. In addition, some end-user systems may be attached to the Fibre Channel network, and may access SAN storage devices directly. Storage subsystems are connected using the Fibre Channel network to servers, end-user platforms, and to each other. The Fibre Channel network is made up of various interconnect components, such as switches, hubs, and bridges, as shown in Figure 21.

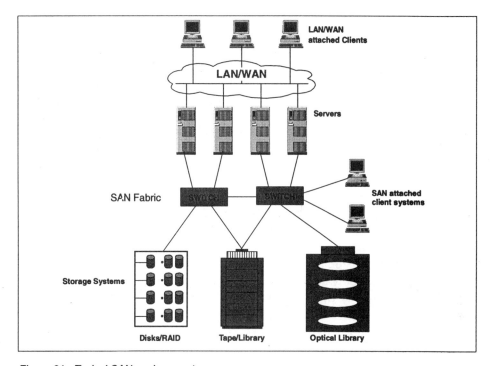

Figure 21. Typical SAN environment

SAN logical view

The logical view identifies and understands the relationships between SAN entities. These relationships are not necessarily constrained by physical connectivity, and they play a fundamental role in the management of SANs. For instance, a server and some storage devices may be classified as a logical entity. A logical entity group forms a private virtual network, or zone, within the SAN environment with a specific set of connected members. Communication within each zone is restricted to its members.

Network Management is concerned with the efficient management of the Fibre Channel SAN. This is especially in terms of physical connectivity mapping, fabric zoning, performance monitoring, error monitoring, and predictive capacity planning.

2.2.5 Element management

The elements that make up the SAN infrastructure include intelligent disk subsystems, intelligent removable media subsystems, Fibre Channel switches, hubs and bridges, meta-data controllers, and out-board storage management controllers. The vendors of these components provide proprietary software tools to manage their individual elements, usually comprising software, firmware and hardware elements such as those shown in Figure 22. For instance, a management tool for a hub will provide information regarding its own configuration, status, and ports, but will not support other fabric components such as other hubs, switches, HBAs, and so on. Vendors that sell more than one element commonly provide a software package that consolidates the management and configuration of all of their elements. Modern enterprises, however, often purchase storage hardware from a number of different vendors.

Fabric monitoring and management is an area where a great deal of standards work is being focused. Two management techniques are in use, - inband and outband management.

2.2.5.1 Inband management

Device communications to the network management facility is most commonly done directly across the Fibre Channel transport, using a protocol called SCSI Enclosure Services (SES). This is known as inband management. It is simple to implement, requires no LAN connections, and has inherent advantages, such as the ability for a switch to initiate a SAN topology map by means of SES queries to other fabric components. However, in the event of a failure of the Fibre Channel transport itself, the management information cannot be transmitted. Therefore, access to devices is lost, as is the ability to detect, isolate, and recover from network problems. This problem can be minimized by provision of redundant paths between devices in the fabric.

Inband developments

Inband management is evolving rapidly. Proposals exist for low level interfaces such as Return Node Identification (RNID) and Return Topology Identification (RTIN) to gather individual device and connection information, and for a Management Server that derives topology information. Inband management also allows attribute inquiries on storage devices and configuration changes for all elements of the SAN. Since inband management is performed over the SAN itself, administrators are not required to make additional TCP/IP connections.

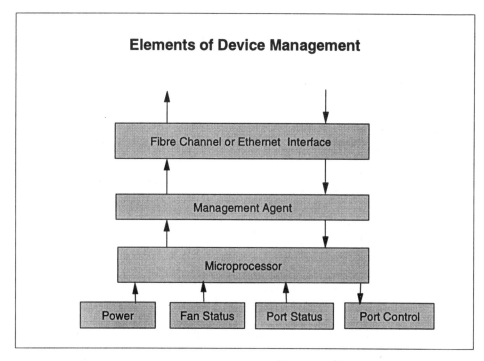

Figure 22. Device management elements

2.2.5.2 Outband management

Outband management means that device management data are gathered over a TCP/IP connection such as Ethernet. Commands and queries can be sent using Simple Network Management Protocol (SNMP), Telnet (a text only command line interface), or a web browser Hyper Text Transfer Protocol (HTTP). Telnet and HTTP implementations are more suited to small networks.

Outband management does not rely on the Fibre Channel network. Its main advantage is that management commands and messages can be sent even if a loop or fabric link fails. Integrated SAN management facilities are more easily implemented, especially by using SNMP. However, unlike inband management, it cannot automatically provide SAN topology mapping.

Outband developments

Two primary SNMP MIBs are being implemented for SAN fabric elements that allow outband monitoring. The ANSI Fibre Channel Fabric Element MIB provides significant operational and configuration information on individual devices. The emerging Fibre Channel Management MIB provides additional link table and switch zoning information that can be used to derive information about the physical and logical connections between individual devices. Even with these two MIBs, outband monitoring is incomplete. Most storage devices and some fabric devices don't support outband monitoring. In addition, many administrators simply don't attach their SAN elements to the TCP/IP network.

Simple Network Management Protocol (SNMP)

This protocol is widely supported by LAN/WAN routers, gateways, hubs and switches, and is the predominant protocol used for multi vendor networks. Device status information (vendor, machine serial number, port type and status, traffic, errors, and so on) can be provided to an enterprise SNMP manager. This usually runs on a UNIX or NT workstation attached to the network. A device can generate an alert by SNMP, in the event of an error condition. The device symbol, or icon, displayed on the SNMP manager console, can be made to turn red or yellow, and messages can be sent to the network operator.

Management Information Base (MIB)

A management information base (MIB) organizes the statistics provided. The MIB runs on the SNMP management workstation, and also on the managed device. A number of industry standard MIBs have been defined for the LAN/WAN environment. Special MIBs for SANs are being built by the SNIA. When these are defined and adopted, multi-vendor SANs can be managed by common commands and queries.

Element management is concerned with providing a framework to centralize and automate the management of heterogeneous elements and to align this management with application or business policy.

2.3 SAN status today

SANs are in the same situation in which LANs and WANs were when these technologies began to emerge in the late 1980's. SAN technology is still relatively immature. Accepted industry standards are still under development in a number of key areas. However, vendors are working together in the standards organizations described, with the intention to rapidly improve this situation. For instance, in March 2000 Brocade Communications Systems announced that it would release elements of its Silkworm Fibre Channel interconnection protocol to the Technical Committee of the primary ANSI Fibre Channel standards group. Known as Fabric Shortest Path First (FSPF), this specifies a common method for routing and moving data among Fibre

Channel switches. For details of FSPF, see 9.3.2.4, "Fabric Shortest Path First (FSPF)" on page 190.

As a result the situation is fluid, and changing quickly. What may be impractical today may be ready for prime time next week, next month, or next year. But, you can be confident that the industry standards initiatives will deliver effective cross platform solutions within the near term.

Many of the SAN solutions on the market today are restricted to specific applications. Interoperability is also often restricted, and currently available software management tools are limited in scope. But these considerations need not prevent you from actively planning and implementing SANs now. They do mean that you need to take care in selecting solutions. You should try to ensure that your choices are not taking you in a direction which could be a dead end route, or locking you in to limited options for the future.

Chapter 3. Fibre Channel basics

Fibre Channel (FC) is a technology standard that allows data to be transferred from one network node to another at very high speeds. Fibre Channel is simply the most reliable, highest performing solution for information storage, transfer, and retrieval available today. Current implementations transfer data at 100 MB/second, although, 200 MB/second and 400 MB/second data rates have already been tested.

This standard is backed by a consortium of industry vendors and has been accredited by the American National Standards Institute (ANSI). Many products are now on the market that take advantage of FC's high-speed, high-availability characteristics.

In the topics that follow, we introduce Fibre Channel basic information to complement the solutions that we describe later in this redbook. We cover areas that are internal to Fibre Channel and show how data is moved and the medium upon which it travels.

3.1 SAN components

The industry considers Fibre Channel as the architecture on which most SAN implementations will be built, with FICON as the standard protocol for S/390 systems, and Fibre Channel Protocol (FCP) as the standard protocol for non-S/390 systems.

Based on this implementation, there are three main categories of SAN components:

- SAN servers
- SAN storage
- SAN interconnects

We show the typical SAN components that are likely to be encountered in Figure 23.

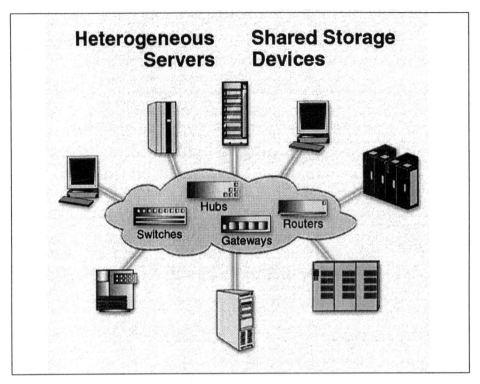

Figure 23. SAN components

3.1.1 SAN servers

The server infrastructure is the underlying reason for all SAN solutions. This infrastructure includes a mix of server platforms, such as Windows NT, UNIX and its various flavors, and mainframes. With initiatives, such as server consolidation and e-business, the need for a SAN has become very strong. Although most current SAN solutions are based on a homogeneous server platform, future implementations will take into account the heterogeneous nature of the IT world.

3.1.2 SAN storage

The storage infrastructure is the foundation on which information relies, and must support the business objectives and business model. In this environment, simply deploying more and faster storage devices is not enough; a new kind of infrastructure is needed, one that provides network availability, data accessibility, and system manageability. The SAN meets this challenge. It is a high-speed subnet that establishes a direct connection between storage resources and servers. The SAN liberates the storage device, so it is not on a particular server bus, and attaches it directly to the network. In other words, storage is externalized, and functionally distributed to the organization. The SAN also enables the centralization of storage devices and the clustering of servers, which makes for easier and less expensive administration.

3.1.3 SAN interconnects

The first element that must be considered in any SAN implementation is the connectivity of components of storage and servers using technologies such as Fibre Channel. The components listed here are typically used in LAN and WAN implementations. SANs, like LANs, interconnect the storage interfaces into many network configurations and across long distances.

- Cables and connectors
- Gigabit Link Model (GLM)
- Gigabit Interface Converters (GBIC)
- Media Interface Adapters (MIA)
- Adapters
- Extenders
- Multiplexors
- Hubs
- Routers
- Bridges
- Gateways
- Switches
- ESCON Directors
- FICON Directors

We go into greater depth on interconnection components in Chapter 5, "Fibre Channel products" on page 97.

3.2 Jargon terminology shift

Much of the terminology used for SAN has its origin in Internet Protocol (IP) network terminology. In some cases, companies in the industry use different terms that mean the same thing, and in some cases, the same terms meaning different things. In this book we will attempt to define some of the terminology that is used and its changing nature among vendors.

3.3 Vendor standards and main vendors

This section gives an overview of the major SAN vendors in the industry:

- **Systems/storage SAN providers**
  - IBM (Sequent), SUN, HP, EMC (DG Clariion), STK, HDS, Compaq, and Dell
- **Hub providers**
  - Gadzoox, Vixel and Emulex
- **Switch providers**
  - Brocade, Ancor, McDATA, Vixel, STK/SND and Gadzoox
- **Gateway and Router providers**
  - ATTO, Chaparrel Tech, CrossRoads Tech, Pathlight, Vicom
- **Host bus adapters (HBA) providers**
  - Ancor, Compaq, Emulex, Genroco, Hewlett-Packard, Interphase, Jaycor Networks, Prisia, Qlogic and Sun Microsystems
- **Software providers**
  - IBM/Tivoli, Veritas, Legato, Computer Associates, DataDirect, Transoft (HP), Crosstor and Retrieve

3.4 Physical characteristics

This section describes the components and technology associated with the physical aspects of Fibre Channel. We describe the supported cables and give an overview of the types of connectors that are generally available and are implemented in a SAN environment.

3.4.1 Cable

As with parallel SCSI and traditional networking, different types of cable are used for Fibre Channel configurations. Two types of cables are supported:

- Copper
- Fiber-optic

Fibre Channel can be run over optical or copper media, but fiber-optic enjoys a major advantage in noise immunity. It is for this reason that fiber-optic cabling is preferred. However, copper is also widely used and it is likely that in the short term a mixed environment will need to be tolerated and supported. Figure 24 shows fiber-optical data transmission.

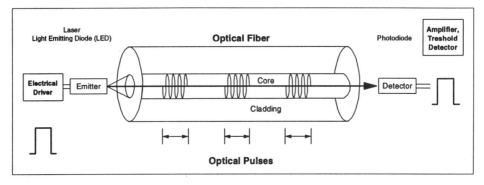

Figure 24. Fiber optical data transmission

In addition to the noise immunity, fiber-optic cabling provides a number of distinct advantages over copper transmission lines that make it a very attractive medium for many applications. At the forefront of the advantages are:

- Greater distance capability than is generally possible with copper
- Insensitive to induced electro-magnetic interference (EMI)
- No emitted electro-magnetic radiation (RFI)
- No electrical connection between two ports
- Not susceptible to crosstalk
- Compact and lightweight cables and connectors

However, fiber-optic and optical links do have some drawbacks. Some of the considerations are:

- Optical links tend to be more expensive than copper links over short distances
- Optical connections don't lend themselves to backplane printed circuit wiring
- Optical connections may be affected by dirt and other contamination

Overall, optical fibers have provided a very high-performance transmission medium which has been refined and proven over many years.

Mixing fiber-optical and copper components in the same environment is supported, although not all products provide that flexibility and this should be taken into consideration when planning a SAN. Copper cables tend to be used for short distances, up to 30 meters, and can be identified by their DB-9, 9 pin, connector.

Normally fiber-optic cabling is referred to by mode or the frequencies of light waves that are carried by particular cable type. Fiber cables come in two distinct types, as shown in Figure 25.

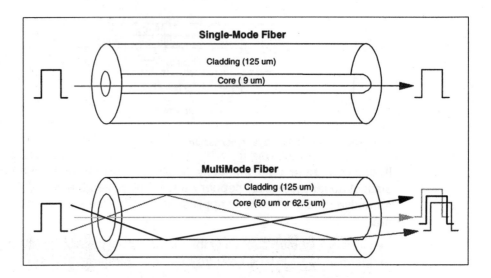

Figure 25. Multi-mode and single-mode propagation

- **Multi-mode fiber (MMF)** for short distances, up to 500m using FCP

  Multi-mode cabling is used with shortwave laser light and has either a 50 micron or a 62.5 micron core with a cladding of 125 micron. The 50 micron or 62.5 micron diameter is sufficiently large for injected light waves to be reflected off the core interior.

- **Single-mode fiber (SMF)** for long distances

  Single-mode is used to carry longwave laser light. With a much smaller 9 micron diameter core and a single-mode light source, single-mode fiber supports much longer distances, currently up to 10 km at gigabit speed.

Fibre Channel architecture supports both short wave and long wave optical transmitter technologies, as follows:

- **Short wave laser** — this technology uses a wavelength of 780 nanometers and is only compatible with multi-mode fiber.

- **Long wave laser** — this technology uses a wavelength of 1300 nanometers. It is compatible with both single-mode and multi-mode fiber.

IBM will support the following distances for FCP as shown in Table 1.

Table 1. FCP distances

Diameter (Microns)	Cladding (micron)	Mode	Laser type	Distance
9	125	Single mode	Longwave	=< 10 km
50	125	Multi mode	Shortwave	<= 500 m
62.5	125	Multimode	Shortwave	<= 175 m

Campus

A campus topology is nothing more than "cabling" buildings together, so that data can be transferred from a computer system in one building to storage devices, whether they are disk storage, or tape storage for backup, or other devices in another building. We show a campus topology in Figure 26.

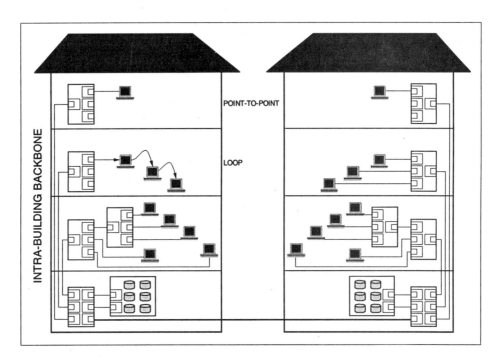

Figure 26. Campus topology

3.4.2 Connectors

Three connector types are generally available. Fiber-optic connectors are usually provided using dual subscriber connectors (SC). Copper connections can be provided through standard DB-9 connectors or the more recently developed high speed serial direct connect (HSSDC) connectors. We show a selection of connectors in Figure 27.

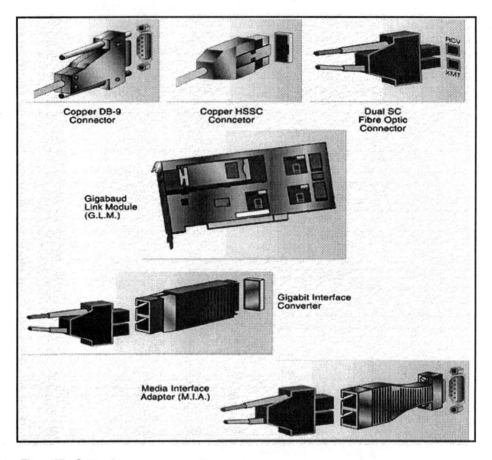

Figure 27. Connectors

Fibre Channel products may include a fixed, embedded copper or fiber-optic interface, or they may provide a media-independent interface. There are three media-independent interfaces available:

- **Gigabit Link Modules (GLMs)** — convert parallel signals to serial, and vice versa. GLMs include the serializer/de-serializer (SERDES) function and provide a 20-bit parallel interface to the Fibre Channel encoding and control logic. GLMs are primarily used to provide factory configurability, but may also be field exchanged or upgraded by users.

- **Gigabit Interface Converters (GBICs)** — provide a serial interface to the SERDES function. GBICs can be hot inserted or removed from installed devices. These are particularly useful in multiport devices, such as switches and hubs, where single ports can be reconfigured without affecting other ports.

- **Media Interface Adapters (MIAs)** — allow users to convert copper DB-9 connectors to multi-mode fibre optics. The power to support the optical transceivers is supplied by defined pins in the DB-9 interface.

3.5 Fibre Channel layers

Fibre Channel (FC) is broken up into a series of five layers. The concept of layers, starting with the ISO/OSI seven-layer model, allows the development of one layer to remain independent of the adjacent layers. Although, FC contains five layers, those layers follow the general principles stated in the ISO/OSI model.

The five layers are divided into two parts:

- Physical and signaling layer
- Upper layer

The five layers are illustrated in Figure 28.

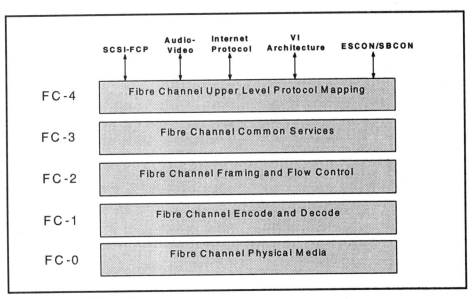

Figure 28. Fibre Channel layers

3.5.1 Physical and Signaling Layers

The physical and signaling layers include the three lowest layers: FC-0, FC-1, and FC-2.

3.5.1.1 Physical interface and media: FC-0

The lowest layer (FC-0) defines the physical link in the system, including the cabling, connectors, and electrical parameters for the system at a wide range of data rates. This level is designed for maximum flexibility, and allows the use of a large number of technologies to match the needs of the desired configuration.

A communication route between two nodes may be made up of links of different technologies. For example, in reaching its destination, a signal may start out on copper wire and become converted to single-mode fibre for longer distances. This flexibility allows for specialized configurations depending on IT requirements.

Laser safety

Fibre Channel often uses lasers to transmit data, and can, therefore, present an optical health hazard. The FC-0 layer defines an open fibre control (OFC) system, and acts as a safety interlock for point-to-point fibre connections that use semiconductor laser diodes as the optical source. If the fibre connection is broken, the ports send a series of pulses until the physical connection is re-established and the necessary handshake procedures are followed.

3.5.1.2 Transmission protocol: FC-1

The second layer (FC-1) provides the methods for adaptive 8B/10B encoding to bind the maximum length of the code, maintain DC-balance, and provide word alignment. This layer is used to integrate the data with the clock information required by serial transmission technologies.

3.5.1.3 Framing and signaling protocol: FC-2

Reliable communications result from Fibre Channel's FC-2 framing and signaling protocol. FC-2 specifies a data transport mechanism that is independent of upper layer protocols. FC-2 is self-configuring and supports point-to-point, arbitrated loop, and switched environments.

FC-2, which is the third layer of the FC-PH, provides the transport methods to determine:

- Topologies based on the presence or absence of a fabric
- Communication models
- Classes of service provided by the fabric and the nodes
- General fabric model

- Sequence and exchange identifiers
- Segmentation and reassembly

Data is transmitted in 4-byte ordered sets containing data and control characters. Ordered sets provide the availability to obtain bit and word synchronization, which also establishes word boundary alignment.

Together, FC-0, FC-1, and FC-2 form the Fibre Channel physical and signaling interface (FC-PH).

3.5.2 Upper layers

The Upper layer includes two layers: FC-3 and FC-4.

3.5.2.1 Common services: FC-3

FC-3 defines functions that span multiple ports on a single-node or fabric. Functions that are currently supported include:

- **Hunt groups:** A hunt group is a set of associated N_Ports attached to a single node. This set is assigned an alias identifier that allows any frames containing the alias to be routed to any available N_Port within the set. This decreases latency in waiting for an N_Port to become available.

- **Striping:** Striping is used to multiply bandwidth, using multiple N_Ports in parallel to transmit a single information unit across multiple links.

- **Multicast:** Multicast delivers a single transmission to multiple destination ports. This includes the ability to broadcast to all nodes or a subset of nodes.

3.5.2.2 Upper layer protocol mapping (ULP): FC-4

The highest layer (FC-4) provides the application-specific protocols. Fibre Channel is equally adept at transporting both network and channel information and allows both protocol types to be concurrently transported over the same physical interface.

Through mapping rules, a specific FC-4 describes how ULP processes of the same FC-4 type interoperate. A channel example is sending SCSI commands to a disk drive, while a networking example is sending IP (Internet Protocol) packets between nodes.

3.6 The movement of data

To move data bits with integrity over a physical medium, there must be a mechanism to check that this has happened and integrity has not been compromised. This is provided by a reference clock which ensures that each bit is received as it was transmitted. In parallel topologies this can be accomplished by using a separate clock or strobe line. As data bits are transmitted in parallel from the source, the strobe line alternates between high or low to signal the receiving end that a full byte has been sent. In the case of 16- and 32-bit wide parallel cable, it would indicate that multiple bytes have been sent.

The reflective differences in fiber-optic cabling mean that modal dispersion may occur. This may result in frames arriving at different times. This bit error rate (BER) is referred to as the jitter budget. No products are entirely jitter free, and this is an important consideration when selecting the components of a SAN.

As serial data transports only have two leads, transmit and receive, clocking is not possible using a separate line. Serial data must carry the reference timing which means that clocking is embedded in the bit stream.

Embedded clocking, though, can be accomplished by different means. Fibre Channel uses a byte-encoding scheme, which is covered in more detail in 3.7, "Data encoding" on page 56, and clock and data recovery (CDR) logic to recover the clock. From this, it determines the data bits that comprise bytes and words.

Gigabit speeds mean that maintaining valid signaling, and ultimately valid data recovery, is essential for data integrity. Fibre Channel standards allow for a single bit error to occur only once in a trillion bits (10^{-12}). In the real IT world, this equates to a maximum of one bit error every 16 minutes, however actual occurrence is a lot less frequent than this.

3.7 Data encoding

In order to transfer data over a high-speed serial interface, the data is encoded prior to transmission and decoded upon reception. The encoding process ensures that sufficient clock information is present in the serial data stream to allow the receiver to synchronize to the embedded clock information and successfully recover the data at the required error rate. This 8b/10b encoding will find errors that a parity check cannot. A parity check will not find even numbers of bit errors, only odd numbers. The 8b/10b encoding logic will find almost all errors.

First developed by IBM, the 8b/10b encoding process will convert each 8-bit byte into two possible 10-bit characters.

This scheme is called 8b/10b encoding, because it refers to the number of data bits input to the encoder and the number of bits output from the encoder.

The format of the 8b/10b character is of the format Ann.m, where:

- A represents 'D' for data or 'K' for a special character
- nn is the decimal value of the lower 5 bits (EDCBA)
- '.' is a period
- m is the decimal value of the upper 3 bits (HGF)

We illustrate an encoding example in Figure 29.

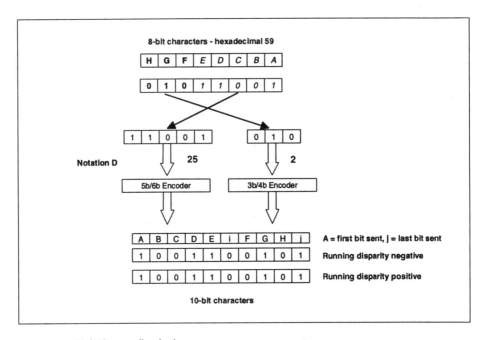

Figure 29. 8b/10b encoding logic

In the encoding example the following occurs:

1. Hexadecimal representation x'59' is converted to binary: 01011001

2. Upper three bits are separated from the lower 5 bits: 010 11001

3. The order is reversed and each group is converted to decimal: 25 2

4. Letter notation D (for data) is assigned and becomes: D25.2

As we illustrate, the conversion of the 8-bit data bytes has resulted in two 10-bit results. The encoder needs to choose one of these results to use. This is achieved by monitoring the running disparity of the previously processed character. For example, if the previous character had a positive disparity, then the next character issued should have an encoded value that represents negative disparity.

You will notice that in our example the encoded value, when the running disparity is either positive or negative, is the same. This is legitimate. In some cases it (the encoded value) will differ, and in others it will be the same.

3.8 Ordered sets

Fibre Channel uses a command syntax, known as an ordered set, to move the data across the network. The ordered sets are four byte transmission words containing data and special characters which have a special meaning. Ordered sets provide the availability to obtain bit and word synchronization, which also establishes word boundary alignment. An ordered set always begins with the special character K28.5. Three major types of ordered sets are defined by the signaling protocol.

The frame delimiters, the start-of-frame (SOF) and end-of-frame (EOF) ordered sets, establish the boundaries of a frame. They immediately precede or follow the contents of a Frame. There are 11 types of SOF and 8 types of EOF delimiters defined for the Fabric and N_Port Sequence control.

The two primitive signals: idle and receiver ready (R_RDY) are ordered sets designated by the standard to have a special meaning. An Idle is a primitive signal transmitted on the link to indicate an operational port facility ready for frame transmission and reception. The R_RDY primitive signal indicates that the interface buffer is available for receiving further frames.

A primitive sequence is an ordered set that is transmitted and repeated continuously to indicate specific conditions within a port or conditions encountered by the receiver logic of a port. When a primitive sequence is received and recognized, a corresponding primitive sequence or Idle is transmitted in response. Recognition of a primitive sequence requires consecutive detection of three instances of the same ordered set. The primitive sequences supported by the standard are:

- Offline state (OLS)
- Not operational (NOS)
- Link reset (LR)
- Link reset response (LRR)

Offline (OLS): The offline primitive sequence is transmitted by a port to indicate one of the following conditions: The port is beginning the link initialization protocol, or the port has received and recognized the NOS protocol or the port is entering the offline status.

Not operational (NOS): The not operational primitive sequence is transmitted by a port in a point-to-point or fabric environment to indicate that the transmitting port has detected a link failure or is in an offline condition, waiting for the OLS sequence to be received.

Link reset (LR): The link reset primitive sequence is used to initiate a link reset.

Link reset response (LRR): Link reset response is transmitted by a port to indicate that it has recognized a LR sequence and performed the appropriate link reset.

3.9 Frames

Frames are the basic building blocks of an FC connection. The frames contain the information to be transmitted, the address of the source and destination ports, and link control information. Frames are broadly categorized as Data frames and Link_control frames. When the frame is defined as a link control frame the length of the data field is zero bytes. If the frame is defined as a data frame, the data field may be any number of words between zero and 528 (0 and 2112 bytes). Data frames may be used as Link_Data frames and Device_Data frames. Link control frames are classified as Acknowledge (ACK) and Link_Response (Busy and Reject) frames.

The primary function of the fabric is to receive the frames from the source port and route them to the destination port. It is the FC-2 layer's responsibility to break the data to be transmitted into frame size, and reassemble the frames. The frame structure is shown in Figure 30.

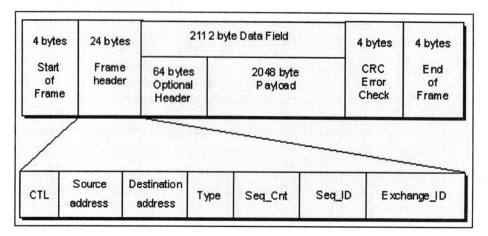

Figure 30. Frame structure

Each frame begins and ends with a frame delimiter. The frame header immediately follows the SOF delimiter. The frame header is used to control link applications and control device protocol transfers, and to detect missing or out of order frames. An optional header may contain further link control information. A maximum 2112 byte long field contains the information to be transferred from a source N_Port to a destination N_Port. The 4 bytes cyclic redundancy check (CRC) precedes the EOF delimiter. The CRC is used to detect transmission errors.

3.10 Framing classes of service

Fibre Channel provides a logical system of communication called class of service that is allocated by various login protocols. Fibre Channel provides six different classes of service:

- Class 1: Acknowledged connection service
- Class 2: Acknowledged connectionless service
- Class 3: Unacknowledged connectionless service
- Class 4: Fractional bandwidth connection-oriented service
- Class 5: Reserved for future development
- Class 6: Uni-directional connection service

Each class of service has a specific set of delivery attributes involving characteristics, such as:

- Is a connection or circuit established?

- Is the in-order delivery of frames guaranteed?

- If a connection is established, how much bandwidth is reserved for that connection?

- Is confirmation of delivery or notification of non-delivery provided?

- Which flow control mechanisms are used?

The answers to the above questions form the basis for the different classes of service provided and are shown in Table 2.

Table 2. Classes of service

Attribute	Class 1	Class 2	Class 3	Class 4	Class 6
Connection or circuit established	Yes			Yes	Yes
In order frame delivery	Yes			Yes	Yes
Amount of link bandwidth	Full				
Confirmation of delivery	Yes	Yes		Yes	Yes
Support Multicast			Yes		Yes
Flow Control used: - End-to-End - Buffer-to-Buffer(R_RDY) - Virtual Circuit (virtual circuit_RDY)	Yes SOFc1 only No	Yes Yes No	No Yes No	Yes No Yes	Yes SOFc1 only No

Class 1: Acknowledged connection service
Class 1 provides true connection service. The result is circuit-switched, dedicated bandwidth connections.

An end-to-end path between the communicating devices is established through the switch. Fibre Channel Class 1 service provides an acknowledgment of receipt for guaranteed delivery. Class 1 also provides full-bandwidth, guaranteed delivery, and bandwidth for applications like image transfer and storage backup and recovery. Some applications use the guaranteed delivery feature to move data reliably and quickly without the overhead of a network protocol stack.

Camp On is a Class 1 feature that enables a switch to monitor a busy port and queue that port for the next connection. As soon as the port is free, the switch makes the connection. This switch service speeds connect time, rather than sending a "busy" signal back to the originating N_Port and requiring the N_Port to retry to make the connection.

Stacked connect is a Class 1 feature that enables an originating N_Port to queue sequential connection requests with the switch. Again, this feature reduces overhead and makes the switch service more efficient.

Another form of Class 1 is called dedicated simplex service. Normally, Class 1 connections are bi-directional; However, in this service, communication is in one direction only. It is used to separate the transmit and receive switching. It permits one node to transfer to another node while simultaneously receiving from a third node.

We show this in Figure 31.

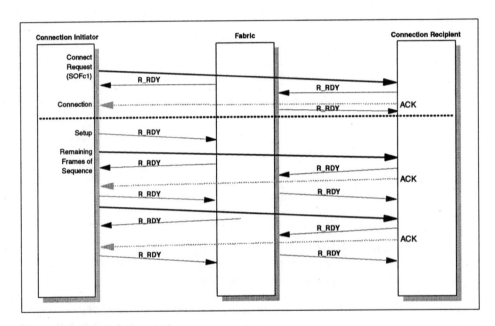

Figure 31. Class 1 flow control

Class 2: Acknowledged connectionless service

Class 2 is a connectionless service, independently switching each frame and providing guaranteed delivery with an acknowledgment of delivery. The path between two interconnected devices is not dedicated. The switch multiplexes traffic from N_Ports and NL_Ports without dedicating a path through the switch.

Class 2 credit-based flow control eliminates congestion that is found in many connectionless networks. If the destination port is congested, a "busy" signal is sent to the originating N_Port. The N_Port will then resend the message.

This way, no data is arbitrarily discarded just because the switch is busy at the time.

We show this in Figure 32.

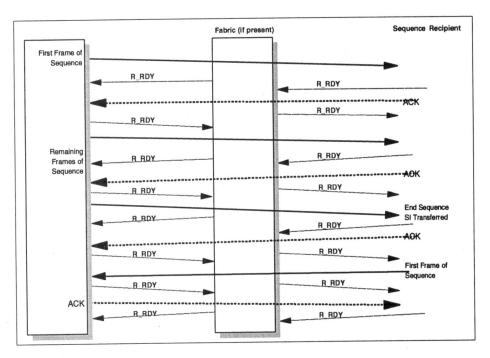

Figure 32. Class 2 flow control

Class 3: Unacknowledged connectionless service
Class 3 is a connectionless service, similar to Class 2, but no confirmation of receipt is given. This unacknowledged transfer is used for multicasts and broadcasts on networks, and for storage interfaces on Fibre Channel loops. The loop establishes a logical point-to-point connection and reliably moves data to and from storage.

Class 3 arbitrated loop transfers are also used for IP networks. Some applications use logical point-to-point connections without using a network layer protocol, taking advantage of Fibre Channel's reliable data delivery.

We show this in Figure 33.

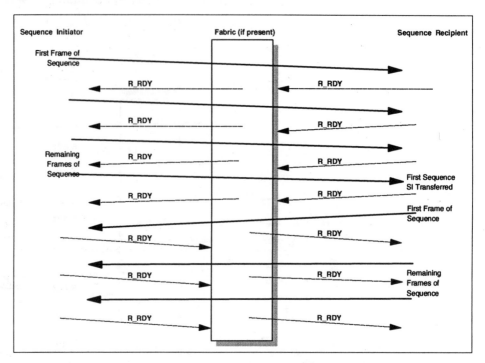

Figure 33. Class 3 flow control

Class 4: Fractional bandwidth acknowledged

Class 4 is a connection-oriented class of service which provides a virtual circuit. Virtual connections are established with bandwidth reservation for a predictable quality of service. A Class 4 connection is bi-directional, with one virtual circuit operational in each direction, and it supports a different set of quality of service parameters for each virtual circuit. These quality of service (QoS) parameters include guaranteed bandwidth and bounded end-to-end delay. A quality of service facilitator (QoSF) function is provided within the switch to manage and maintain the negotiated quality of service on each virtual circuit.

A node may reserve up to 256 concurrent Class 4 connections. Separate functions of Class 4 are the setup of the quality of service parameters and the connection itself.

When a Class 4 connection is active, the switch paces frames from the source node to the destination node. Pacing is the mechanism used by the switch to regulate available bandwidth per virtual circuit. This level of control permits congestion management for a switch and guarantees access to the destination node. The switch multiplexes frames belonging to different virtual circuits between the same or different node pairs.

Class 4 service provides in-order delivery of frames. Class 4 flow control is end-to-end and provides guaranteed delivery. Class 4 is ideal for time-critical and real-time applications like video.

We show this in Figure 34.

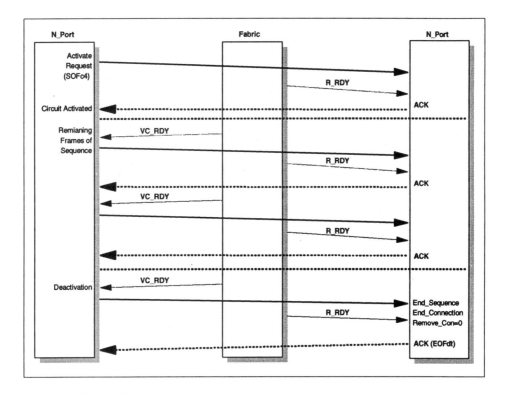

Figure 34. Class 4 flow control

Class 5: Still under development
Class 5 is still under development. This service allow for simultaneous (isochronous) data transfer to several participants and is especially applicable for audio and video servers in broadcast mode.

Class 6: Uni-directional connection service
Class 6 is similar to Class 1, providing uni-directional connection service. However, Class 6 also provides reliable multicast and pre-emption. Class 6 is ideal for video broadcast applications and real-time systems that move large quantities of data.

3.11 Naming and addressing

In a Fibre Channel environment the unique identity of participants is maintained through a hierarchy of fixed names and assigned addresses identifiers.

In Fibre Channel terminology, a communicating device is a node. Each node has a fixed 64-bit Node_name assigned by the manufacturer. The node name will be unique if the manufacturer has registered a range of addresses with the IEEE, and so is normally referred to as a World-Wide Name. An N_Port within a parent (WWN) node is also assigned a unique 64-bit Port_Name, which aids the accessibility of the port and is known as the World-Wide Port Name (WWPN).

The WWN is a registered, unique 64-bit identifier assigned to nodes and ports. An example of a registration authority is the registration service support of the Media Access Control (MAC) address associated with the network interface card. In the IEEE understanding, a MAC address consists of 48 bits, 24 of which are assigned to a particular company through the registration process with the remaining 24 bits assigned by the user.

An example of the node and port name correlation is shown in Figure 35.

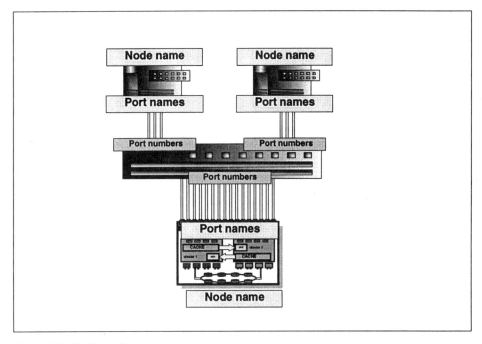

Figure 35. Nodes and ports

For more information on the governing body and the WWN, go to:

`standards.ieee.org/regauth/oui/index.html`

This naming convention allows each node and its associated N_Ports to be unique and accessible, even in a complex SANs.

The Fibre Channel naming convention allows either global or locally administered uniqueness to be assigned to a device. However, the administered name or WWN is not used for transporting frames across the network. In addition to a Fibre Channel WWN, a communicating device is dynamically assigned a 24-bit port address, or N_Port ID that is used for frame routing. As well as providing frame routing optimization, this 24-bit port address strategy removes the overhead of manual administration of addresses by allowing the topology to assign address.

In fabric environments, the switch is responsible for assigning a 24-bit address to each device as it logs on.

Allowing the topology to manage the assignment of addresses has the advantage that control of the addresses is now performed by the entity that is responsible for the routing of information. This means that address assignments can be made in a manner that results in the most efficient routing of frames within that topology. This approach mimics the behavior of the telephone system, where the telephone number (address) of a particular telephone is determined by where it is attached to the telephone system.

We describe this in greater detail in 4.3.2, "Name and addressing" on page 82.

Fibre Channel ports

There is more than one kind of port, though, and its designation represents the use which is being made of it. We show some port designations in Figure 36.

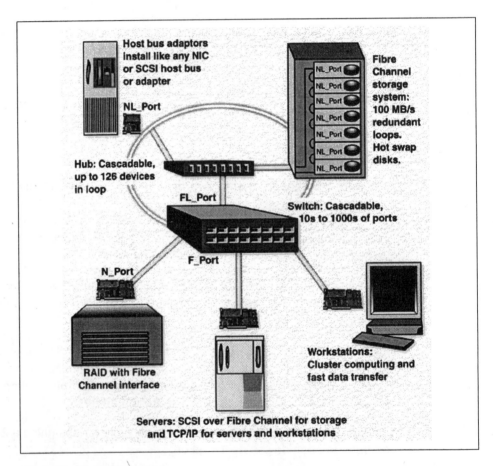

Figure 36. Fibre Channel ports

There are six kinds of ports that we are concerned with in this redbook. They are:

- **Loop port (L_Port)**

  This is the basic port in a Fibre Channel arbitrated loop (FC-AL) topology. If an N_Port is operating on a loop it is referred to as an NL_Port. If a fabric port is on a loop it is known as an FL_Port. To draw the distinction, throughout this book we will always qualify L_Ports as either NL_Ports or FL_Ports.

- **Node ports (N_Port)**

  These ports are found in Fibre Channel nodes, which are defined to be the source or destination of information units (IU). I/O devices and host systems interconnected in point-to-point or switched topologies use N_Ports for their connection. N_Ports can only attach to other N_Ports or to F_Ports.

- **Node-loop ports (NL_Port)**

  These ports are just like the N_Port described above, except that they connect to a Fibre Channel abritrated loop (FC-AL) topology. NL_Ports can only attach to other NL_Ports or to FL_Ports

- **Fabric ports (F_Port)**

  These ports are found in Fibre Channel switched fabrics. They are not the source or destination of IU's, but instead function only as a "middle-man" to relay the IUs from the sender to the receiver. F_Ports can only be attached to N_Ports.

- **Fabric-loop ports (FL_Port)**

  These ports are just like the F_Ports described above, except that they connect to an FC-AL topology. FL_Ports can only attach to NL_Ports.

- **Expansion ports (E_Port)**

  These ports are found in Fibre Channel switched fabrics and are used to interconnect the individual switch or routing elements. They are not the source or destination of IUs, but instead function like the F_Ports and FL_Ports to relay the IUs from one switch or routing elements to another. E_Ports can only attach to other E_Ports.

We show all these ports and how they interconnect in Figure 37.

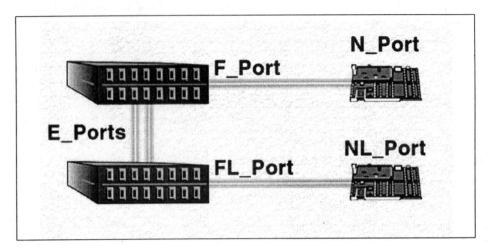

Figure 37. Port interconnections

The Fibre Channel architecture specifies the link characteristics and protocol used between N_Ports, between N_Ports and F_Ports, an between NL_Ports and FL_Ports.

Chapter 4. The technical topology of a SAN

Fibre Channel provides three distinct and one hybrid interconnection topologies. By having more than one interconnection option available, a particular application can choose the topology that is best suited to its requirements. The three fibre channel topologies are:

- Point-to-point
- Arbitrated loop
- Switched — referred to as a fabric

The three topologies are shown in Figure 38.

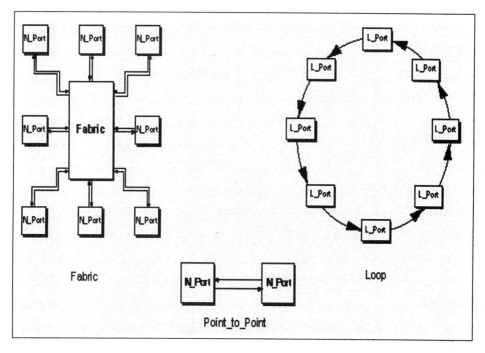

Figure 38. SAN topologies

4.1 Point-to-point

A *point-to-point* connection is the simplest topology. It is used when there are exactly two nodes, and future expansion is not predicted. There is no sharing of the media, which allows the devices to use the total bandwidth of the link. A simple link initialization is needed before communications can begin.

We illustrate a simple point-to-point connection in Figure 39.

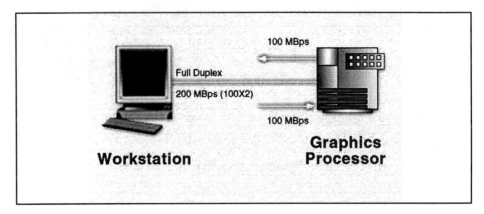

Figure 39. Point-to-point

An extension of the point-to-point topology is the logical start topology. This is a collection of point-to-point topology links and both topologies provide 100 MB/s full duplex bandwidth.

4.2 Arbitrated loop

The second topology is Fibre Channel Arbitrated Loop (FC-AL). FC-AL is more useful for storage applications. It is a loop of up to 126 nodes (NL_Ports) that is managed as a shared bus. Traffic flows in one direction, carrying data frames and primitives around the loop with a total bandwidth of 100 MB/s. Using arbitration protocol, a single connection is established between a sender and a receiver, and a data frame is transferred around the loop. When the communication comes to an end between the two connected ports, the loop becomes available for arbitration and a new connection may be established. Loops can be configured with hubs to make connection management easier. Up to 10 km distance is supported by the Fibre Channel standard for both of these configurations. However, latency on the arbitrated loop configuration is affected by the loop size.

A simple loop, configured using a hub, is shown in Figure 40.

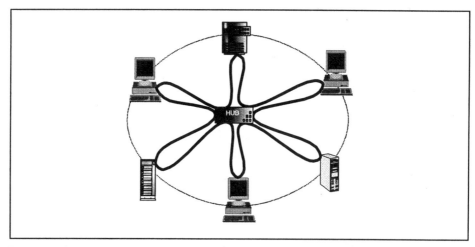

Figure 40. Arbitrated loop

4.2.1 Loop protocols

To support the shared behavior of the arbitrated loop, a number of loop-specific protocols are used. These protocols are used to:

- Initialize the loop and assign addresses

- Arbitrate for access to the loop

- Open a loop circuit with another port in the loop

- Close a loop circuit when two ports have completed their current use of the loop

- Implement the access fairness mechanism to ensure that each port has an opportunity to access the loop

4.2.2 Loop initialization

Loop initialization is a necessary process for the introduction of new participants on to the loop. Whenever a loop port is powered on or initialized, it executes the loop initialization primitive (LIP) to perform loop initialization. Optionally, loop initialization may build a positional map of all the ports on the loop. The positional map provides a count of the number of ports on the loop, their addresses and their position relative to the loop initialization master.

Following loop initialization, the loop enters a stable monitoring mode and begins with normal activity. An entire loop initialization sequence may take only a few milliseconds, depending on the number of NL_Ports attached to the loop. Loop initialization may be started by a number of causes. One of the most likely reasons for loop initialization is the introduction of a new device. For instance, an active device may be moved from one hub port to another hub port, or a device that has been powered on could re-enter the loop.

A variety of ordered sets have been defined to take into account the conditions that an NL_Port may sense as it starts the initialization process. These ordered sets are sent continuously while a particular condition or state exists. As part of the initialization process, loop initialization primitive sequences (referred to collectively as LIPs) are issued. As an example, an NL_Port must issue at least three identical ordered sets to start initialization. An ordered set transmission word always begins with the special character K28.5.

Once these identical ordered sets have been sent, and as each downstream device receives the LIP stream, devices enter a state known as open-init. This causes the suspension of any current operation and enables the device for the loop initialization procedure. LIPs are forwarded around the loop until all NL_Ports are in an open-init condition.

At this point, the NL_Ports need to be managed. In contrast to a Token-Ring, the Arbitrated Loop has no permanent master to manage the topology.

Therefore, loop initialization provides a selection process to determine which device will be the temporary loop master. After the loop master is chosen it assumes the responsibility for directing or managing the rest of the initialization procedure. The loop master also has the responsibility for closing the loop and returning it to normal operation.

Selecting the loop master is carried out by a subroutine known as the Loop Initialization Select Master (LISM) procedure. A loop device can be considered for temporary master by continuously issuing LISM frames that contain a port type identifier and a 64-bit World-Wide Name. For FL_Ports the identifier is x'00' and for NL_Ports it is x'EF'.

When a downstream port receives a LISM frame from a upstream partner, the device will check the port type identifier. If the identifier indicates an NL_Port, the downstream device will compare the WWN in the LISM frame to its own. The WWN with the lowest numeric value has priority. If the received frame's WWN indicates a higher priority, that is to say it has a lower numeric value, the device stops its LISM broadcast and starts transmitting the received LISM. Had the received frame been of a lower priority, the receiver would have thrown it away and continued broadcasting its own.

At some stage in proceedings, a node will receive its own LISM frame, which indicates that it has the highest priority, and succession to the throne of 'temporary loop master' has taken place. This node will then issue a special ordered set to indicate to the others that a temporary master has been selected.

4.2.3 Hub cascading

Since an arbitrated loop hub supplies a limited number of ports, building larger loops may require linking another hub. This is called hub cascading. A server with an FC-AL, shortwave, host bus adapter can connect to an FC-AL hub 500 meters away. Each port on the hub can connect to an FC-AL device up to 500 meters away. Cascaded hubs use one port on each hub for the hub-to-hub connection and this increases the potential distance between nodes in the loop by an additional 500 meters. In this topology the overall distance is 1500 meters. Both hubs can support other FC-AL devices at their physical locations. Stated distances assume a 50 micron multimode cable.

4.2.4 Loops

There are two different kinds of loops, the private and the public loop.

4.2.4.1 Private loop

The private loop does not connect with a fabric, only to other private nodes using attachment points called NL_Ports. A private loop is enclosed and known only to itself. In Figure 41 we show a private loop.

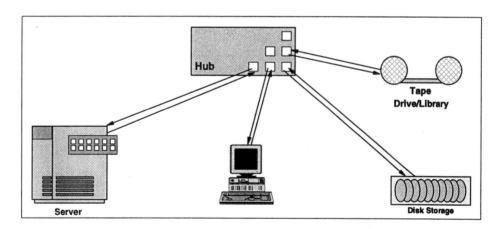

Figure 41. Private loop implementation

4.2.4.2 Public loop

A public loop requires a fabric and has at least one FL_Port connection to a fabric. A public loop extends the reach of the loop topology by attaching the loop to a fabric. Figure 42 shows a public loop.

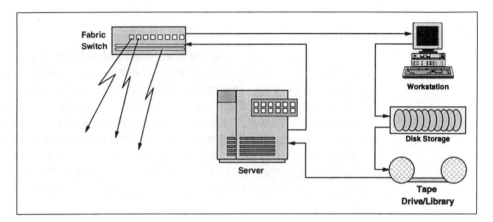

Figure 42. Public loop implementation

4.2.5 Arbitration

When a loop port wants to gain access to the loop, it has to arbitrate. When the port wins arbitration, it can open a loop circuit with another port on the loop; a function similar to selecting a device on a bus interface. Once the loop circuit has been opened, the two ports can send and receive frames between each other. This is known as "loop tenancy".

If more than one node on the loop is arbitrating at the same time, the node with the lower Arbitrated Loop Physical Address (AL_PA) gains control of the loop. Upon gaining control of the loop, the node then establishes a point-to-point transmission with another node using the full bandwidth of the media. When a node has finished transmitting its data, it is not required to give up control of the loop. This is a channel characteristic of Fibre Channel. However, there is a "fairness algorithm", which states that a device cannot regain control of the loop until the other nodes have had a chance to control the loop.

4.2.6 Loop addressing

An NL_Port, like a N_Port, has a 24-bit port address. If no switch connection exists, the two upper bytes of this port address are zeroes (x'00 00') and referred to as a private loop. The devices on the loop have no connection with the outside world. If the loop is attached to a fabric and an NL_Port supports a fabric login, the upper two bytes are assigned a positive value by the switch. We call this mode a public loop.

As fabric-capable NL_Ports are members of both a local loop and a greater fabric community, a 24-bit address is needed as an identifier in the network. In the case of public loop assignment, the value of the upper two bytes represents the loop identifier, and this will be common to all NL_Ports on the same loop that performed login to the fabric.

In both public and private arbitrated loops, the last byte of the 24-bit port address refers to the arbitrated loop physical address (AL_PA). The AL_PA is acquired during initialization of the loop and may, in the case of fabric-capable loop devices, be modified by the switch during login.

The total number of the AL_PAs available for arbitrated loop addressing is 127. This number is based on the requirements of 8b/10b running disparity between frames.

As a frame terminates with an end-of-frame character (EOF) this will force the current running disparity negative. In the Fibre Channel standard each transmission word between the end of one frame and the beginning of another frame should also leave the running disparity negative. If all 256 possible 8-bit bytes are sent to the 8b/10b encoder, 134 emerge with neutral disparity characters. Of these 134, seven are reserved for use by Fibre Channel. The 127 neutral disparity characters left have been assigned as AL_PAs. Put another way, the 127 AL_PA limit is simply the maximum number, minus reserved values, of neutral disparity addresses that can be assigned for use by the loop. This does not imply that we recommend this amount, or load, for a 100MB/s shared transport, but only that it is possible.

Arbitrated Loop will assign priority to AL_PAs, based on numeric value. The lower the numeric value, the higher the priority is. For example, an AL_PA of x'01' has a much better position to gain arbitration over devices that have a lower priority or higher numeric value. At the top of the hierarchy it is not unusual to find servers, but at the lower end you would expect to find disk arrays.

It is the arbitrated loop initialization that ensures each attached device is assigned a unique AL_PA. The possibility for address conflicts only arises when two separated loops are joined together without initialization.

4.2.7 Logins

There are three different types of login for Fibre Channel. These are:

- Fabric login
- Port login
- Process login

Here we will describe port login and process login. We detail fabric login in 4.3.3, "Fabric login" on page 84.

Port login
Port login is also known as PLOGI.

Port login is used to establish a session between two N_Ports (devices) and is necessary before any upper level commands or operations can be performed. During the port login, two N_Ports (devices) swap service parameters and make themselves known to each other.

Process login
Process login is also known as PRLI.

Process login is used to set up the environment between related processes on an originating N_Port and a responding N_Port. A group of related processes is collectively known as an image pair. The processes involved can be system processes, system images, such as mainframe logical partitions, control unit images, and FC-4 processes. Use of process login is optional from the perspective of Fibre Channel FC-2 layer, but may be required by a specific upper-level protocol as in the case of SCSI-FCP mapping.

We show Fibre Channel logins in Figure 43.

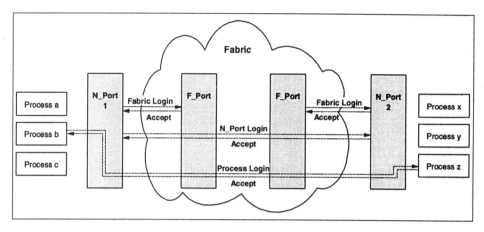

Figure 43. Fibre Channel logins

4.2.8 Closing a loop circuit

When two ports in a loop circuit complete their frame transmission, they may close the loop circuit to allow other ports to use the loop. The point at which the loop circuit is closed depends on the higher-level protocol, the operation in progress, and the design of the loop ports.

4.2.9 Supported devices

An arbitrated loop may support a variety of devices, including HBAs installed in the following servers:

- Individual Fibre Channel disk drives
- JBOD
- Fibre Channel RAID
- Native Fibre Channel tape sub-systems
- Fibre Channel to SCSI bridges

4.2.10 Broadcast

Arbitrated loop, in contrast to Ethernet, is a non-broadcast transport. When an NL_Port has successfully won the right to arbitration, it will open a target for frame transmission. Any subsequent loop devices in the path between the two will see the frames and forward them on to the next node in the loop.

It is this non-broadcast nature of arbitrated loop, by removing frame handling overhead from some of the loop, which enhances performance.

4.2.11 Distance

As stated before, arbitrated loop is a closed-ring topology. The total distance requirements being determined by the distance between the nodes. At gigabit speeds, signals propagate through fiber-optic media at five nanoseconds per meter and through copper media at four nanoseconds per meter. This is the delay factor.

Calculating the total propagation delay incurred by the loop's circumference is achieved by multiplying the length — both transmit and receive — of copper and fiber-optic cabling deployed by the appropriate delay factor. For example, a single 10 km link to an NL_Port would cause a 50 microsecond (10 km x 5 nanoseconds delay factor) propagation delay in each direction and 100 microseconds in total. This equates to 1 MB/s of bandwidth used to satisfy the link.

4.2.12 Bandwidth

For optical interconnects for SANs, the bandwidth requirements are greatly influenced by the capabilities of:

- The system buses
- Network switches
- The interface adapters that interface with them
- Traffic locality

The exact bandwidth required is somewhat dependent on implementation, but are currently in the range of 100 to 1000 MB/s. Determining bandwidth requirements is difficult and there is no exact science that can take into account the unpredictability of sporadic bursts of data, for example. Planning bandwidth based on peak requirements could be wasteful. Designing for sustained bandwidth requirements, with the addition of safety margins, may be less wasteful.

4.3 Switched fabric

The third topology used in SAN implementations is Fibre Channel Switched Fabric (FC-SW). A Fibre Channel fabric is one or more fabric switches in a single, sometimes extended, configuration. Switched fabrics provide full 100MB/s bandwidth per port, compared to the shared bandwidth per port in Arbitrated Loop implementations.

If you add a new device into the arbitrated loop, you further divide the shared bandwidth. However, in a switched fabric, adding a new device or a new connection between existing ones actually increases the bandwidth. For example, an 8-port switch with three initiators and three targets can support three concurrent 100 MB/s conversations or a total 300 MB/s throughput (600 MB/s if full-duplex applications were available). A switched fabric configuration is shown in Figure 44.

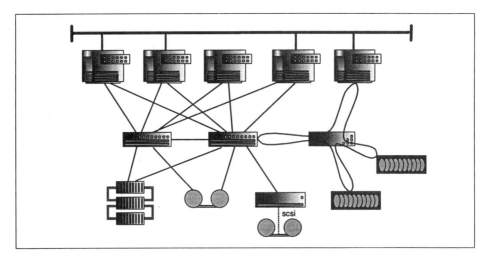

Figure 44. Sample switched fabric configuration

4.3.1 Addressing

As we know from 3.11, "Naming and addressing" on page 66, each participant in the Fibre Channel environment has a unique ID. This ID is called the World Wide Name (WWN). This WWN is a 64-bit address and if two WWN addresses are put into the frame header, this leaves 16 bytes of data just for identifying destination and source address. So 64-bit addresses can impact routing performance.

Because of this there is another addressing scheme used in Fibre Channel networks. This scheme is used to address the ports in the switched fabric. Each port in the switched fabric has its own unique 24-bit address. With this 24-bit addressing scheme we get a smaller frame header and this can speed up the routing process. With this frame header and routing logic the Fibre Channel fabric is optimized for high-speed switching of frames.

With a 24-bit addressing scheme this allows for up to 16 million addresses, which is an address space larger than any practical SAN design in existence in today's world. Who knows what the future will bring? Maybe Fibre Channel addressing will have the same problems in the future as the internet does today, which is a lack of addresses. This 24-bit addressing has to be connected with the 64-bit addressing associated with World Wide Names. We explain this in the section that follows.

4.3.2 Name and addressing

The 24-bit address scheme also removes the overhead of manual administration of addresses by allowing the topology itself to assign addresses. This is not like WWN addressing, in which the addresses are assigned to the manufacturers by the IEEE standards committee, and are built in to the device at build time, similar to naming a child at birth. If the topology itself assigns the 24-bit addresses, then somebody has to be responsible for the addressing scheme from WWN addressing to port addressing.

In the switched fabric environment, the switch itself is responsible for assigning and maintaining the port addresses. When the device with its WWN is logging into the switch on a specific port, the switch will assign the port address to that port and the switch will also maintain the correlation between the port address and the WWN address of the device on that port. This function of the switch is implemented by using a Simple Name Server (SNS).

The Simple Name Server is a component of the fabric operating system, which runs inside the switch. It is essentially a database of objects in which fabric-attached device registers its values.

Dynamic addressing also removes the potential element of human error in address maintenance, and provides more flexibility in additions, moves, and changes in the SAN.

4.3.2.1 Port address
A 24-bit port address consists of three parts:

- Domain (bits from 23 to 16)
- Area (bits from 15 to 08)
- Port or arbitrated loop physical address - AL_PA (bits from 07 to 00)

We show how the address is built up in Figure 45.

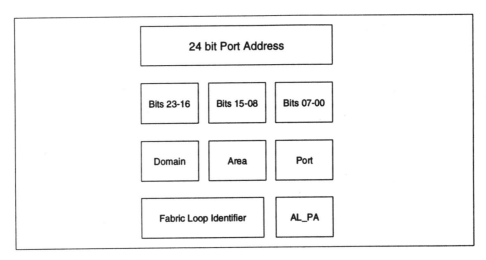

Figure 45. Fabric port address

We explain the significance of some of the bits that make up the port address in the following sections.

Domain

The most significant byte of the port address is the domain. This is the address of the switch itself. One byte allows up to 256 possible addresses. Because some of these are reserved (like the one for broadcast) there are only 239 addresses actually available. This means that you can have as many as 239 switches in your SAN environment. The domain number allows each switch to have a unique identifier if you have multiple interconnected switches in your environment.

Area

The area field provides 256 addresses. This part of the address is used to identify the individual FL_Ports supporting loops or it can be used as the identifier for a group of F_Ports; for example, a card with more ports on it. This means that each group of ports has a different area number, even if there is only one port in the group.

Port

The final part of the address provides 256 addresses for identifying attached N_Ports and NL_Ports.

To arrive at the number of available addresses is a simple calculation based on:

Domain x Area x Ports

This means that there are 239 x 256 x 256 = 15,663,104 addresses available.

4.3.3 Fabric login

After the fabric capable Fibre Channel device is attached to a fabric switch, it will carry out a fabric login (FLOGI).

Similar to port login, FLOGI is an extended link service command that sets up a session between two participants. With FLOGI a session is created between an N_Port or NL_Port and the switch. An N_Port will send a FLOGI frame that contains its Node Name, its N_Port Name, and service parameters to a well-known address of 0xFFFFFE.

A public loop NL_Port first opens the destination AL_PA 0x00 before issuing the FLOGI request. In both cases the switch accepts the login and returns an accept (ACC) frame to the sender. If some of the service parameters requested by the N_Port or NL_Port are not supported, the switch will set the appropriate bits in the ACC frame to indicate this.

When the N_Port logs in it uses a 24-bit port address of 0x000000. Because of this the fabric is allowed to assign the appropriate port address to that device, based on the Domain-Area-Port address format. The newly assigned address is contained in the ACC response frame.

When the NL_Port logs in a similar process starts, except that the least significant byte is used to assign AL_PA and the upper two bytes constitute a fabric loop identifier. Before an NL_Port logs in it will go through the LIP on the loop, which is started by the FL_Port, and from this process it has already derived an AL_PA. The switch then decides if it will accept this AL_PA for this device or not. If not a new AL_PA is assigned to the NL_Port, which then causes the start of another LIP. This ensures that the switch assigned AL_PA does not conflict with any previously selected AL_PAs on the loop.

After the N_Port or public NL_Port gets its fabric address from FLOGI, it needs to register with the SNS. This is done with port login (PLOGI) at the address 0xFFFFFC. The device may register values for all or just some database objects, but the most useful are its 24-bit port address, 64-bit Port Name (WWPN), 64-bit Node Name (WWN), class of service parameters, FC-4 protocols supported, and port type, such as N_Port or NL_Port.

4.3.4 Private devices on NL_Ports

It is easy to explain how the port to World Wide Name address resolution works when a single device from an N_Port is connected to an F_Port, or when a public NL_Port device is connected to FL_Port in the switch. The SNS will add an entry for the device World Wide Name and connects that with the port address which is selected from the selection of free port addresses for that switch. Problems may arise when a private Fibre Channel device is attached to the switch. Private Fibre Channel devices were designed to only to work in private loops.

When the arbitrated loop is connected to the FL_Port, this port obtains the highest priority address in the loop to which it is attached (0x00). Then the FL_Port performs a LIP. After this process is completed, the FL_Port registers all devices on the loop with the SNS. Devices on the arbitrated loop use only 8-bit addressing, but in the switched fabric, 24-bit addressing is used. When the FL_Port registers the devices on the loop to the SNS, it adds two most significant bytes to the existing 8-bit address.

The format of the address in the SNS table is 0xPPPPLL, where the PPPP is the two most significant bytes of the FL_Port address and the LL is the device ID on the arbitrated loop which is connected to this FL_Port. Modifying the private loop address in this fashion, all private devices can now talk to all public devices, and all public devices can talk to all private devices.

Because we have stated that private devices can only talk to devices with private addresses, some form of translation must take place. We show an example of this in Figure 46.

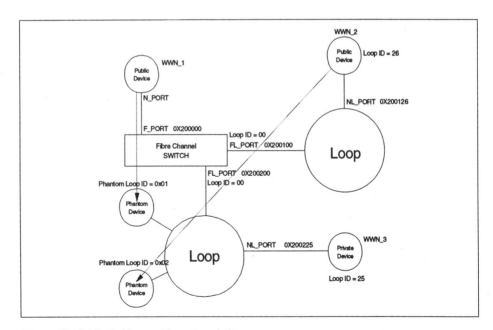

Figure 46. Arbitrated loop address translation

As you can see, we have three devices connected to the switch:

- Public device N_Port with WWN address WWN_1 on F_Port with the port address 0x200000
- Public device NL_Port with WWN address WWN_2 on FL_Port with the port address 0x200100. The device has AL_PA 0x26 on the loop which is attached on the FL_Port
- Private device NL_Port with WWN address WWN_3 on FL_Port with the port address 0x200200. The device has AL_PA 0x25 on the loop which is attached to the FL_Port

After all FLOGI and PLOGI functions are performed the SNS will have the entries shown in Table 3.

Table 3. Simple name server entries

24 bit port address	WWN	FL_Port address
0x200000	WWN_1	n/a
0x200126	WWN_2	0x200100
0x200225	WWN_3	0x200200

We now explain some possible scenarios.

Public N_Port device accesses private NL_Port device
The communication from device to device starts with PLOGI to establish a session. When a public N_Port device wants to perform a PLOGI to a private NL_Port device, the FL_Port on which this private device exists will assign a "phantom" private address to the public device. This phantom address is known only inside this loop, and the switch keeps track of the assignments.

In our example, when the WWN_1 device wants to talk to the WWN_3 device, the following, shown in Table 4, is created in the switch.

Table 4. Phantom addresses

Switch port address	Phantom Loop Port ID
0x200000	0x01
0x200126	0x02

When the WWN_1 device enters into the loop it represents itself with AL_PA ID 0x01 (its phantom address). All private devices on that loop use this ID to talk to that public device. The switch itself acts as a proxy, and translates addresses in both directions.

Usually the number of phantom addresses is limited, and this number of phantom addresses decreases the number of devices allowed in the Arbitrated loop. For example, if the number of phantom addresses is 32 this limits the number of physical devices in the loop to 126 - 32 = 94.

Public N_Port device accesses public NL_Port device
If an N_Port public device wants to access an NL_Port public device, it simply performs a PLOGI with the whole 24-bit address.

Private NL_Port device accesses public N_Port or NL_Port device
When a private device needs to access a remote public device, it uses the public device's phantom address. When the FL_Port detects the use of a phantom AL_PA ID, it translates that to a switch port ID using its translation table similar to that shown in Table 4.

4.3.5 QuickLoop

As we have already explained above, private devices can cooperate in the fabric using translative mode. However, if you have a private host (server), this is not possible. To solve this, switch vendors, including IBM, support a QuickLoop feature. The QuickLoop feature allows the whole switch or just a set of ports to operate as an arbitrated loop. In this mode, devices connected to the switch do not perform a fabric login, and the switch itself will emulate the loop for those devices. All public devices can still see all private devices on the QuickLoop in the translative mode. This is described in 4.3.4, "Private devices on NL_Ports" on page 84.

4.3.6 Switching mechanism and performance

In a switched fabric, a "cut-through" switching mechanism is used. This is not unique to switched fabrics and it is also used in Ethernet switches. The function is to speed packet routing from port to port.

When a frame enters the switch, cut-through logic examines only the link level destination ID of the frame. Based on the destination ID, a routing decision is made, and the frame is switched to the appropriate port by internal routing logic contained in the switch. It is this cut-through which increases performance by reducing the time required to make a routing decision. The reason for this is that the destination ID resides in the first four bytes of the frame header, and this allows the cut-through to be accomplished quickly. A routing decision can be made at the instant the frame enters the switch.

An important criterion in selecting a switch is the number of frames that can be buffered on the port. During periods of high activity and frame movement, the switch may not be able to transmit a frame to its intended destination.

This is true if two ports are sending data to the same destination. Given this situation, but depending on the class of service, the switch may sacrifice the frames it is not able to process. Not only does frame buffering reduce this likelihood, it also enhances performance.

Another great performance improvement can be realized in the way in which the 24-bit port address is built. Because the address is divided into domain, area and port, it is possible to make the routing decision on a single byte. An example of this would be if the domain number of the destination address indicates that the frame is intended for a different switch, the routing process can forward the frame to the appropriate interconnection without the need to process the entire 24-bit address and the associated overhead.

4.3.7 Data path in switched fabric

A complex switched fabric can be created by interconnecting Fibre Channel switches. Switch to switch connections are performed by E_Port connections. This mean that if you want to interconnect switches they need to support E_Ports. Switches may also support multiple E_Port connections to expand the bandwidth.

In such a configuration with interconnected switches, known as a meshed topology, multiple paths from one N_Port to another can exist.

An example of a meshed topology is shown in Figure 47.

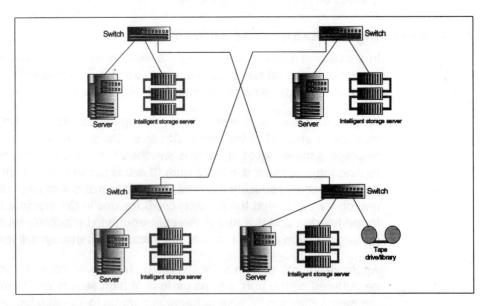

Figure 47. Meshed topology switched fabric

4.3.7.1 Spanning tree

In case of failure, it is important to consider having an alternative path between source and destination available. This will allow the data still to reach its destination. However, having different paths available could lead to the delivery of frames being out of the order of transmission, due to a frame taking a different path and arriving earlier than one of its predecessors.

A solution to this, which can be incorporated into the meshed fabric, is called a spanning tree and is an IEEE 802.1 standard. This means that switches keep to certain paths as the spanning tree protocol will block certain paths to produce a simply connected active topology. Then the shortest path in terms of hops is used to deliver the frames and, most importantly, only one path is active at a time. This means that all associated frames go over the same path to the destination. The paths that are blocked can be held in reserve and used only if, for example, a primary path fails. The fact that one path is active at a time means that in the case of a meshed fabric, all frames will arrive in the expected order.

4.3.7.2 Path selection

For path selection, link state protocols are popular and extremely effective in today's networks. Examples of link state protocol are OSPF for IP and PNNI for ATM.

The most commonly used path selection protocol is Fabric Shortest Path First (FSPF). This type of path selection is usually performed at boot time and no configuration is needed. All paths are established at start time and only if the inter switch link (ISL) is broken or added will reconfiguration take place.

In the case that multiple paths are available if the primary path goes down, the traffic will be rerouted to another path. If the route fails this can lead to congestion of frames, and any new frames delivered over the new path could potentially arrive at the destination first. This will cause an out of sequence delivery.

One possible solution for this is to prevent the activation of the new route for a while, (this can be configured from milliseconds to a few seconds), so the congested frames are either delivered or rejected. Obviously, this can slow down the routing, so it should only be used when the devices connected to the fabric are not in a position to, or cannot tolerate occasional out of order delivery. For instance, video can tolerate out of sequence delivery, but financial and commercial data cannot.

But today, Fibre Channel devices are much more sophisticated, and this is a feature that is not normally required. FSPF allows a fabric still to benefit from load balancing the delivery of frames by using multiple paths.

4.3.7.3 Route definition

Routes are usually dynamically defined. The fabric itself usually keeps only eight possible paths to the destination.

Static routes can also be defined. In the event that a static route fails, a dynamic route will take over. Once the static route becomes available, frames will return to utilizing that route.

If dynamic paths are used, FSPF path selection is used. This guarantees that only the shortest and fastest paths will be used for delivering the frames.

We show an example of FSPF in Figure 48.

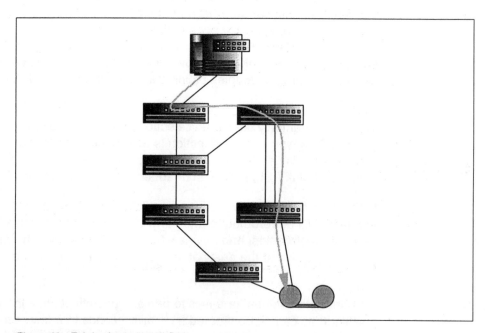

Figure 48. Fabric shortest path first

4.3.8 Adding new devices

Switched fabrics, by their very nature, are dynamic environments. They can handle topology changes as new devices are attached, or previously active devices are removed or taken offline. For these reasons it is important that notification of these types of events can be provided to participants (nodes) in the switched fabric.

Notification is provided by two functions:

- State Change Notification - SCN
- Registered State Change Notification - RSCN

These two functions are not obligatory, so each N_Port or NL_Port must register its interest in being notified of any topology changes, or if another device alters its state.

The original SCN service allowed an N_Port to send a notification change directly to another N_Port. This is not necessarily an optimum solution, as no other participants on the fabric will know about this change. RSCN offers a solution to this and will inform all registered devices about the change.

Perhaps the most important change that you would want to be notified about, is when an existing device goes offline. This information is very meaningful for participants which communicate with that device. For example, a server in the fabric environment would want to know if their resources are powered off or removed, or as and when new resources became available for its use.

Changed notification provides the same functionality for the switched fabric as loop initialization provides for arbitrated loop.

4.3.9 Zoning

Zoning allows for finer segmentation of the switched fabric. Zoning can be used to instigate a barrier between different environments. Only the members of the same zone can communicate within that zone and all other attempts from outside are rejected.

For example, it may be desirable to separate a Windows NT environment from a UNIX environment. This is very useful because of the manner in which Windows attempts to claim all available storage for itself. Because not all storage devices are capable of protecting their resources from any host seeking for available resources, it makes sound business sense to protect the environment in another manner.

Looking at zoning in this way, it could also be considered as a security feature and not just for separating environments. Zoning could also be used for test and maintenance purposes. For example, not many enterprises will mix their test and maintenance environments with their production environment. Within a fabric, you could easily separate your test environment from your production bandwidth allocation on the same fabric using zoning.

We show an example of zoning in Figure 49.

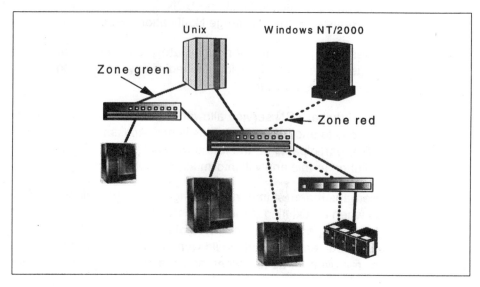

Figure 49. Zoning

Zoning also introduces the flexibility to manage a switched fabric to meet different user groups objectives.

4.3.10 Implementing zoning

Zoning can be implemented in two ways:

- Hardware zoning
- Software zoning

Hardware zoning

Hardware zoning is based on the physical fabric port number. The members of a zone are physical ports on the fabric switch. It can be implemented in the following configurations:

- One to one
- One to many
- Many to many

A single port can also belong to multiple zones. We show an example of hardware zoning in Figure 50.

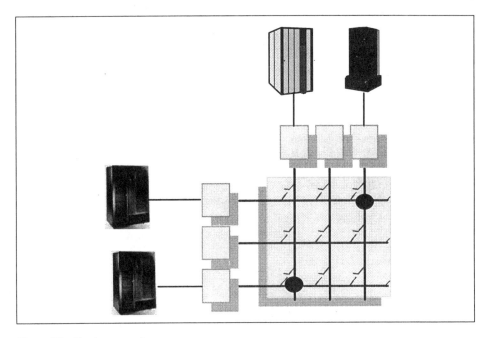

Figure 50. Hardware zoning

One of the disadvantages of hardware zoning is that devices have to be connected to a specific port, and the whole zoning configuration could become unusable when the device is connected to a different port. In cases where the device connections are not permanent the use of software zoning is recommended.

The advantage of hardware zoning is that it can be implemented into a routing engine by filtering. As a result, this kind of zoning has a very low impact on the performance of the routing process.

Software zoning

Software zoning is implemented within the SNS running inside the fabric switch. When using software zoning the members of the zone can be defined with:

- Node WWN
- Port WWN

Usually zoning software also allows you to create symbolic names for the zone members and for the zones themselves.

The number of members possible in a zone is limited only by the amount of memory in the fabric switch. A member can belong to multiple zones. You can define multiple sets of zones for the fabric, but only one set can be active at any time. You can activate another zone set any time you want, without the need to power down the switch.

With software zoning there is no need to worry about the physical connections to the switch. If you use WWNs for the zone members, even when a device is connected to another physical port, it will still remain in the same zoning definition, because the device's WWN remains the same.

There is a potential security leak with software zoning. When a specific host logs into the fabric and asks for available storage devices, the SNS will look into the software zoning table to see which storage devices are allowable for that host. The host will only see the storage devices defined in the software zoning table. But the host can also make a direct connection to the storage device, while doing device discovery, without asking SNS for the information it has.

> **Note**
>
> For maximum security, hardware zoning is recommended. But as the standards are evolving and the industry is following them, it is likely that in the future, software zoning will probably be the preferred solution.

4.3.11 LUN masking

Another approach to securing storage devices from hosts wishing to take over already assigned resources is logical unit number (LUN) masking. Every storage device offers its resources to the hosts by means of LUNs. For example, each partition in the storage server has its own LUN. If the host (server) wants to access the storage, it needs to request access to the LUN in the storage device. The purpose of LUN masking is to control access to the LUNs. The storage device itself accepts or rejects access requests from different hosts.

The user defines which hosts can access which LUN by means of the storage device control program. Whenever the host accesses a particular LUN, the storage device will check its access list for that LUN, and it will allow or disallow access to the LUN.

4.3.12 Expanding the fabric

As the demand for the storage grows, a switched fabric can be expanded to service these needs. Not all storage requirements can be satisfied with fabrics alone. For some applications, the 100 MB/s per port and advanced services are overkill, and they amount to wasted bandwidth and unnecessary cost. When you design a storage network you need to consider the application's needs and not just rush to implement the latest technology available. SANs are often combinations of switched fabric and arbitrated loops.

4.3.12.1 Cascading

Expanding the fabric is called switch cascading. Cascading is basically interconnecting Fibre Channel switches. The cascading of switches provides the following benefits to a SAN environment:

- The fabric can be seamlessly extended. Additional switches can be added to the fabric, without powering down existing fabric.

- You can easily increase the distance between various SAN participants.

- By adding more switches to the fabric, you increase connectivity by providing more available ports.

- Cascading provides high resilience in the fabric.

- With Inter Switch Links (ISL) you can increase the bandwidth. The frames between the switches are delivered over all available data paths. So the more ISL you create, the faster the frame delivery will be, but careful consideration must be employed to ensure that a bottleneck is not introduced.

- When the fabric grows, the SNS is fully distributed across all the switches in fabric.

- With cascading, you also provide greater fault tolerance within the fabric.

4.3.12.2 Hops

As we stated in 4.3.2, "Name and addressing" on page 82, the maximum number of switches allowed in the fabric is 239. The other limitation is that only seven hops are allowed between any source and destination. However, this is likely to change between vendors and over time.

We show a sample configuration that illustrates this in Figure 51.

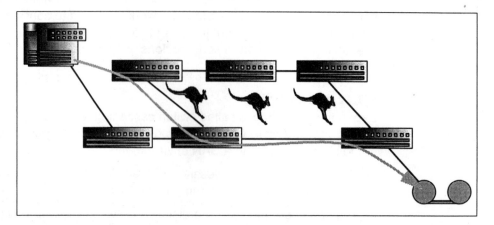

Figure 51. Cascading in switched fabric

The hop count limit is set by the fabric operating system and is used to derive a frame holdtime value for each switch. This holdtime value is the maximum amount of time that a frame can be held in a switch before it is dropped (Class 3) or the fabric is busy (F_BSY, Class 2) is returned. A frame would be held if its destination port is not available. The holdtime is derived from a formula using the error detect time-out value (E_D_TOV) and the resource allocation time-out value (R_A_TOV).

The value of seven hops is not 'hard-coded', and if manipulation of E_D_TOV or R_A_TOV was to take place, the reasonable limit of seven hops could be exceeded. However, be aware that this seven hop suggestion was not a limit that was arrived at without careful consideration of a number of factors. In the future the number of hops is likely to increase.

Chapter 5. Fibre Channel products

This chapter describes the Fibre Channel products which are used and are likely to be encountered in an IBM Enterprise SAN implementation. This does not mean that you cannot implement other SAN compatible products, including those from other vendors.

5.1 Fiber optic interconnects

In Fibre Channel technology, frames are moved from source to destination using Gigabit transport, which is a requirement to achieve fast transfer rates. To communicate with Gigabit transport, both sides have to support this type of communication. This can be accomplished by installing this feature into the device or by using specially designed interfaces which can convert other communication transport into Gigabit transport. Gigabit transport can be used in a copper or fiber-optic infrastructure. We recommend that you consider using a fiber-optic implementation if you need to avoid the distance limitation of 30 meters with copper, or are likely to in the future.

The interfaces that are used to convert the internal communication transport of Gigabit transport are named Gigabit Interface Converters (GBIC), Gigabit Link Modules (GLM), 1x9 Transceivers and Media Interface Adapters (MIA). We provide a brief description of their functions in the topics that follow.

5.1.1 Gigabit Interface Converters

Gigabit interface converters are data communication transceivers which convert data coming in from the device on one side to an optical signal on the other side. GBICs can be used for Fibre Channel, Gigabit Ethernet and 1394b applications. The devices usually supply a differential serial data signal as input and the GBIC converts this signal into an optical or copper signal. As we stated before, if you need to achieve long distances, you should use fiber-optic as the transport layer.

If the GBIC is receiving an optical signal, this signal is then converted to an electrical signal which is delivered to the host device as a differential serial data signal. The data format on the device side is standardized to 8b/10b. There are two types of connection on the service side:

- DB-9
- HSSDC

Cables are connected with industry-standard SC connectors.

On the optical side there are two modes of operation. The difference between them is in the laser wave length. The two modes are:

- ShortWave mode - SW
- LongWave mode - LW

The distances that can be achieved are shown in Table 5.

Table 5. Distances using fiber-optic

Type of fiber	SW	LW
9 micron optical fiber	n/a	10 km
50 micron optical fiber	2 - 500 m	2 - 550 m
62.5 micron optical fiber	2 - 175 m	2 - 550 m

GBICs are usually hot pluggable, easy to configure and replace. On the optical side they use low-loss, SC type, push-pull, optical connectors. They are mainly used in:

- Hubs
- Switches
- Gateways

The transfer rates are from 1063 MB/s and above. A GBIC is shown in Figure 52.

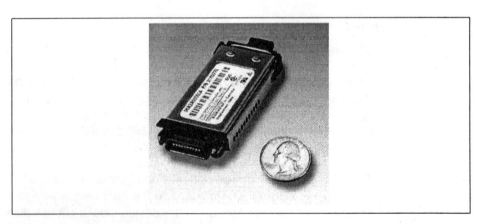

Figure 52. Gigabit Interface Converter

The selection of a GBIC for SAN interconnection is just as important a consideration as choosing a hub or a switch and should not be overlooked or taken lightly.

5.1.2 Gigabit Link Modules

Gigabit Link Modules (sometimes referred to as Gigabaud Link Modules) were used in early Fibre Channel applications. GLMs are a low cost alternative to GBICs, but they sacrifice the ease of use and hot pluggable installation and replacement characteristics that GBICs offer. This means that you need to power down the device for maintenance, replacement, or repair.

GLMs enable computer manufacturers to integrate low-cost, high-speed fiber-optic communications into devices. They use the same fiber-optic for the transport of optical signal as GBICs. GLMs also use two types of lasers, ShortWave and LongWave, to transport the information across the fiber-optic channel. The transfer rates that are available are 266 MB/s and 1063 MB/s.

The 266 MB/s and 1063 MB/s GLM cards support continuous, full-duplex communication. The GLM converts encoded data that has been serialized into pulses of laser light for transmission into the optical fiber. A GLM at a second optical link, running at the same speed as the sending GLM, receives these pulses, along with the requisite synchronous clocking signals.

With 1063 MB/s you can achieve the distances shown in Table 5.

A GLM is shown in Figure 53.

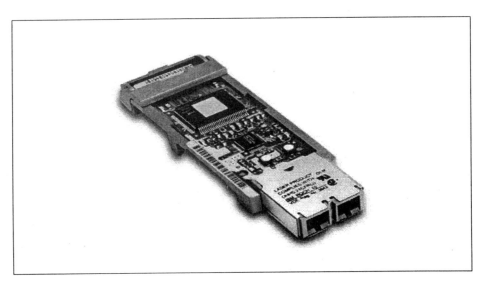

Figure 53. Gigabit Link Module

5.1.3 Media Interface Adapters

Media Interface Adapters can be used to facilitate conversion between optical and copper interface connections. Typically, MIAs are attached to host bus adapters, but they can also be used with switches and hubs. If a hub or switch only supports copper or optical connections, MIAs can be used to convert the signal to the appropriate media type, copper or optical.

A MIA is shown in Figure 54.

Figure 54. Media Interface Adapter

5.1.4 1x9 Transceivers

Some of the switch manufacturers prefer to use 1x9 transceivers for providing SC connection to their devices. 1x9 transceivers have some advantages over GBICs which are the most widely used in switch implementations:

- Easier to cool
- Better air flow
- More reliable (2.5 times that of a GBIC)

We show a picture of 1x9 transceivers in Figure 55.

Figure 55. 1x9 Transceivers

5.2 Host bus adapters

Host bus adapters (HBAs) are used to connect server or storage devices to the Fibre Channel (FC) network. HBAs control the electrical protocol for communications. Several variations are possible depending on:

- Type of cable supported: single or multi-mode fiber, copper

- Fibre Topology support: point-to-point, loop, switch attachment capabilities

- Protocol support: FCP-SCSI, IP, and SCSI concurrently; other FC-4 protocols: IPI-3, SB-2

IBM has announced two FC adapters:

- The Netfinity Fibre Channel PCI Adapter, which is in fact the Qlogic 2100F adapter.

- The RS/6000 (TM) Giga Fibre Channel Adapter for PCI Bus (FC #6227), which is the Emulex LP7000 adapter.

- IBM has also announced, as part of the IBM Fibre Channel RAID Storage Server announcement, support for FC Adapters on SUN and HP UNIX servers.

- The Qlogic 2100F adapter is also available for non-Netfinity Windows NT hosts.

You can reach the Qlogic Web page at:

www.qlc.com

You can reach the Emulex Web page at:

www.emulex.com

These two FC adapters have the characteristics shown in Table 6.

Table 6. FC adapter characteristics

Adapter	Topologies	Cabling	Protocols
RS/6000 Giga Fibre Adapter for PCI	Point-to-point Arbitrated loop Switch fabric	Fiber Copper	SCSI FCP
Netfinity Fibre Channel PCI Adapter	Arbitrated loop	Fiber	SCSI

A pair of HBAs are shown in Figure 56.

Figure 56. Host Bus Adapters

5.3 Hubs

Fibre Channel Hubs are used to implement Fibre Channel arbitrated loop (FC-AL) connections. The three most common implementations of hubs are:

- Unmanaged hubs
- Managed hubs
- Switched hubs

We describe these hubs in the following sections.

5.3.1 Unmanaged hubs

Fibre Channel Hubs are seen as entry level components for the SAN fabric. Usually they are used for homogeneous server failover applications. They can also be used to extend distance, for example, to enable extended distance disaster recovery.

IBM offers the IBM Fibre Channel Storage Hub (2103-H07) in the unmanaged hubs arena. It was announced on February 16, 1999, as part of the IBM Fibre Channel RAID Storage Server announcement.

The specification sheet can be viewed at:

www.storage.ibm.com/hardsoft/products/fchub/fchub.htm

It is also part of the IBM Netfinity Fibre Channel Storage Solutions.

The IBM Fibre Channel Storage Hub, which allows for up to a 7-port central interconnection for FC-AL, adheres to the ANSI FC-AL standard. Each Fibre Channel Storage Hub port receives serial data from an attached node and retransmits the data out of the next hub port to the next node attached in the loop. Each reception includes data regeneration (both signal timing and amplitude), supporting full-distance optical links.

The Fibre Channel Storage Hub detects any loop node that is missing or is inoperative and automatically routes the data to the next operational port and attached node in the loop.

Each port requires a Gigabit Interface Converter (GBIC) to connect to each attached node. The FC Storage Hub provides four short-wave optical GBIC ports, and the option to add up to three additional long-wave or short-wave optical GBIC ports.

The GBICs are hot-pluggable into the Fibre Channel Storage Hub, which means that you can add servers and storage devices to the arbitrated loop dynamically, without powering off the Fibre Channel Storage Hub or any connected devices. If you remove a GBIC from a Fibre Channel Storage Hub, that port is automatically bypassed. Conversely, if you plug a GBIC into the Fibre Channel Storage Hub, it will automatically be inserted and become a node on the loop.

Hubs can also be used as distance extenders, in connection with the IBM SAN Data Gateway.

You can see the IBM Fibre Channel Hub in Figure 57.

Figure 57. IBM Fibre Channel Hub

5.3.2 Managed hubs

Fibre Channel managed hubs are also viewed as entry level components of a SAN fabric. They are similar to non-managed hubs in their function, but they have in built software to manage them. Because of their manageability, they offer better fault isolation, planning and controlling. Usually they are used for entry level homogeneous server implementations. Some of the possible uses of these hubs are clustering, LAN-free backup, storage consolidation and remote disk mirroring. IBM offers the IBM Fibre Channel Managed Hub (3534-1RU).

More information and the specifications are available at:

www.pc.ibm.com/ww/netfinity/san

The Fibre Channel managed Hub is also part of IBM's Netfinity Fibre Channel Storage Solutions.

The IBM Fibre Channel Managed Hub offers eight hot-pluggable FC-AL ports. The loop can be extended by cascading the hubs and by connection to IBM Fibre Channel Switches. Unlike other products where the 100 MB/s transfer rate is shared among all the ports in the IBM Fibre Channel Managed Hub, all ports have pure 100 MB/s transfer rate. The non-blocking architecture guarantees full-speed data delivery irrespective of traffic conditions.

Managed hubs are designed as field replaceable units (FRUs) to provide optimal price performance. Highly reliable components, continuous monitoring of environmental components (fan status and temperature), and a streamlined design maximize the hub's reliability. Power-on self test (POST) and online diagnostics allow monitoring and thorough port-level testing while the hub is running. Per-port statistics help in diagnosing and isolating problem ports. A port can be removed from a loop, and the hub will continue to operate. Embedded port-monitoring facilities automatically disable failing ports and restart them when the problem has cleared.

Hot-pluggable ports enable the attachment of new systems without requiring server downtime. Seven ports incorporate fixed short wave laser optical media for device interconnection at a maximum distance of Fibre Channel Managed Hub of 500 meters. A single GBIC slot accommodates an optional GBIC, which supports either short wave or long wave laser fibre optic cabling with a maximum distance of 10 km.

The Managed Hub provides a single FC-AL loop. This simple loop configuration can be expanded by cascading to another Managed Hub. The Managed Hub may also be interconnected with the IBM SAN Fibre Channel Switch for more advanced SAN requirements.

Configuration management is performed using a command line interface or the graphical administrative capability offered by the StorWatch Fibre Channel Managed Hub Specialist.

A picture of the IBM Fibre Channel Managed Hub is shown in Figure 58.

Figure 58. IBM Fibre Channel Managed Hub

5.3.3 Switched hubs

Fibre Channel switched hubs can also cover the same SAN fabric implementations as unmanaged and managed hubs. The main differentiation is the speed of the intercommunication between the ports in the hub. In Fibre Channel switched hubs each port uses a fixed, dedicated amount of bandwidth. In the case of Fibre Channel switched hubs, this is 100 MB/s. Usually Fibre Channel switched hubs are also manageable. IBM does not have any special product in this segment, because the IBM Fibre Channel Managed Hub is also a switched hub. Refer to 5.3.2, "Managed hubs" on page 104 for more information.

5.4 Fabric switches

Fibre Channel switches are used to implement a Fibre Channel fabric topology. Fibre Channel fabric can consist of point to point and Fibre Channel arbitrated loop connections to Fibre Channel switches. Switches can also be cascaded for creating high availability and larger topologies. Fibre Channel switches can be used in entry level enterprise heterogeneous implementations, and also in the largest of enterprise environments. Any Fibre Channel enabled device can be connected to any Fibre Channel switch.

5.4.1 IBM SAN Fibre Channel Switch

The IBM SAN Fibre Channel Switch offers two models, an 8-port and a 16-port model (2109-S08 and 2109-S16 respectively). It uses a non-blocking switch architecture, therefore, delivering multiple, concurrent 100 MB/s connections.

The IBM SAN Fibre Channel Switch supports the following types of Fibre Channel connections:

- Fabric (F_Port)
- Arbitrated Loop — public and private (FL_Port)
- Interswitch Connection (E_Port)
  - At this moment in time, only same vendor switch interconnection is available.

The IBM Fibre Channel Switch also provides advanced management capabilities for:

- Automatic discovery and registration of host and storage devices
- Intelligent re-routing of connection paths, should a port problem occur

Other features of the IBM Fibre Channel Switch include:

- A Web browser interface to help you configure and manage the switch

- Cascading of switches, for scaling to larger configurations and to provide resiliency for high data availability

- An option for a second power supply

- Configuration with hot pluggable port GBICs for shortwave or longwave optical connections of up to 10 kilometers

The IBM Fibre Channel Switch supports attachments to multiple host systems:

- IBM Netfinity and Intel-based servers running Microsoft's **Windows NT** or Novell Netware

- IBM RS/6000 running AIX

- SUN servers running Solaris

The SAN connectivity products and storage systems that can be attached are:

- IBM SAN Data Gateway with IBM Magstar and Magstar MP libraries, and the IBM Versatile Storage Server

- IBM DLT tape libraries

- IBM Fibre Channel Hub and Netfinity Channel Hub

- IBM Fibre Channel RAID Storage Server and the Netfinity **Fibre Channel** RAID Controller Unit

We show a picture of both the IBM Fibre Channel Switches in **Figure 59.**

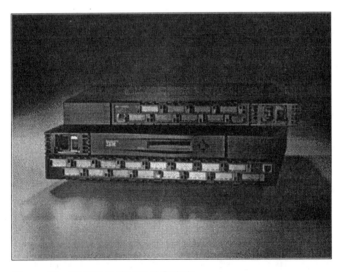

Figure 59. IBM Fibre Channel Switch

More information and product specifications are available at:

www.storage.ibm.com/hardsoft/products/fcswitch/fcswitch.htm

5.4.2 McDATA Enterprise Fibre Channel Director

For high end e-business and other mission-critical business applications, IBM offers the McDATA Enterprise Fibre Channel Director (ED-5000 or IBM 2032-001). The Fibre Channel Director offers 32 port switching capability.

Each port delivers 100 MB/s, full-duplex data transfer. Industry-leading 3,200 MB/s transmission bandwidth supports full non-blocking 32-port switch performance.

The Fibre Channel Director is based upon the IBM ESCON Director which, over a number of years has provided industry leading data availability, performance and the data integrity required by the most demanding data centers.

The McDATA Enterprise Fibre Channel Director supports the following types of Fibre Channel connections:

- Fabric (F_Port)
- Interswitch Connection (E_Port)

The McDATA Enterprise Fibre Channel Director offers excellent redundancy and maintenance capabilities such as:

- All active components are redundant
- Active components provide support for automatic failover
- Redundant power and cooling
- Hot swapping of all field replacable units
- Automatic fault detection and isolation
- Non-disruptive firmware updates

The Fibre Channel Director offers multiple configuration options for Fibre Channel connectivity. There can be up to eight four port cards in each Fibre Channel Director combining together to total 32 ports. The port cards can have the following configurations:

- All four ports with short-wave laser
- All four ports with long-wave laser
- Combo card with three short-wave and one long-wave laser

All ports are hot-pluggable.

Cascading using the E_Port is supported up to a maximum of four directors and two hops.

The McDATA Enterprise Fibre Channel Director also offers advanced management capabilities:

- Enterprise Fabric Connectivity (EFC) Management provides centralized control for managing multiple, distributed Fibre Channel Directors in an enterprise-wide Fibre Channel fabric

- EFC Management can be operated remotely from anywhere using Java based software
- EFC Management is designed to add managed Fibre Channel Directors as the enterprise Fibre Channel fabric grows
- EFC Management tools provide continuous Fibre Channel Director monitoring, logging, and alerting

Each Fibre Channel Director features two Ethernet ports if it is configured in high availability (HA) mode, otherwise one Ethernet port, for access from the LAN for management purposes.

The McDATA Enterprise Fibre Channel Director is shown in Figure 60.

Figure 60. McDATA Enterprise Fibre Channel Director

5.5 Bridges

Fibre Channel bridges in the SAN environment are used to connect and integrate SCSI and SSA legacy devices into the Fibre Channel network. They will allow you to easily migrate from your SCSI or SSA disk subsystem to SAN oriented storage.

IBM offers these products:
- IBM SAN Data Gateway
- IBM SAN Data Gateway Router

- VICOM Fibre Channel SLIC Router

We describe these products in the following sections.

5.5.1 IBM SAN Data Gateway

The IBM SAN Data Gateway (2108-G07) is one of the first components of the IBM SAN solution that allows an easy migration to the SAN environment using Fibre Channel technology. The SAN Data Gateway connects SCSI and Ultra SCSI storage devices to Fibre Channel environments. It attaches new or existing SCSI storage products to the SAN using an industry standard Fibre Channel arbitrated loop (FC-AL) interface. The SAN Data Gateway solves three immediate problems:

- The 25m cable length restriction for SCSI - the cable can extend up to 500m

- The increased bandwidth demand that Ultra SCSI storage products can place on the SCSI bus

- The address limitations of SCSI

IBM Fibre Channel Storage Hubs and Managed Hubs, IBM SAN Fibre Channel Switches and McDATA Enterprise Fibre Channel Directors expand the connectivity options, enabling hundreds of server and storage connections. This any-to-any switched fabric capability supports large and rapidly growing storage consolidation and data sharing requirements.

The use of hubs in SAN configurations increases the device connectivity, but hubs have some impact with respect to multiple hosts on the FC-AL loop. These include loop initialization process and arbitration. If a system is turned off and then on, or rebooted, it might impact the operation of other systems in the FC-AL loop. Many integrators will not support multi-host loop at all.

The use of switches increases the host fan-out which is another way of saying the number of host connections of SAN configurations.

The SAN Data Gateway utilizes Fibre Channel and Ultra SCSI channel bandwidth for high-performance attachment of the following devices:

- IBM Enterprise Storage Server

- IBM Magstar 3590 Tape Subsystem in stand-alone, Magstar 3494 Tape Library, and Magstar 3590 Silo Compatible Tape Subsystem environments

- IBM Magstar MP 3570 Tape Subsystem or Magstar MP 3575 Tape Library Dataserver

- IBM 3502 DLT Tape Library

For the latest and most up-to-date list of supported servers, adapters, disk and tape subsystems on the SAN Data Gateway visit:

www.storage.ibm.com/hardsoft/products/sangateway/supserver.htm

Sharing the Gateway between disk and tape products is currently not supported or practical, because:

- The Enterprise Storage Server needs all the SCSI attachments.
- The levels of the HBA driver required for disk and for tape are different, which makes it impossible to use Gateway-attached disks and tapes on the same host. This will eventually be fixed, but is a nice illustration of an interoperability problem.

The Gateway can either be used as a stand-alone table top unit or mounted in a standard 19" rack. The rack can be either the IBM 2101 Seascape Solutions rack or an industry standard rack.

The SAN Data Gateway is equipped with:

- Four Ultra SCSI Differential ports
- One to six FC-AL short-wave and long-wave ports and Fibre Channel optic cables
- StorWatch SAN Data Gateway Specialist (included on CD)

Features and functions of the SAN Data Gateway

- **SAN connectivity:** Creates reliable SAN solutions without needing hubs, switches and bridges. The SAN Data Gateway provides a distance or connectivity solution for SCSI attached storage devices.
- **Heterogeneous systems and storage:** Provides seamless support for different host platforms and multiple device types.
- **SAN resource sharing:** Zoning or partitioning enables a simple and effective resource sharing solution. Zones are created by controlling the access between different channels or ports and are implemented with the StorWatch SAN Data Gateway Specialist access control function.
- **SAN value added functions:**
  - Supports up to 256 LUNs across multiple interfaces
  - Persistent Address Maps are preserved in non-volatile memory
  - Full awareness of SCSI 3 protocol for disk and tape
  - 'SCSI over TCP' for remote transfer, management and control. SCSI commands and data are encapsulated in TCP packets

- Support for SNIA Extended Copy Command specification; This is the basis for Server-free Backup solutions in the future

- **Transparent SAN performance:** The total bandwidth of the SAN Data Gateway is 120 MB/s; The overall performance is driven by the maximum available device performance.

- **SAN Management:** The SAN Data Gateway is remotely managed and controlled by the StorWatch SAN Data Gateway Specialist.

- **SAN Scalability**

- The SAN Data Gateway is offered with up to **six FC ports** to provide 6x4 configurations.

Zoning or access control

The SAN Data Gateway has the ability to connect to more than one host. In the default configuration, there is no restriction between the channels for access to the target devices. Without additional controls, host operating systems do not handle multiple systems using the same target devices simultaneously. The result is corrupted file systems when two hosts try to use the same disk drives or LUN. Or, tape backup and restore operations might be interrupted. The IBM StorWatch SAN Data Gateway Specialist Channel Access options can be used to disable access between the SAN Connections and individual SCSI channels.

IBM StorWatch SAN Data Gateway Specialist

The SAN Data Gateway provides access between its Fibre Channel ports and its SCSI ports. Channel zoning provides access control between ports. While channel zoning provides control of paths between host adapters and SCSI storage ports, it does not limit access to specific devices (LUNs) within the storage system. Virtual Private SAN (VP SAN) provides "LUN masking" to limit access between host adapters and LUNs attached to SAN Data Gateway SCSI ports. The IBM StorWatch SAN Gateway Specialist, an easy to use graphical user interface, provides the tools to define SAN Data Gateway channel zoning, the VP SAN LUN-masking, and control which host systems have access to specific storage devices.

This Access Control function, also called zoning, partitions the SAN configuration by either allowing or denying access between the FC and SCSI ports of the Gateway.

Figure 61 shows a zoning example for the SAN Data Gateway with two FC ports.

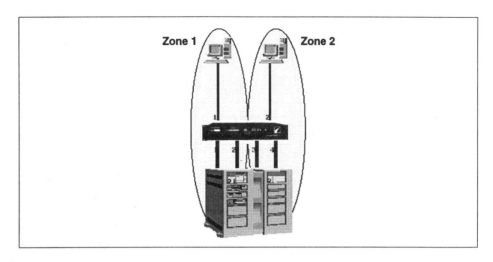

Figure 61. SAN Data Gateway zoning

In this example, we have implemented two zones. Zone 1, with a host on FC adapter 1, sees only the devices attached to SCSI adapter 1 and 2. Zone 2 contains a different host attached to FC adapter 2 and the devices attached to SCSI adapter 3 and 4.

The SAN Data Gateway supports one server per FC-AL adapter in point to point connections. Each host must have its own drives or tape libraries. This means that there is no drive sharing possible at all. To use a drive on a different host requires you to reconfigure the Gateway.

Advantages of SAN Data Gateway versus a hub

- Concurrency - aggregate throughput is not limited to one loop.

- Zoning - access control available based on FC and SCSI ports.

- Hosts are each point-to-point and they can be heterogeneous.

- Smaller configurations with fewer devices lower administration cost for customer and lower service/support cost for IBM (easier to isolate problems).

- Avoids the inherent multi-host issues of the FC-AL loop, such as loop initialization process (LIP) and arbitration. If a system is turned OFF/ON or rebooted it might impact the operation of other systems in the FC-AL loop. Many integrators will not support multi-host loop at all.

Advantages of SAN Data Gateway versus a switch

- Defers or completely avoids the high entry cost of a switch.

- Smaller configurations with fewer devices lower administration cost for customer and lower service/support cost for IBM (easier to isolate problems).
- Interoperability issues with switches: fabric support is limited, resource sharing requires middleware.

The IBM SAN Data Gateway is shown in Figure 62.

Figure 62. IBM SAN Data Gateway

5.5.2 IBM SAN Data Gateway Router

The IBM SAN Data Gateway Router is a SCSI to Fibre Channel protocol converter for tape libraries, with one Fibre Channel adapter and up to two SCSI ports. It is a low-cost solution, compared to the IBM SAN Data Gateway product, which offers up to three FC x four SCSI ports configurations.

The IBM SAN Data Gateway Router (2108-R03) can accommodate either Ultra SCSI single-ended ports or Ultra SCSI differential ports.

The Router supports full mapping of SCSI ids and LUNs between the Fibre Channel attached host and the SCSI tape library. Also, a StorWatch Specialist for centralized configuration and management support is available.

The IBM SAN Data Gateway Router can be attached to an IBM Fibre Channel Switch for extended connectivity.

For supported attachments, refer to:

www.storage.ibm.com/hardsoft/products/tape/ro3superserver.htm

5.5.3 Vicom Fibre Channel SLIC Router

The Vicom Fibre Channel SLIC (Serial Loop IntraConnect) Router Model FC-SL (7139-111) enables all IBM 7133, 7131, and 3527 Serial Disk Systems to attach to host systems using Fibre Channel host adapters and drivers.

The Fibre Channel SLIC Router replicates data across or within serial disk systems — simultaneously mirroring two or three copies of data without host involvement. With global hot disk sparing, data is automatically rebuilt if a mirrored disk fails. In this way, the Fibre Channel SLIC Router improves performance and data availability while simplifying storage operations.

The Instant Copy function can create a separately addressable copy of mirrored data that can be used for tape backup. After the backup has completed, data is re-synchronized with the primary copy. To support remote storage operations, mirrored 7133 Advanced Models D40 or T40 can be separated by up to 10 km with serial storage fiber-optic extenders.

With 36.4 GB disks, logical volume groups or partitions as large as 580 GB can be created for Windows NT servers, which have limited volume addressing. The Fibre Channel SLIC Router can also create composite drives by concatenating up to 16 physical disks. These capabilities provide excellent configuration flexibility for growing storage environments.

Simplified management
The SLIC Manager is a Windows NT based management tool that provides configuration and service functions, including mirror group definition, the ability to create composite drives, and Instant Copy disk management. The SLIC Manager can manage multiple Fibre Channel SLIC Routers across the enterprise.

A highly scalable solution
The Fibre Channel SLIC Router supports up to 64 serial disk drives in a single loop and enables non-disruptive growth in disk capacity from 18.2 GB to 2.3 TB. Up to eight UNIX and Windows NT host systems can be attached to a single loop. Performance scales up as more Fibre Channel SLIC Routers are added to the serial loop.

A standalone, tabletop Fibre Channel SLIC Router unit provides one fibre channel port and two SSA ports. Short- and long-wave laser optical interfaces are supported. An optional rack-mounted enclosure can hold up to four Fibre Channel SLIC Routers in a compact 2U-high space in an industry-standard 19-inch rack.

Fully utilized bandwidth potential

The Fibre Channel SLIC Router enables fibre channel servers to benefit from high-performance, non-arbitrated serial disk technology. The fibre channel host-based adapter views the Fibre Channel SLIC Router as a single FC-AL target, which minimizes loop arbitration overhead. Vicom has measured up to 90 MB/s sustained throughput, or up to 25,000 I/Os per second per logical channel in full-duplex, simultaneous read/write mode.

Investment protection

The 7133 Advanced Model D40 is a key component in the Enterprise Storage Server. You may attach your serial disk to the ESS as your requirements change.

The Vicom SLIC Router is shown in Figure 63.

Figure 63. Vicom SLIC Router

5.6 RAID and JBOD

All these devices are used to store data. RAID is an acronym for redundant array of independent disks and JBOD represents just a bunch of disks. Both RAID and JBOD devices are primarily used to store directly used data and tapes are used for backing up this data. If you want to attach these devices directly to the SAN fabric components they must have Fibre Channel attachment built in. However, all SCSI attachable devices can be connected using the SAN Data Gateway which is described 5.5.1, "IBM SAN Data Gateway" on page 110.

We will show the devices that are offered in the IBM portfolio of Fibre Channel capable devices in the following topics.

5.6.1 IBM Fibre Channel RAID Storage Server

The IBM Fibre Channel RAID Storage Server (2102-F10) is a robust storage solution for environments that require Fibre Channel attachment. This storage system can be attached to servers running AIX, Sun Solaris, HP/UX, Windows NT, or Novell NetWare — and it can be shared simultaneously by two operating systems, such as UNIX and Windows NT. Multiple server attachments can be implemented by incorporating the attachment of the IBM SAN Fibre Channel Switch or the IBM Fibre Channel Storage Hub.

For enterprises with multiple platforms that share a storage system, this configuration can help protect storage and server investments while potentially reducing the overall cost of ownership. The Fibre Channel RAID Storage Server supports heterogeneous environments by enabling each RAID controller to work independently.

Redundancy
The Fibre Channel RAID Storage Server has dual-active RAID controllers that provide high throughput and redundancy. Both controllers can be simultaneously active to provide seamless failover capability in case of emergency.

To increase availability, each RAID controller supports up to 256 MB of battery-backed cache and can mirror write operations. Dual fans and power supplies further support 24x7 operations and continuous availability.

Extended distances
The IBM SAN Fibre Channel Switch and the IBM Fibre Channel Storage hub provide greater flexibility and extended distances across Fibre Channel SAN topologies — enabling the Fibre Channel RAID Storage Server to be configured at distances of up to 500m using short-wave fiber connections or up to 10km using long-wave fiber connections.

Bandwidth
The Fibre Channel RAID Storage Server has dual Fibre Channel ports that provide an aggregate bandwidth of 200 MB/s. With dual Fibre Channel Windows NT hosts, sustained data transfer rates of up to 179 MB/s can be achieved with 256 KB sequential reads (up to 190 MB/s for 256 KB sequential writes for 100 percent cache hits). Approximately 16,200 I/O operations per second may be reached with 4 KB, 100 percent cache hits in certain environments.

Simplified management

The StorWatch Fibre Channel RAID Specialist is a network-based integrated storage management tool that helps storage administrators configure, monitor, dynamically change, and manage multiple Fibre Channel RAID Storage Servers from a single Windows 95 or Windows NT workstation. High availability and full redundancy are provided with the host-specific Fibre Channel Storage Manager software, which resides on the host system and provides automatic I/O path failover if a host adapter, IBM SAN Fibre Channel Switch, IBM Fibre Channel Storage Hub, or a storage controller fails.

More product information is available at:

www.storage.ibm.com/hardsoft/products/fcss/fcss.htm

We show a picture of the FCSS in Figure 64.

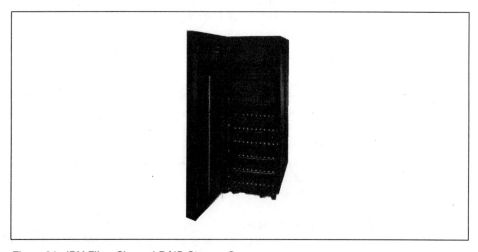

Figure 64. IBM Fibre Channel RAID Storage Server

5.6.2 Netfinity Fibre Channel RAID Controller

The Netfinity Fibre Channel RAID Controller is similar to the FCSS from a technology perspective. It provides similar functionality as FCSS does. However, the Netfinity Fibre Channel storage solution is designed and optimized for, and only supported on Netfinity Servers. The Netfinity Fibre Channel storage server is available for Netfinity servers on NT, Novell and SCO Unix platforms. Just like FCSS, it has dual controllers, redundant power supplies and fans. This is an ideal solution for Netfinity users that would like to implement high-performance Fibre Channel storage solutions.

We show a picture of the Netfinity Fibre Channel RAID Controller in Figure 65.

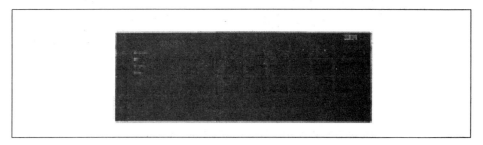

Figure 65. IBM Netfinity Fibre Channel RAID Controller

For more product information visit:

www.pc.ibm.com/us

5.6.3 Enterprise Storage Server

The IBM Enterprise Storage Server (ESS), affectionately and otherwise known as 'Shark', is a member of the Seascape family. It consists of a storage server and attached disk storage devices. The ESS (2105-F10 or 2105-F20) provides integrated caching and RAID support for the attached disk devices. The disk devices are attached using a serial interface. The ESS can be configured in a variety of ways to provide scalability in capacity and performance.

Redundancy
Redundancy within the ESS provides continuous availability. It is packaged in one or more enclosures, each with dual line cords and redundant power. The redundant power system allows the ESS to continue normal operation when one of the line cords is deactivated.

Device presentation
The ESS provides an image of a set of logical disk devices to attached servers. The logical devices are configured to emulate disk device types that are compatible with the attached servers. The logical devices access a logical volume that is implemented using multiple disk drives.

Supported attachments
The following host I/O interface attachments are supported:

- Up to 32 SCSI-3 Parallel Interface ports
- Up to 32 ESCON ports
- Any FC topology (up to 16 FC ports using the SAN Data Gateway)

On SCSI-3 interfaces, the ESS emulates a variety of fixed-block devices with either 512 or 520 byte blocks. SCSI-3 is, in general, a superset of SCSI-2. A SCSI-3 disk device can be attached to a SCSI-2 initiator, provided the cabling can be interfaced. Many SCSI-2 initiators attach directly to the cabling specified for the SCSI-3 parallel interface, but are referred to as SCSI-2 initiators because they limit their use of the command set to the SCSI-2 subset. Host systems with SCSI-2 or SCSI-3 interfaces can attach to the ESS. The ESS provides multiple SCSI I/O interfaces (busses), each with multiple SCSI targets, and each with multiple disk logical units. The storage provided by the ESS for SCSI interfaces can be configured so that it is shared among multiple SCSI interfaces if desired.

On ESCON interfaces, the ESS emulates one or more IBM 3990 control units attaching variable size IBM 3390 devices in either 3390 or 3380 track format. The ESS provides multiple ESCON interfaces that provide a set of control unit images, each with multiple disk devices. The storage provided by the ESS for ESCON interfaces is configured so that it is accessible from any ESCON interface.

On a FC interface, the ESS allows you to connect any Fibre Channel capable host. The following Fibre Channel connections can be used:

- Fibre Channel Arbitrated Loop
- Point-to-point
- Switched Fabric (IBM 2109 Fibre Channel Switch)
- Switched Fabric (McDATA ED-5000 Enterprise Fibre Channel Director)

When connected over Fibre Channel, ESS also supports LUN masking.

Components
The ESS is composed of the following components:

- The storage server is composed of two clusters that provide advanced functions to control and manage data transfer. Should one cluster fail, the remaining cluster can take over the functions of the failing cluster. A cluster is composed of the following subcomponents:

  - Host adapters — Each cluster has one or more host adapters (HAs). Each host adapter provides one or more host I/O interfaces. A host adapter can communicate with either cluster complex.

  - Device adapters — Each cluster has one or more device adapters (DAs). Each device adapter provides one or more storage device interfaces. Disk drives are attached to a pair of device adapters, one in each cluster, so that the drives are accessible from either cluster. At any given time, a disk drive is managed by only one device adapter.

- Cluster complex — The cluster complex provides the management functions for the ESS. It consists of cluster processors, cluster memory, cache, nonvolatile storage (NVS) and related logic.

  - Cluster processor — The cluster complex contains four cluster processors (CP) configured as symmetrical multiprocessors (SMP). The cluster processors execute the licensed internal code that controls operation of the cluster.

  - Cluster memory/cache — This is used to store instructions and data for the cluster processors. The cache memory is used to store cached data from the disk drives. The cache memory is accessible by the local cluster complex, by device adapters in the local cluster, and by host adapters in either cluster.

  - Nonvolatile storage (NVS) — this used to store a nonvolatile copy of active written data. The NVS is accessible to either cluster-processor complex and to host adapters in either cluster. Data may also be transferred between the NVS and cache.

- Disk drives — These provide the primary nonvolatile storage medium for any host data stored within the ESS Storage devices. They are grouped into ranks and are managed by the clusters.

SAN integration

As a member of the IBM Seascape family, the ESS provides the outboard intelligence required by SAN solutions, off-loading key functions from host servers, which frees up valuable processing power for applications. As a comprehensive SAN-based storage solution, the ESS provides considerable management flexibility to meet the fast-paced requirements of the next century.

Among the many factors that make the IBM ESS ideal SAN solution are:

- Supports all major server platforms including S/390, AS/400, Windows NT, and many other varieties of UNIX

- Fibre Channel attachment capability

- Extensive StorWatch management capabilities through a Web interface

- Excellent scalability:

  - From 400 GBs to over 11 TBs

  - Simple selection from 16 standard configurations to meet the most voracious capacity and performance appetites

- Performance optimized to your heterogeneous environment needs
  - High bandwidth and advanced transaction processing capabilities provide solutions for both online and batch applications
  - Innovations, for example, Parallel Access Volumes, to reduce S/390 resource contention and dramatically improve performance
- Availability required to support e-business applications
  - Non-disruptive access to data while making a copy using Concurrent Copy
  - Business continuity through remote copy services — PPRC and XRC
  - Rapid data duplication through FlashCopy, providing extensive capabilities to exploit, manage, and protect your information in a 24x7 environment
  - Storage server availability through redundancy and nondisruptive service with design for no single point of failure or repair

More information about the ESS can be seen at:

www.storage.ibm.com/hardsoft/products/ess/ess.htm

We show a picture of the ESS in Figure 66.

Figure 66. IBM Enterprise Storage Server

In the future, native Fibre Channel attachment will be provided in the ESS.

5.7 New Netfinity Fibre Channel products

The IBM Netfinity division has announced that the following **new products for SAN** will be available by the end of March 2000:

- Netfinity Fibre Channel Raid Controller Unit (3552-1RU)

  - Includes redundant RAID controllers, hot-plug fans, **and redundant** power supplies
  - Two Fibre Channel (FC) to arbitrated loop (AL) loop **host buses and** four FC to AL loop drive buses — supports RAID 0, 1, 3, **and 5**
  - Support for up to 200 disk drives, per controller unit, **using Netfinity** EXP500 FC storage units

- Netfinity Fibre Channel PCI Adapter (00N6881)

  - Active PCI (hot-plug and hot-add)
  - 64/32-bit PCI host adapter
  - Supports FC to SCSI and IP protocols
  - Supports FC to arbitrated loop (AL) public loop profile

- Netfinity EXP500 Fibre Channel (3560-1RU)

  - Fully redundant base unit includes hot-plug redundant **power supplies,** fans, and 10 drive bays
  - Supports high-speed Fibre Channel hard disk drives **(HDDs)**

- High-Speed 10,000 RPM Fibre Channel HDDs

  - Netfinity 9.1 GB(1) 10K-3 FC Hot-Swap HDD
  - Netfinity 18.2 GB 10K-3 FC Hot-Swap HDD
  - Netfinity 36.4 GB 10K-3 FC Hot-Swap HDD

- Netfinity Fibre Channel Advanced Storage Manager Version **7.0**

  - Supports up to eight storage partitions
  - Java-based can manage Netfinity Fibre Channel storage **remotely from** single or multiple locations

These are important additions to the IBM SAN family.

Chapter 6. Physical connectivity for Storage Area Networks

This chapter discusses the physical connection of Storage Area Network (SAN) devices. Background of the Physical Interface portion of the Fibre Channel specification is presented and practical elements are discussed in some detail. Also, the concept of a structured approach to physical connectivity is presented with some emphasis on the SAN environment. This generic approach to connectivity leads to a short discussion of the IBM structured cabling solutions for the data center environment, called Fiber Transport Services (FTS).

FTS is explained and some discussion as to its application in a SAN environment is included. Finally, an example of how to plan a connection of SAN devices in a practical example is presented.

6.1 Background

Storage Area Networks have employed many technologies to provide businesses with the ability to pool or share data between multiple servers and storage devices. The technologies include application and operating system capabilities, hardware design, and a protocol mechanism to connect the elements. The industry participants in the SAN arena have settled on the American National Standards Institute (ANSI) Fibre Channel standard as the lowest cost, most flexible, and scalable solution applicable to their requirements.

Fibre Channel standards work has been underway for nearly 10 years. Its original application was high performance graphics and design workstation communications. This technology, therefore has had time to mature and now offers a robust, standards based solution for the data storage environment. For example, the physical interface layer (FC-PI) of the ANSI Fibre Channel standard has just circulated revision 6.5 for industry comment.

6.2 Fibre Channel in the SAN environment

Inevitably, a discussion of SAN will lead to a discussion of Fibre Channel. We explore this subject in some depth from the view point of the physical connectivity issues. We address these topics:

- Fibre Channel background
- Why fiber has replaced copper
- The optical link budgets for SAN products
- A discussion of current infrastructures and other protocol link budgets

• Planning considerations and recommendations for SAN fiber-optic links

6.2.1 Fibre Channel background

The history of this technology and standard was to provide a scalable high-speed technology for the networking environment. Technologies available at the time of its inception were not robust, scalable, or cost effective. Therefore, the standards group and interested industry participants looked at lower cost lasers, originally from the CD-ROM marketplace, to determine if highly reliable and low cost solutions were possible. Within a short time, suitable technologies were adopted for short and long wavelength implementation.

Subsequent work by the ANSI T11 technical committee refined the specifications and increased the bandwidth levels, while maintaining the 10-to-12 bit error rate (BER) of the link. These serial full-duplex links have 1000 times better BER than asynchronous transfer mode (ATM) and synchronous optical network (SONET). All of the experience of prior protocols, such as Fiber Distributed Data Interface (FDDI) and fiber interfaces for Token Ring and Ethernet, as well as IBM System 390's Enterprise Systems Connectivity (ESCON), have been brought to bear on this newer standard.

Fibre Channel is a high speed, scalable, protocol stack that provides for the interconnection of network elements while simultaneously providing for traffic management and data flow control, as well as reliable and highly available links. The technology has been mapped into three topologies:

• Point-to-point
• Arbitrated loop
• Switched fabric

We show these topologies in Figure 67:

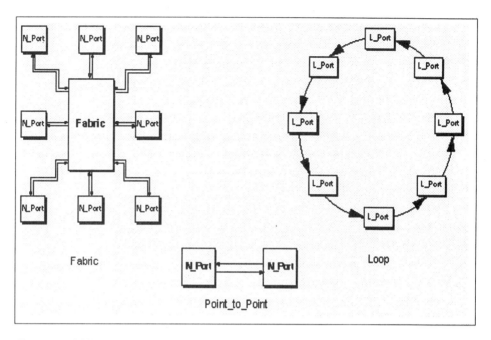

Figure 67. SAN topologies

These topologies, though similar to earlier standards, such as FDDI, ESCON, or Ethernet, employ new methods to manage the transportation of information. However, unlike these other standards, all three topologies use the same physical interfaces that are configurable for the individual function. The physical interfaces in Fibre Channel, and therefore the SAN arena, are either short wavelength or long wavelength lasers. Further, the specifications provide for minimum distances and power budgets for connections with 50 micron or 62.5 micron multi-mode, and single-mode fiber cable plants. The result of the standard committee's work is a scalable solution in bit rate and in complexity of the cabling infrastructure.

For example, point to point solutions between server and storage may simply be a matter of appropriate jumper cables. However, a switched fabric used in pooling of resources may require a more sophisticated structured cabling system.

All topologies lend themselves to the star wiring scheme found in a structured system. Point to point can contain two patch panels connected by a trunk. An arbitrated loop using a hub and the switched fabric may both have various main and zone cabinets.

Also, consideration needs to be given to connections that leave a building or campus for such activities as remote mirroring or backup.

The standard also provides for recommended device interface connectors (SC Duplex) as well as providing guidance for the use of the emerging "small form factor" connectors (SG, LC Duplex, and MT-RJ).

Though the implementations may be physically different, the emphasis continues to be on robust, highly reliable, and cost effective solutions that will continue to offer value and flexibility as higher signaling rates are adopted.

In Figure 68 we show typical connectors from various manufacturers as identified in the standard. It should be noted that other connectors exist and may be used in supporting a structured cabling system. These connectors are specifically identified to connect to the SAN devices. For a definitive explanation as to a connectors application, it is important to reference the manufacturer's installation guide to determine which connector is used in their product.

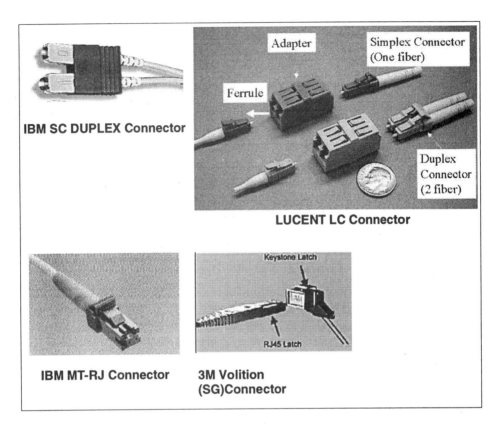

Figure 68. Typical connectors

6.2.2 Why fiber has replaced copper

One of the observations that can be made is the obvious reliance on a fiber-optic based solution in the SAN environment as well as in the Fibre Channel arena. Though a copper standard for Fibre Channel exists for various types of balanced and unbalanced coax transmission links, manufacturers have embraced fiber-optics for SAN products.

Though this would seem to be a more expensive solution, the user's need for simplicity, repeatability, and reliability makes fiber-optic links the best choice. Also, the use of low cost laser devices for both single mode and multi-mode links increases manufacturing volumes and experience to provide the lowest cost, highest performance optical transmitter-receiver assemblies possible.

Ultimately the scalability of Fibre Channel to the currently defined speed of 4.25GBs on fiber-optic links provides a growth path with minimum impact to the connecting infrastructure unmatched by copper.

As the selection of technologies required to implement SAN progressed, both copper and fiber solutions were examined. For example, Gigabit Ethernet has fiber and a copper implementation to 100 meters. Other protocols, such as Asynchronous Transfer Mode (ATM) or FDDI with high speed copper options, do not have scalable copper solutions above 100 MB/s. Therefore, fiber-optic was selected to allow scalability, reliability, and cost.

Specifically, Fibre Channel was selected because it provided the most functionality and maturity for the SAN environment. Also, the upper layers of the protocol stack allow for easy transportation of other protocols found in the storage arena such as Small Computer Systems Interface (SCSI), Serial Storage Architecture (SSA), High Performance Parallel Interface (HIPPI), Intelligent Peripheral Interface (IPI-3), ESCON, and even Internet Protocol (IP). SAN has become one more reason that fiber-optic connectivity is becoming pervasive.

6.2.3 Optical link budgets for SAN products

As mentioned earlier, multiple connectors are recognized by the standard giving the physical installation design flexibility and some assurances of repeatability. The performance of the different fiber-optic cable types is also identified in the standard. Therefore, flexibility is provided to the physical infrastructure designer. The achievable link distances for the different cable types is identified in Table 7.

Table 7. Fibre Channel distance and link losses

	Singlemode			Multimode - 50			Multimode - 62.5		
Data rate (MB/second)	400	200	100[a]	400	200	100[a]	400	200	100[a]
Modal bandwidth (MHz km)	N/A	N/A	N/A	500 / 500	500 / 500	500 / 500	200 / 500	200 / 500	200 / 500
Cable plant dispersion (Ps/nm km)	12	12	12	N/A	N/A	N/A	N/A	N/A	N/A
Transmitter spectral center wavelength (nm)	1310	1310	1310	770 -860	830 -860	830 -860	770 -860	830 -860	830 -860
Operating range (m)	2- 10,000	2- 10,000	2- 10,000	2-150	2-300	2-500	2-70	2-150	2-300
Loss budget (db)	7.8	7.8	7.8	2.06	2.62	3.85	1.78	2.1	3.01

a. 100 MB/s products were available at time of writing. Other baud rate information is included for growth planning purposes.

The overriding trend is decreased distance and loss budgets as the data rate increases for the same type of cable. Looking at the multi-mode cables, 50 micron fiber enables significantly longer links than the 62.5 micron fiber at the same data rate. Lastly, the single mode distances are generally not affected by the increased data rates. It is also noted in the standard that lower performance multi-mode fibers have been installed in the past and performance will be affected. It should also be noted that higher performance multi-mode cables have been available since the beginning of 1999 which allows increased distances. The actual performance will need to be obtained from the manufacturer.

The bandwidths, distances, and losses identified in Table 7, are those specified in the ANSI Fibre Channel Physical Interface document. The current and complete standard can be obtained from the publisher: Global Engineering, 15 Inverness Way East, Englewood, CO 80112-5704; telephone (800) 854-7179. Current versions being circulated for industry ballot or comment are available at:

www.t11.org

Search for the Physical Interface title.

6.2.4 Current infrastructures and other protocol link budgets

Whenever new technologies are introduced, the first consideration tends to be whether it will work on the existing installed infrastructure. In the case of fiber-optic cabling, most industry consultants and designers, including IBM Connectivity consultants, recommended the installation of 62.5 multi-mode and single-mode fibers in the campus and building backbones, with 62.5 micron multi-mode fiber recommended for the horizontal unless a specific product required single-mode. In most large data center installations, fiber was usually installed to support ESCON connectivity, and, therefore, was also predominantly 62.5 micron multi-mode cable. Therefore, when evaluating whether the new Fibre Channel products will operate over existing cable, the answer is, "it depends".

Today, as the bandwidth requirements increase and the shift from light emitting diode (LED) transmitters to lasers is completed, the existing infrastructure must be scrutinized. Often the requirements for correct operation of new equipment are much more restrictive than those they replace. This will result in previously installed optical fiber infrastructures possibly not supporting the new protocols being installed on the network. Gigabit Ethernet is a case in point. If the distance or the link loss of the cable plant is too great, customers could find that they have no choice between a 1000BASE-LX or 1000BASE-SX, and must implement the SX solution of Gigabit Ethernet on single-mode fiber for the distances required. The increased cost of the SX devices may be less expensive than the cost of new cabling.

Currently, industry standards groups are re-examining optical fiber specifications. This includes the re-introduction of 50 micron fiber into the TIA-568B Premises Wiring standard. Committee consensus has specified 50 micron fiber to have a performance of 3.5/1.5 dB/km with a bandwidth of 500 MHz*km at 850/1300 nm.

Working with the IEEE 802.3z committee on Gigabit Ethernet, TIA recognizes the deficiency of 62.5 micron fiber with short wavelength devices, an implementation likely to be more cost effective and popular with customers. It is important to understand that 62.5 micron multimode fiber provides the best link performance for LED transmitters that have dominated the customer network and data center in the recent past.

Now, new protocol technologies are moving to laser sources where a smaller diameter core is key to the enhanced performance, and hence the reintroduction of 50 micron multimode fiber. To provide a smoother transition, some manufacturers are introducing higher bandwidth 62.5 micron fibers to extend the distances the laser signals can travel. Specific performance parameters need to be obtained from the manufacturer for the fiber being considered.

In the continually improving paradigm in which we find ourselves, it is valuable for clients to install the communication media that allows maximum data rate, distance, and longevity.

Table 8 provides a quick summary comparison of protocol specifications.

Table 8. Optical link comparison

Connection	Fiber type	Connector	Data rate	Distance (m)	Link budget (db)
ESCON	9/125 SM	SC duplex	200 MB/s	20000	14
	62.5/125 MM	ESCON duplex	200 MB/s	3000	8
	50/125 MM	ESCON duplex	200 MB/s	2000	8
Sysplex timer	62.5/125 MM	ESCON duplex	8 MB/s	3000	8
ATM 155	9/125 SM	SC duplex	155 MB/s	20000	15
	62.5/125 MM	SC duplex	155 MB/s	2000	11
Gigabit ethernet	9/125 SM	SC duplex	1.25 GB/s	5000	7.5
	62.5/125 MM	SC duplex	1.25 GB/s	275	7.5
	62.5/125 MM[a]	SC duplex	1 GB/s	550	7.5
	50/125 MM	SC duplex	1.25 GB/s	550	7.5
	50/125 MM[a]	SC duplex	1 GB/s	550	7.5
FDDI	62.5/125 MM	SC duplex or MIC	100 MB/s	2000	9
FICON	9/125 SM	SC duplex	1 GB/s	10000	7
	62.5/125 MM[a]	SC duplex	1 GB/s	550	5
	50/125 MM[a]	SC duplex	1 GB/s	550	5
Intra-system coupler[b]	9/125 SM	SC duplex	1 GB/s	10000	7

a. Requires use of a mode conditioner
b. 50 micron multimode is supported by RPQ for links of 550m and 3db

It is interesting to note the different drive distances and link budgets for the many protocols over the same fiber types. Consideration should be given to these different options as more network protocols make their way onto the same fiber cable infrastructure.

Also, it should be pointed out that fibers with higher modal bandwidth than specified in the various standards are now available, and, therefore, will allow longer distance links. Exact performance details will have to be obtained from the manufacturers. When this increased capability is used in planning a link ensure that appropriate documentation is provided for future reference.

The link budget for the different bit rates in Fibre Channel makes designing systems that have room for growth significantly difficult. Therefore, a thorough assessment and understanding of current and future goals must be considered and all designed capabilities be clearly communicated. Furthermore, the decision between multi-mode and single-mode solutions may require cost analyses in more cases to offer solutions that meet current needs and provide for future growth.

One other consideration to assess with an installed fiber-optic system is the issue of polarity. Many systems designed with the idea of a duplex connector system enforce the correct polarity to ensure the transmitter of one device connects to the receiver of the other. FTS, for example, provides this feature throughout. Other generic fiber-optic cabling systems that provide connectivity within a building, on a campus, or distance connections such as "dark fiber" from a local exchange carrier, may not provide this feature automatically. So any design needs to identify to the installers that polarity be maintained throughout the system.

To summarize the situation with existing infrastructure, there essentially is no easy answer. Each currently installed system would need to be assessed for applicability with Fibre Channel. If the data for the fiber-optic cables and connectors is known, then the decision can be made relatively easily. If the information is not known, bandwidth and loss measurements may be required of each link in question.

Since there are no simple methods to measure bandwidth in the field, as of yet, loss measurements may be the only information that will be useful with 100MBs multi-mode solutions. When the cost of testing is weighed against the cost of installing a new cabling, a new system may actually cost less than measuring and replacing the currently installed system. In conclusion, each situation will need to be decided on its own merits between the client and the connectivity specialist.

6.2.5 Planning considerations and recommendations

Many miscellaneous considerations are needed to successfully install fiber-optic links for any protocol. However, the higher data rate and lower optical link budgets of Fibre Channel lends itself to more conservative approaches to link design. Some of the key elements to consider are:

- All links must use the currently predominant "physical contact" connectors for smaller losses, better back reflectance, and more repeatable performance.

- The use of either fusion or mechanical splices is left to the designer to determine the desired losses weighed against the cost of installation.

- Multi-mode links cannot contain mixed fiber diameters (62.5 and 50 micron) in the same link. The losses due to the mismatch may be as much as 4.8 dB with a variance of 0.12 dB. This would more than exceed the small power budgets available by this standard.

- The use of high quality factory terminated jumper cables is also recommended to ensure consistent performance and loss characteristics throughout the installation.

- The use of a structured cabling system is strongly recommended even for small installations.

- A structured cabling system provides a protected solution that serves current requirements as well as allows for easy expansion.

- The designer of a structured system should consider component variance affects on the link if applicable.

Much of the discussion so far has been centered around single floor or single room installation. Unlike earlier FDDI or ESCON installations that had sufficient multi-mode link budgets to span significant distances, Fibre Channel multi-mode solutions for the most part do not. Though the Fibre Channel standard allows for extend distance links and handles distance timing issues in the protocol the link budgets are the limiting factor.

Therefore, installations that need to span between floors or buildings will need any proposed link to be evaluated for its link budget closely. Degradation over time, environmental effects on cables run in unconditioned spaces, as well as variations introduced by multiple installers need to be closely scrutinized. The choice between single-mode and multi-mode devices may need to be made for many more links. Repeating the signal may also provide a cost effective solution if intermediary conditioned space can be found.

Since Fibre Channel provides a built in mirroring capability to SAN, in addition to its 10 km link distances using single-mode fiber, there will be more consideration for off-campus or across city links. In these cases, right-of-way issues, leasing of "dark" fiber (no powered devices provided by the lessors) issues, service level agreements, and other factors associated with leaving the client owned premises needs to be planned for and negotiated with local providers. The industry has also announced interest in providing wide area network (WAN) interfaces similar to those employed in the networking world of today. When these devices are made available, then connections to these devices will need to be included in the designs as well.

6.3 Structured cabling

Because of access to the Internet, the data centers of today are changing rapidly. Both e-business and e-commerce are placing increasing demands on access to and reliance on the data center. No longer is the data center insulated from the rest of the company and just used to perform batch processing.

Now, access and processing is a 24x7 necessity for both the company and its customers. The cabling that connects servers to the data storage devices has become a vital part of corporate success. Few companies can function without a computer installation supported by an efficiently structured and managed cabling system.

There are many important factors to consider when planning and implementing a computer data center. Often, the actual physical cabling is not given enough planning and is considered only when the equipment arrives. The result of this poor planning is cabling that is hard to manage when it comes to future moves, adds, and changes due to equipment growth and changes.

Planning a manageable cabling system requires knowledge about the equipment being connected, the floor layout of the data center(s), and, most importantly, how the system requirements will change. Questions that should be considered include:

- Will the data center grow every year?
- Will you need to move the equipment around the floor(s)?
- Will you upgrade the equipment?
- Will you add new equipment?
- What type of cabling do you require?
- How will you run the cables?
- How will you label the cables?
- Can you easily trace the cables if there is a problem?

Answers to these important questions should be obtained as part of the early planning for the cabling installation.

6.3.1 Data center fiber cabling options

The most prevalent data center connectivity environment that uses fiber cabling is IBM's ESCON architecture. However, the same structured fiber cabling principles can be applied in the SAN environment, and to other fiber connectivity environments such as IBM's Fiber Connection (FICON), Parallel Sysplex(R), and Open Systems Adapters (OSA). The examples throughout this chapter apply to structured fiber optic cabling systems designed to support multiple fiber-optic connectivity environments. This is illustrated in Figure 69.

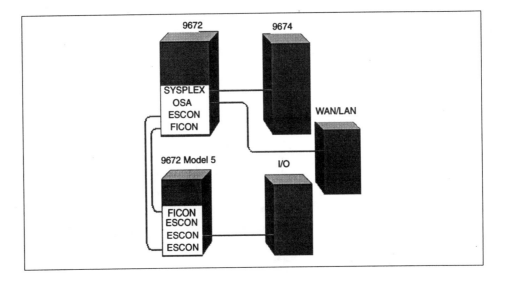

Figure 69. Connectivity environments

The need for data center fiber cabling implementation arises from the following three scenarios:

- Establishing a new data center
- Upgrading an existing data center by replacing the cabling
- Adding new equipment to an existing data center

Fundamentally, two options exist when implementing fiber cabling in this environment:

- Jumper cables
- Structured cabling

6.3.2 Jumper cable option

The jumper cable option uses discrete fiber jumper cables, where each jumper cable connects one machine port directly to another (for example, one 9672 server channel port to one ESCON Director port or one SAN Data Gateway to a SAN Fibre Channel Switch).

In a small data center installation, this starts out as a simple installation. However, as the data center grows, the number of jumper cables running under the floor increases rapidly. Moves, adds, and changes also become harder as the number of jumpers under the floor grows. The jumpers get tangled up beneath the machines and become very hard to move, relocate or reuse. As the number of jumpers continues to grow, it becomes impossible to manage where they all connect.

Figure 70 shows a typical jumper cable installation in an ESCON environment.

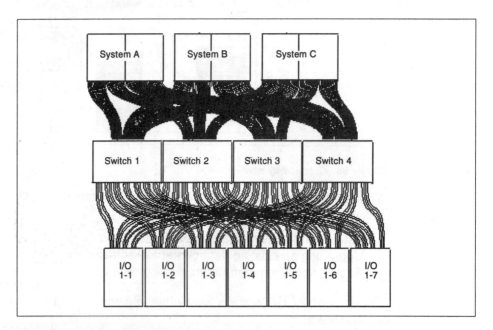

Figure 70. A typical jumper cable installation

In this example:

- The systems are 9672 Enterprise Servers with 80 ESCON channels each.
- The switches are 9032 ESCON Directors with 108 ports each.
- Each I/O is any I/O control unit with 16 ports.

6.3.3 Structured cabling system option

The second choice for fiber cabling is a structured cabling system. A structured cabling system utilizes fiber trunk cables, local patch panels (zone panels) and short, local patch cables to greatly reduce the number of discrete jumper cables running under the raised floor. For example, instead of having 216 fiber jumpers connecting to a 9672 Enterprise Server, three 72-channel trunk cables do the same job. The fiber trunk cables connect the machine ports to the back of patch panels that are located in the Central Patching Location (CPL). We show an example of this in Figure 71.

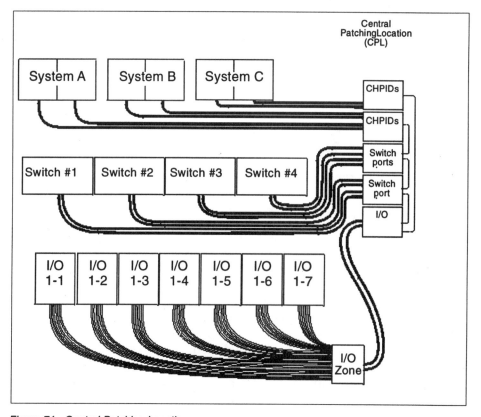

Figure 71. Central Patching Location

The CPL is usually made up of cabinets or racks that hold the patch panels. The front of the patch panels have individual duplex ports that now represent the machine ports. Connections between two machine ports can be made quickly and easily by running a short jumper to connect the two patch panel's duplex ports. Connections for I/O devices are provided from the zone patch panels to the I/O, with zones being strategically placed around the data center to accommodate hardware concentrations. Finally, trunk cables can be installed with diverse routes to provide some level of redundancy for the connectivity.

As the data center expands to multiple buildings, the structured cabling system approach can be scaled to accommodate the connectivity requirements. Trunk cables can be provided between buildings to support local patch panels in facilities where concentrations of hardware require connectivity.

With the expanded distances supported by multimode and single mode fiber optic cable, the traditional data center can now exist in multiple buildings on a campus or across town if required. Finally, with diverse routing between facilities, redundant connectivity can be provided between data center facilities.

In those instances where the path between the remote facilities is not owned by the end user, right-of-way or fiber-optic lines may need to be procured from the local telephone company, cable television provider or other local exchange carrier. However, the structured cabling system approach remains constant as the connectivity requirements are scaled up to support geographically disperse operations.

6.3.4 Benefits of structured cabling

The most apparent benefit of the structured trunking system is the large reduction in the number of fiber cables under the raised floor. Fewer cables make tracking the destination of each cable easier, and facilitates the tracing of a fiber link during problem determination and for future growth planning. Also, a well planned structured cabling system provides for cost effective moves, adds and changes while minimizing disruption under the raised floor.

With individual hardware devices, (SAN storage devices, tape, DASD, communication controllers, LAN equipment), connecting to local patch panels (zones) with short patch cables, hardware connectivity is handled in the vicinity of the hardware/patch panels, rather than across the entire floor.

Structured cabling provides for faster, less disruptive installation and removal of equipment, ease of reconfiguration of equipment and more efficient use of the under-floor space (with the potential to improve air movement and air conditioning needs).

6.4 IBM Fiber Transport Services

Fiber Transport Services (FTS) is an IBM Global Services (IGS) Connectivity offering that provides a structured, flexible fiber cabling system. This offering incorporates planning and design, fiber trunking components, and installation activities, all performed by IBM personnel. It consists of a variety of connectivity solutions including leading edge, Small Form Factor, SC-DC Connectivity Solutions, as pictured in Figure 72 and, Modular Panel-Mount Connectivity Solutions.

FTS solutions use fiber trunks, jumpers, direct-attach harnesses, trunk-mounting kits, and patch panels for the Central Patching Location (CPL) and Zone Patching Location (ZPL) that are sold under the IBM logo. Patch panels in FTS are panels of optical couplers attached to boxes containing the termination connection to trunks or MTP connectors to be attached to trunk cables.

FTS is developed in partnership with IBM S/390 products to ensure that the FTS cabling system works with the S/390 products. The FTS connectivity solutions support both multi-mode 62.5 micron and single-mode fiber. Custom 50 micron solutions are available from IBM as well.

Figure 72 shows a picture of the FTS SC-DC connector.

Figure 72. FTS SC-DC connector

6.4.1 FTS overview

With the proliferation of industry-standard fiber-optic interfaces and connector types, the management of a large-systems fiber cable environment and the network fiber cable environment is becoming increasingly important. FTS offers complete end-to-end connectivity of a fiber cable plant for all data center, S/390, and SAN applications. It provides the products, design, and installation for a successful data center cabling infrastructure.

The FTS system organizes fiber cabling for the large-system data center and network. It is based on a quick connect/disconnect trunking strategy using the 12-fiber MTP connector such as that pictured in Figure 73.

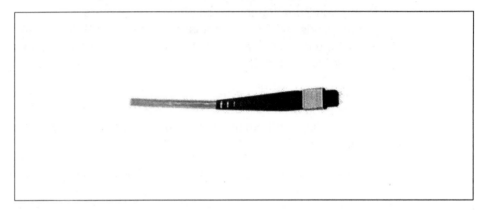

Figure 73. 12-fiber MTP connector

It is possible to attach 12 fibers (six duplex channels) with a single connection operation. The MTP connector enables FTS to be disconnected and relocated very quickly. The FTS trunk cables have one MTP connector for the 6-channel trunk, three MTPs for the 18-channel trunk, six MTPs for the 36-channel trunk, and 12 MTPs for the 72-channel trunk.

6.4.2 FTS design elements

There are a number of elements that constitute the design. We discuss them in the topics that follow.

Direct-attach trunking
The MTP connector also enables FTS to bring its fiber trunk cables directly under the covers of the S/390 data center equipment. This is known as direct-attach trunking, and it eliminates the need for discrete fiber jumper cables connecting to the processors and directors.

The direct-attach trunk cables connect to direct-attach harnesses inside the equipment. Direct-attach harnesses have one MTP connector that breaks out to six duplex connectors, for example, ESCON.

We show a picture of a fiber-optic harness in Figure 74.

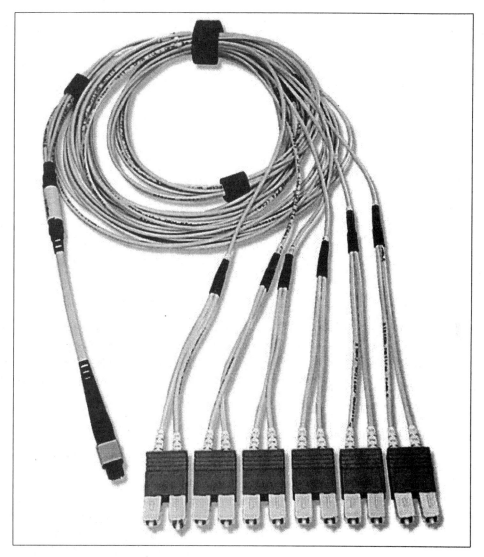

Figure 74. Direct-attach harness

The direct-attach harnesses connect the trunk cable to the individual machine ports and accommodate the different industry-standard optical connectors used on data processing equipment. The direct-attach harnesses and trunk cables enable you to efficiently relocate the machine ports to a Central Patching Location (CPL).

Central Patching Location
The CPL, shown in Figure 75, contains patch panels with duplex, 2 fiber ports in the front and trunk cable connections in the rear. The FTS trunk cables connect to the rear of the patch panel, and the duplex ports in the front are the relocated machine ports.

Typically, the processor channels are relocated to one set of patch panels, the ESCON director ports to another set of panel-mount boxes, and the I/O storage control unit ports to a third set. This allows you to make all the connections between the different machines by connecting the duplex ports in the different patch panels with short jumper cables (patch cords).

We show a schematic drawing of a typical CPL in Figure 75.

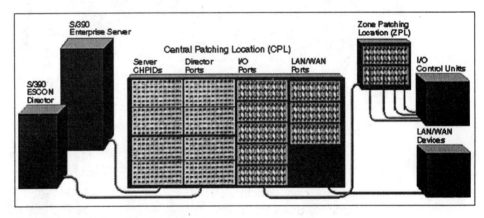

Figure 75. Central patching location

Zone Patching Location
For I/O storage control unit cabling, where the smaller number of device ports can make direct-attach trunking less critical, you can also make use of a Zone Patching Location (ZPL). The ZPL, which is also shown in Figure 75, is a kind of mini-CPL. It is used to relocate I/O ports to the CPL by means of a trunk cable running from a patch panel in the ZPL to a patch panel in the CPL. Then, I/O device ports are connected to the patch panel in the ZPL using jumper cables.

FTS connectivity solutions

FTS offers two main, leading edge, connectivity solutions for the CPL. The first of which is the Small Form Factor SC-DC Connectivity Solution and uses trunk cables that have MTP connectors on one end, and SC-DC two fiber connectors on the other. With this solution, the machine ports at the SC-DC patch panels are arranged in sequential order, and you can order the boxes with the machine addresses factory labeled. We show this in Figure 76.

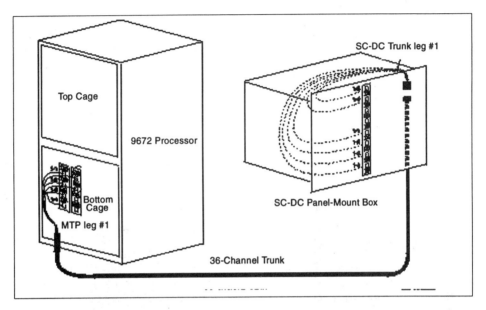

Figure 76. Panel mount boxes with MT terminated trunking

The second connectivity solution for the CPL, is the Modular Panel-Mount Connectivity Solution. It uses MTP-to-MTP trunk cables that connect to modular patch panels in the CPL. The modular patch panels are designed around the ability to change the port type in the patch panel by unplugging the trunk and changing the modular inserts in the patch panel. We illustrate this in Figure 77.

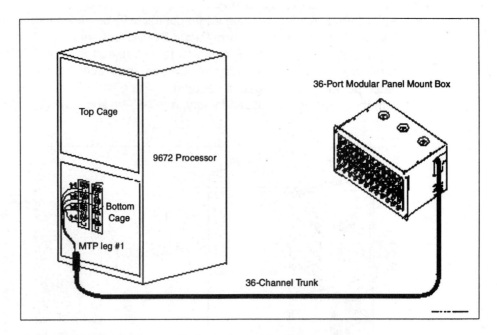

Figure 77. Panel mount boxes with direct-attached trunking

6.4.3 Why choose FTS?

The technologies and products required to build storage area networks with Fibre Channel are just becoming available. In very short order, clients will move from the investigation and testing stage to full implementations. When this happens, IBM has the products and services to design, and install a reliable and flexible cable infrastructure that will continue to add value to a network and accommodate business expansion.

In Figure 78, we provide a view of an installation in progress. The design has been completed and cabling is being installed to the plan.

Figure 78. An FTS installation in progress

6.4.4 SAN connectivity example

This section attempts to take a typical example and show how the physical link information can be mapped into a structured cabling solution. It is noted that specific site information was not built into this plan. This type of information would include items, such as:

- Specific lengths for each and every link

- Physical location of the equipment laid out on a grid

- The pathways, routing, and locations for the structured cabling system components on the machine room floor, within the building, or on the campus

- The layout for the patch panels including specific labeling information

- Bills-of-material identifying the lengths, termination choices, and performance of all trunk and jumper cables as well as other system components that are required

- Any other specific limitations or detail instructions required to actually install a design

Figure 79 shows a depiction of an IBM Enterprise Storage Server (ESS) with a storage area network of servers attached and the connection to the network. This serves as the conceptual direction that needs a connectivity solution.

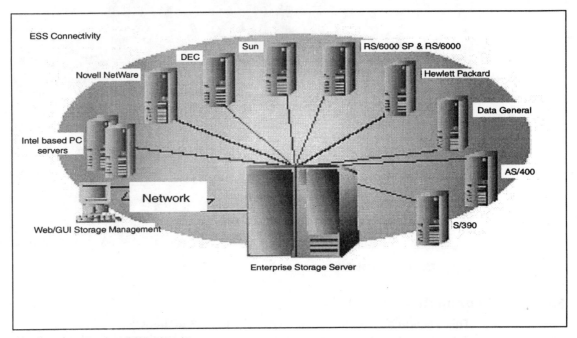

Figure 79. Conceptual SAN example

After the appropriate strategy, architectural, and design steps are completed, the physical design takes all this information and builds a series of drawings and details.

These documents are then used to build an implementation plan. This would then be translated into specific architectural drawings and associated details for the building(s) located on the premises. Since these detailed documents require specific site information before they can developed, they are not included here. A conceptual drawing of a structured physical connectivity solution is shown in Figure 80.

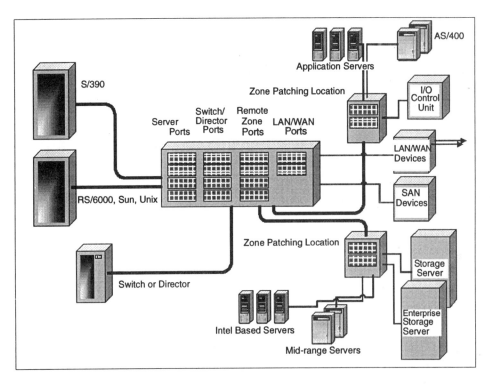

Figure 80. Structured cabling system for SAN example

The physical connectivity example shows a structured fiber-optic cabling system supporting a multi-vendor, multi-protocol environment. The structured fiber optic cabling systems consists of a CPL that acts as the focal point for all connectivity.

Fiber-optic patch cables are used within the CPL to connect specific devices together, whether the devices are directly connected to the CPL or remotely connected by trunks from remote zone patching locations.

ZPLs connect areas of high equipment or connectivity concentration to the CPL using fiber-optic trunk cables, to allow for connectivity from any device to any other device. The ZPLs are strategically located to provide convenient connectivity access using jumper cables, for the devices local to the ZPL.

Trunks connecting the ZPL to the CPL are appropriately sized to accommodate current and future requirements. Additional trunking can easily be added from a CPL to ZPL to accommodate unexpected growth, with no impact to the overall operation. Additional ZPLs may be added for connectivity to the CPL as more equipment or sites are added to the overall system. By creating a structured fiber-optic backbone network that can easily adapt to changes in the processing environment, the fiber infrastructure becomes another utility in the facility, similar to the critical electrical and HVAC systems.

Since reuse is a key factor of any "utility", careful planning for the cabling infrastructure during the early introduction period of SAN products will ensure migration and growth capabilities. IBM consultants will provide an optimum solution that applies to a particular situation.

Chapter 7. IBM SAN initiatives

In June 1999, IBM made a corporate-wide announcement defining a comprehensive Enterprise SAN strategy. All IBM hardware (servers, networking and storage) and software divisions, including IBM Tivoli Systems, participated in the announcement, together with IBM International Global Services.

This chapter outlines the basis of that strategy, and describes how IBM and Tivoli Systems will deliver "end-to-end" management facilities for SANs.

7.1 IBM's Enterprise SAN design objectives

IBM understands that every business has unique requirements. IBM also recognizes that investment protection and minimization of operational disruption and risk are key factors influencing an organization's SAN decisions.

IBM's Enterprise SAN is designed to:

- Use current investments in hardware, software and skills.

- Enable the integration of new technologies as they emerge, mature, and become more affordable, by deploying a building-block infrastructure.

- Apply to the open systems environment the experience and lessons learned from the mainframe arena, such as systems-managed storage concepts and switched fabric management.

- Support multi-platform, multi-vendor hardware and software interoperability.

- Minimize the risks of unproven technologies by providing "mix and match" freedom of choice to deploy what makes the most sense for each unique environment.

IBM's Enterprise SAN strategy is an "end to end" approach that delivers technology, support, consultancy, services, and education throughout the entire SAN solution life cycle. Five basic initiatives form the cornerstone of IBM's strategy: hardware, connectivity, management, exploitation, and support. These initiatives are discussed in the following sections.

7.1.1 Hardware

IBM will provide a base of native Fibre Channel SAN enabled hardware, incorporating servers (S/390, RS/6000, NUMAQ, AS/400, and Netfinity) and storage subsystems. Support of non-IBM servers, such as Sun, HP, and Compaq, will also be enabled, so that they can participate in an IBM Enterprise SAN.

7.1.2 Connectivity

IBM will provide a comprehensive range and hierarchy of components to allow enterprise-wide connectivity within a Fibre Channel switched fabric environment, including hubs, switches, and directors. Since few businesses can afford to implement a complete replacement strategy, IBM will provide a range of "bridges" (routers and gateways), that will permit organizations to bring existing hardware into a Fibre Channel SAN environment, including SCSI to Fibre Channel, ESCON to FICON, and SSA to Fibre Channel.

7.1.3 Management

Without good software management tools, organizations cannot effectively implement SANs. IBM will provide the management functions needed to configure, control and monitor the SAN fabric elements (switches, hubs, gateways, and so on), and the storage devices and hosts attached to the SAN. Initially this will include management tools for individual devices, and ultimately provides a single interface to manage all the SAN resources. IBM and Tivoli Systems will deliver a SAN management infrastructure which is able to accommodate both existing and future systems (see "IBM SAN management solutions" on page 154). Products from IBM, and other storage vendors, such as EMC, STK and Hitachi Data Systems, will be incorporated in this management scheme to provide a closed-loop, "zero-latency" management infrastructure.

7.1.4 Exploitation

The true value of SAN comes from software functions that use the SAN technologies and provide business value.

IBM will deliver a set of business solutions that exploit SAN technology and address today's most pressing IT problems, including tape pooling, disk pooling, third-party copy services, file pooling, clustering and data sharing. IBM Tivoli, for example, delivers tape pooling — which dynamically allocates tape drives and libraries to improve efficiency, enhance productivity, and provide economies of scale. LAN-free backup and serverless backup capabilities are planned to be delivered in the year 2000 (see 7.2.2, "Tivoli data management" on page 156). IBM Tivoli will also deliver true data sharing, for selected open systems environments, using its SANergy File Sharing solution (see Chapter 8, "Tivoli SANergy File Sharing" on page 169). Also, Netfinity has announced an eight-way, high-availability cluster that provides true data sharing with Oracle Parallel Server. Other software solutions will also be delivered over time.

By delivering early business benefits, solutions such as these can help organizations gain a competitive edge with SAN technology.

7.1.5 Support

SAN's promise of any-to-any connectivity, and the complexity it introduces, highlight the critical nature of both system integration and services in any SAN strategy. As the industry's leading service provider, IBM Global Services can provide the support to build end-to-end SAN solutions. This includes education, consulting, installation and maintenance services, as well as interoperability testing facilities. Substantial investments have been made in interoperability testing facilities at Gaithersburg, USA; Mainz, Germany; and Montpelier, France to enable IBM and customers to test and prove multi-vendor hardware and software environments. Additional facilities are planned for Japan.

A summary of the IBM SAN initiatives are shown in Figure 81.

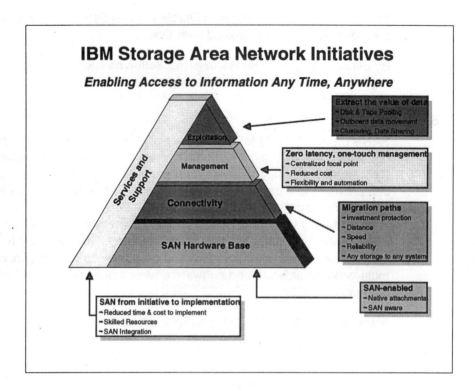

Figure 81. IBM's SAN Initiative: The Value Proposition

7.2 IBM SAN management solutions

IBM's Enterprise SAN initiative involves software solutions from both IBM and Tivoli Systems, designed to provide comprehensive management control of all storage resources.

IBM and Tivoli Storage Management Solutions are designed to address the SAN Management layers described in Chapter 2, "The drive for SAN industry standardization" on page 31. This is shown in Figure 82.

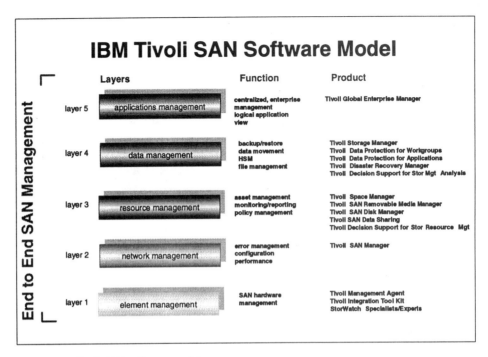

Figure 82. Tivoli SAN software model

The architecture of the IBM and Tivoli SAN and storage management solutions stack is illustrated in Figure 85 on page 161.

We will outline the solutions incorporated within that stack in the topics that follow.

7.2.1 Tivoli application management

Tivoli Global Enterprise Manager (GEM) unifies the management of cross-platform business applications. Tivoli GEM allows you to manage strategic applications from a unique business systems perspective, focusing your IT resources on keeping these systems healthy and productive.

With Tivoli GEM, you can graphically monitor, control, and configure applications residing in distributed and centralized host S/390 environments. You can utilize the concept of business systems management to organize related components and give business context to management decisions. The GEM-Storage Management View provides a single, consolidated application view of storage. This allows administrators to view, monitor and manage the entirety of enterprise storage.

The GEM allows you to define the components necessary for the healthy and productive operation of a business system. It consolidates monitoring information from all of these components, and presents a health view of the applications. GEM not only consolidates information about the applications, systems and networks but also about the file systems, physical storage and SAN fabric required for these applications. As a result, if there is a network failure in the SAN, which prevents access to data that is required for a specific application, GEM will produce an alert. Also, GEM allows administrators to coordinate and monitor the enterprise-wide backup and disaster recovery of a business application. Administrators can get a consolidated view of the backup status of all components of a cross-platform business application.

7.2.2 Tivoli data management

A number of Tivoli products combine to give enterprise-wide management of data.

7.2.2.1 Tivoli Storage Manager

The Tivoli Storage Manager server is the cornerstone of Tivoli's data management architecture. It is constructed on a common, highly portable code base that scales from PC servers through UNIX and mid-range servers to OS/390 mainframe servers. The Storage Manager server is the data management backbone for Tivoli solutions.

The Storage Manager server is a data management application built on top of a relational semantic database. The Storage Manager database was created by IBM research specifically for the task of managing data. All policy information, logging, authentication and security, media management and object inventory information is managed by and driven through the Storage Manager database. It is highly tuned and implements zero-touch administration. No Database Administrator (DBA) interaction is required.

Included with the Storage Manager server is the Storage Manager backup/archive client. This client provides for both operational backup and long-term vital record retention archive. Storage Manager has implemented its patented Progressive Backup methodology for many years, Today the information on over one million computers is being protected in this manner.

> **Note**
>
> The Tivoli backup/archive client included with the Storage Manager server interacts with the Storage Manager server. Associated data management solutions for various environments such as Tivoli Data Protection for Network Attach Storage, Tivoli Data Protection for Mobile, Tivoli Data Protection for Workgroups, Tivoli Data Protection for applications, Tivoli Space Manager and Tivoli Disaster Recovery Manager all interact with the Storage Manager server. This means that administrators are not required to install, manage or monitor multiple servers in order to provide the many data management functions required in an enterprise.

For storing information, the Storage Manager server incorporates a hierarchy of storage capacity which can include any combination of disk, optical, tape or robotic systems. There are built-in drivers for over 340 different device types from every major manufacturer. Devices may operate stand-alone, or be linked together to form one or more storage hierarchies. Based on customer defined policies, information is stored into one of these hierarchies.

7.2.2.2 Tivoli SAN exploitation

Tivoli Storage Manager provides a number of important SAN solutions, and others are under development. These include:

Tape Resource Sharing

The Tape Resource Sharing feature of Tivoli Storage Manager allows administrators to pool tape resources for use by many Storage Manager servers running on heterogeneous platforms. This can improve backup and recovery performance, and tape hardware asset utilization.

LAN-free backup/client transfer

At the direction of the Storage Manager server, tape, optical or disk storage pools are dynamically allocated to clients. This allows backup, archive or HSM information to be sent across the SAN directly to storage pools. In this way the data path completely bypasses the LAN and the Storage Manager server. Less IP communications bandwidth is used, and service levels for end users are improved. This is illustrated in Figure 83.

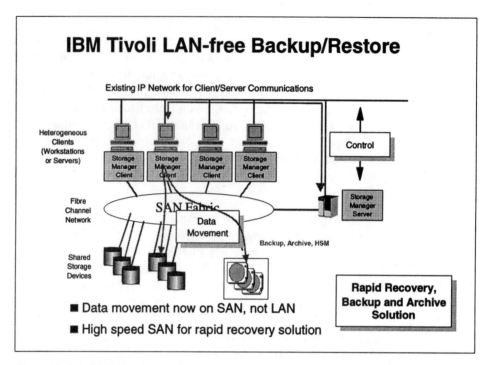

Figure 83. Tivoli LAN-free backup/restore

Server-free data transfer

The Storage Manager directs the SAN to move its data. The data transfer is accomplished wholly within the SAN, for instance from disk to tape, without the data path going through the Storage Manager server. This is illustrated in Figure 84.

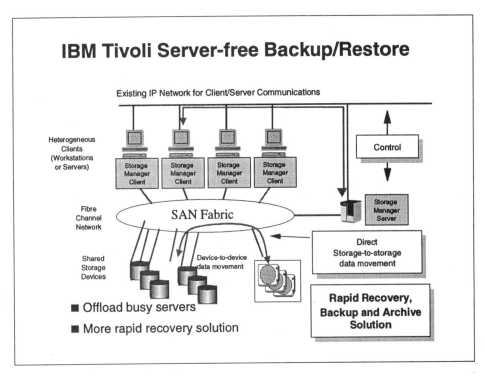

Figure 84. Tivoli server-free backup/restore

When LAN-free backup/client transfer is combined with server-free data transfer, the Storage Manager is transformed into a SAN based controller of all storage management. Administrators use its policy and scheduling capability to direct SAN-based, as well as LAN and WAN based, data management operations.

7.2.2.3 Tivoli SAN Data Manager

The concept of System-Managed Storage (SMS) is one of automated system management of all storage resources and data, done by hardware and software. This automated management is policy-driven to meet the needs of the individual business.

IBM introduced the first incarnation of system-managed storage on the OS/390 platform in 1988 with Data Facility Storage Management Subsystem (DFSMS). From the outset, DFSMS was based on a comprehensive set of customer requirements, documented by user groups.

Tivoli SAN Data Manager implements the system-managed storage concepts on open systems platforms and SANs. This provides applications and users with a view of infinite storage that meets administrator defined service levels for performance, availability and reliability, as well as true, platform independent data sharing.

Beneficial functions which will be enabled with Tivoli SAN Data Manager include:

- Policy based data placement, such as automatic selection of highly available, high performance RAID disk for mission critical database applications.
- Policy based life cycle management, such as automatic movement of aging data to lower performance, lower cost storage without host intervention.
- Server-free data movement — allowing movement of data through the SAN fabric without any interaction with hosts attached to the SAN, for tasks such as replication of files, operational backup, vital-records retention, and cross site disaster recovery backups. Another example is the management of hardware lease expirations and new purchases. Movement of data required due to installation of new disks, and retirement of old storage hardware can be achieved without involving or impacting the application servers.
- True data sharing — enabling all authorized hosts to access and work on the same data files by means of a metadata server.

Decision support for storage management analysis
This facility allows you to consolidate, transform and present your enterprise management data to reveal hidden patterns and natural relationships among the data. This tool organizes common topics and provide your storage administrators with graphical and tabular views. Data from multiple sources is integrated and presented in a variety of views. You can ask additional questions easily, or create new reports covering event, performance, and capacity analysis.

We show the Tivoli Storage Management Solutions Stack in Figure 85 and continue explaining the components in the topics that follow.

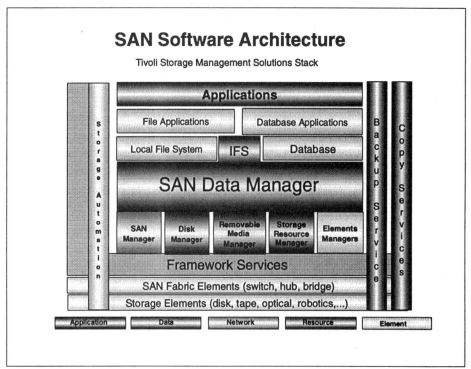

Figure 85. Tivoli Storage Management Solutions Stack

7.2.3 Tivoli resource management

Tivoli is developing a number of products which will provide comprehensive enterprise-wide resource management capabilities.

7.2.3.1 Tivoli Space Manager

This delivers a fully integrated solution for open system Hierarchical Space Management (HSM) using industry standard APIs.

7.2.3.2 Tivoli Removable Media Manager

Tivoli Removable Media Manager allows multiple applications dynamically to share removable media resources (drives, media and automated libraries). This results in more efficient usage of these resources and lower total cost of ownership. It implements the industry standard Removable Storage Management (RSM) API across heterogeneous operating platforms.

The RSM API was created by HighGround Systems and is included in the Microsoft Windows 2000 operating system. This makes Windows 2000 the only operating system, other than IBM OS/390, to natively support removable media sharing. For other open systems platforms, IBM has licensed RSM from HighGround and offers RSM support in the form of Tivoli Removable Media Manager (TRMM). Tivoli Removable Media Manager also integrates with IBM Data Facility Storage Management Subsystem Removable Media Manager (DFSMSrmm) on OS/390 to consolidate removable media management across mainframe and open systems servers.

7.2.3.3 Tivoli SAN Disk Manager

Tivoli SAN Disk Manager allows administrators to create secure, logical connections between host systems and disk Logical Units (LUNs) on a SAN. Administrators can view all of their SAN attached disk storage as a single, virtual pool, and can dynamically add or subtract storage from a host as needed.

Common discovery agent

One of the challenges an administrator faces is the ongoing management and maintenance of the agent software required to perform storage management functions. To simplify this job, Tivoli has made the architectural decision to provide a common discovery agent as part of the common Framework Services available to its Storage Management Solutions. The common discovery agent uses industry standard technologies like SNMP, FE-MIB, return node identification (RNID) and return topology information (RTIN) as well as patented scanner technology, to gather information about systems, storage and the SAN fabric that connects them. The common discovery agent also interacts with hosts participating in the SAN Disk Manager to ensure end-to-end security of the host-to-LUN relationship.

Host to LUN mapping

Tivoli SAN Disk Manager uses information from the common discovery agent to present an administrator with a tabular view of all the hosts and LUNs on a SAN. Detailed information about the hosts and the LUNs are also presented to aid in decision making. The administrator may then create secure logical connections. Scenarios include:

- One LUN with one host for dedicated use
- One LUN with multiple hosts for clustering
- Combinations of the above for multi-host pooling and sharing of SAN disk resources

Hardware-based LUN masking versus SAN Disk Manager

Most vendors of intelligent disk subsystems offer integrated, hardware based LUN masking, as IBM does with the Enterprise Storage Server (ESS). This function provides largely the same function as SAN Disk Manager. The difference is that the hardware-based solutions are proprietary to the hardware platform. In addition, these functions are not available for a JBOD. SAN Disk Manager is hardware independent. It provides a single interface and process that may be used across intelligent disk subsystems from any vendor, as well as JBOD implementations. This presents three major benefits to users of SAN Disk Manager.

- Enterprises are not locked into one hardware vendor or one disk architecture type.

- The common interface and process of SAN Disk Manager remains constant across multiple vendors or as hardware choices change.

- Disk and data security is provided for disk technologies that do not provide their own secure LUN masking.

Decision support for storage resource management
Using the framework services of Tivoli Decision Support important decision-making information is delivered about your enterprise storage resources, including:

- Asset Inventory analysis (for example, summary of physical hardware installed by device type, storage, SAN fabric components, HBAs, hosts, and so on).

- Capacity Analysis (for example, summary of all data growth: by operating system, by file system, by file type, and so on).

Automation for disk allocation
File systems that have violated installation specific free space thresholds are identified, and the process of allocating additional disk space is automated. Administrators can define policies that govern the monitoring of file systems and the proactive actions that are to be taken to avoid out-of-space conditions. For example, an administrator would define the utilization threshold that would trigger action, the amount of disk space that should be added to the file system, and the type of disk to be used. Administrators are then freed from this redundant task, and down time due to an out-of-space condition is avoided.

7.2.4 Tivoli network management
Network computing has become so pervasive that many enterprises simply cannot function when the TCP/IP network is down. Modern LAN and WAN networks can be complicated and confusing. Configuration mistakes and difficulty in problem isolation lead to downtime and reduced performance. This is why powerful network management tools have evolved.

Storage area networks are simply a new network for storage. In the same way that an e-business can't function without the TCP/IP network, it can't function when the SAN that connects it to storage is down. One feature of a network is the ability to create logical subsets or zones in the network.

7.2.4.1 Tivoli SAN Manager

Tivoli SAN Manager is the network manager for the SAN network. It uses the Common Discovery Agent (see "Common discovery agent" on page 162) to perform both in-band and out-band monitoring and management of systems, storage and the SAN fabric elements that connect them. Collected information is also used to build a physical topology map of the SAN. Once a physical map is produced, additional information allows logical views to be overlaid showing zones, host-to-storage and storage-to-host mappings.

SAN Manager also collects and consolidates information about events, and provides for multi-vendor, multi-component fault isolation and problem determination in the SAN. In the event that a device must be manipulated or reconfigured, device specific element management tools, such as IBM StorWatch products, may be launched from the SAN Manager console.

Decision support for SAN management analysis

Important decision-making information is provided about your enterprise SAN deployment in the areas of Event Analysis, Performance Analysis and Capacity Analysis.

Summary

In summary, the Tivoli SAN Manager will provide these functions:

- Discover and present the SAN topology
- Indicate device and interconnect status
- Perform continuous monitoring and fault isolation
- Provide reports and analysis via Tivoli Decision Support
- Launch vendor provided management applications

7.2.5 Tivoli element management

Most vendors today offer specialized software and interfaces for monitoring, configuring and managing their own hardware. In an enterprise that uses hardware from many different vendors, it becomes difficult even to find all of these interfaces, let alone monitor and manage them. Tivoli Storage Management Solutions provide a consolidation point for these hardware specific configuration tools. Through the Tivoli Ready partner program, hardware vendors may integrate their unique interfaces into a common location, allowing centralized monitoring and event forwarding as well as launch and drill-down capabilities (see 7.2.4.1, "Tivoli SAN Manager" on page 164).

7.2.5.1 Tivoli Ready Program

Tivoli's open Tivoli Ready Program is designed specifically to solve the problems of integration and manageability of multi-vendor heterogeneous product environments. Tivoli works with hundreds of industry-leading hardware and software vendors to offer integrated tools and products that can be effectively managed by Tivoli. The Tivoli Ready program extends from business software applications and systems management tools to hardware systems and devices, including storage devices and SAN fabric components. Tivoli Ready manageability can be provided in a variety of methods, such as use of the Tivoli Management Agent or a special management module.

Tivoli Management Agent

The Tivoli Management Agent is a self-updating agent that can be embedded in third-party products. Any new addition to an IT environment that holds the pre-installed Tivoli Management Agent is considered Tivoli Ready, and is instantly manageable by Tivoli software. The Tivoli Management Agent enables IT managers to define and execute management actions from a single point of control, and eliminates the need for manual distribution of complex software to thousands of computers and devices in order to manage them.

The agent was designed to provide an unlimited range of remote management of the end devices. In addition, it allows unprecedented scalability, supporting hundreds of thousands of devices under a single management server. With the agent's ability to automatically update its internal software and receive new functionality, any managed endpoint with the Agent installed will never require a physical visit to that endpoint again — all management can be directed from a single console. This is called "One-Touch Management."

The Tivoli Ready Program eliminates the complex problems presented by multi-vendor, multi-platform implementations, including Storage Area Networks. The major storage hardware and SAN fabric vendors have joined Tivoli Ready program, or announced their intentions to integrate their products into the Tivoli element management framework. Today it is estimated that more than ten million devices are Tivoli Ready, and that this will increase to more than one hundred million by the end of the year 2000. IBM's own Tivoli Ready device specific management tools are known as the StorWatch family.

7.2.5.2 IBM StorWatch software

IBM StorWatch Specialists are storage management tools that are integrated into specific IBM storage products. They provide easy to use, web browser based, management facilities to allow a storage administrator to manage the specific device, or a group of like devices. They include:

- IBM StorWatch Enterprise Storage Server Specialist
- IBM StorWatch Enterprise Storage Server Expert
- IBM StorWatch Fibre Channel RAID Specialist
- IBM StorWatch Serial Storage Expert
- IBM StorWatch SAN Data Gateway Specialist
- IBM StorWatch SAN Data Gateway S20 Specialist
- IBM StorWatch Fibre Channel Managed Hub Specialist
- IBM StorWatch SAN Fibre Channel Switch Specialist
- IBM StorWatch Virtual Tape Server Specialist

Additional StorWatch family members are planned for future delivery.

7.2.5.3 Enterprise-wide element management

The combination of Tivoli storage and SAN management software, IBM StorWatch device management tools, and Tivoli Management Agents running on OEM computers and storage devices, provided through the Tivoli Ready program, enable complete enterprise-wide element management of a multi-vendor, heterogeneous SAN.

7.3 Summary of IBM's "end to end" SAN Management

IBM aims to provide businesses with the ability to integrate SAN technology into their existing IT infrastructure, while protecting investments in storage, server and application resources; and to use new technologies as they mature.

Early deliverables are focusing on Fibre Channel connectivity and device-level management. These provide the basic building blocks to enable IT resource management and information sharing across storage networks. Later deliverables will add additional value to the Fibre Channel infrastructure by delivering storage connectivity solutions and comprehensive fabric management that help organizations manage, track, and more easily share, the complex and ever-increasing volume of data created by the Internet and by e-business applications.

The goals of the IBM corporate SAN initiatives and the Tivoli storage management vision are to achieve:

- Uninterrupted availability
- Scalability
- Access to storage anywhere, anytime
- Improved and expanded performance
- Improved data integrity
- Improved security
- Improved data protection
- True data sharing
- Cost reductions through improved allocation of IT resources and automation

To realize these promises, we believe enterprises will need to implement management capabilities similar to those depicted in Figure 85 on page 161.

IBM will use its enterprise experience, and technology leadership, to help companies make a smooth transition to SANs, and to provide a framework incorporating IBM and non-IBM products and services. IBM will deliver interoperability tested, certified solutions consisting of best-of-breed IBM and non-IBM software, servers, SAN fabric components and storage. IBM Global Services will develop and implement the best practices required to support the new generation of SAN technology. This strategy is designed to protect current investments, to provide a road map for incorporating evolving technology, and to help minimize risks.

For additional information, see the IBM SAN Web site at:

www.storage.ibm.com/ibmsan

And, see the Tivoli Systems SAN Web site at:

www.tivoli.com/products/index/san/

Chapter 8. Tivoli SANergy File Sharing

In the SAN environment, sharing of large files at high speeds with fail safe security is a high priority. Tivoli SANergy File Sharing (SANergy FS) Version 2.1 (formerly SANergyFS from Mercury Computer Systems, Inc.) and its optional High Availability feature (formerly SANergyXA), provide these capabilities.

In the topics that follow, we provide an overview of the functionality and the benefits that Tivoli SANergy brings to the SAN environment.

8.1 Tivoli SANergy software

Tivoli SANergy FS is software that delivers the power to dynamically share files on storage area network (SAN) based storage, using standard networks and file systems. Instead of relying on a LAN that trickles data at 10 megabytes per second or less.

Tivoli SANergy FS enables you to share data among the supported SAN connected systems on your network at the high throughput rates of your storage area network. Different systems can access the same information at the same time, even running different operating systems, and the data arrives substantially faster than with traditional LAN-based file server alternatives.

Tivoli SANergy FS supports virtually any network-aware application without costly programming or systems administration changes. In addition, since it is generally less expensive to purchase a single large array than to buy several smaller ones, the SAN environment leverages the efficiencies of centralized storage to reduce operational costs.

Tivoli SANergy FS is unique, because it is based upon standard file systems and network services. By leveraging existing standards, Tivoli SANergy affords all of the access control and security features that you expect in your network, while enabling greater compatibility with existing and future applications and management utilities.

The features of Tivoli SANergy FS which are specifically aimed at supporting business-critical enterprise environments include:

- Support for several environments — Tivoli SANergy FS is currently available for the following operating systems connected to the SAN: Windows NT, Windows 2000, MacOS, IBM AIX, SGI IRIX, Sun Solaris, DG/UX, and Tru64 UNIX systems. Currently, the only systems that can act as the Meta Data Controller (MDC) for the SAN are those running Windows NT, Windows 2000, or Sun Solaris.

- High Availability feature — This optional feature is an add-on for NT-based Tivoli SANergy systems that serves as an automated failure recovery monitor for MDCs. If an MDC should fail, a new MDC can be assigned automatically from any Windows NT or Windows 2000 client computer. This feature is only available for Windows NT 4.0 or Windows 2000.

8.1.1 Tivoli SANergy at a glance

Tivoli SANergy File Sharing Version 2.1 provides users with file sharing at SAN speeds. Key features include:

- High-speed, file-level sharing in a homogeneous or heterogeneous environment

- A new, open API which allows third party file systems to support and integrate with SANergy 2.1

- Priced optional High Availability feature that acts as an automated failure recovery monitor for Meta Data Controllers (MDCs)

- A custom Tivoli SANergy management information base (MIB) is included to enable management by any SNMP console

With these features, Tivoli SANergy FS offers these advantages to its users:

- Supports the standard user interface, management, access control, and security features native to the host platforms to simplify operation

- Reduces or eliminates the expense of redundant storage

- Enables use of higher bandwidth I/O in a shared environment, enhanced speed of workflow, resulting in increased productivity

- Reduces costly down time, increases data availability

- Reduces network congestion and overhead on LAN

8.1.2 File sharing

Tivoli SANergy File Sharing Version 2.1 benefits applications that demand high bandwidth access to common file storage at speeds faster than the typical LAN. This high speed data access offers benefit to applications such as streaming digital multimedia, complex large-file/multi-server workflow, and multi-system web hosts and/or file servers.

Tivoli SANergy File Sharing enables multiple Windows NT, Macintosh, and UNIX systems to dynamically share files and data on shared SAN-based storage devices using standard network and file systems (for example CIFS, NFS).

Tivoli SANergy FS is software that runs on workstations connected to a storage area network (SAN). Similar to how a LAN with a server works, a SAN using Tivoli SANergy allows all workstations to both read and write all the disk volumes across the SAN at the same time. In fact, Tivoli SANergy makes storage across the SAN appear on the desktop as if it were just more storage across the LAN.

In a Tivoli SANergy FS environment, multiple machines use a LAN layer for various ordinary metadata synchronization. One of the systems (Windows or Solaris) connected to the SAN is designated as the metadata controller (MDC) to handle control information such as the permissions, access rights, and location in the network. The actual file data is not passed over the LAN layer but instead is transparently redirected over the SAN layer. The file system is managed across the LAN while the file data goes down the high speed SAN connection (Fibre Channel, SCSI, or SSA).

8.1.3 High Availability optional feature

A Windows NT system, running the High Availability feature, can automatically step in for a failed MDC; Tivoli SANergy FS NT clients will re-map their SANergy SHAREs to the new MDC without user intervention. This feature allows Tivoli SANergy-based file sharing to avoid the single point of failure risk associated with LAN-based file-servers. With the High Availability priced option, the failure of any system on the SAN has minimal impact on the I/O operations of the systems.

8.1.4 Open standards

Tivoli SANergy FS works with standard networking, security, management and file systems:

- Windows NT network security and NTFS (current)
- SAN- and media- independent
- Fibre Channel, SCSI, or SSA
- Works with most commercial adapters, switches, and hubs
- Heterogeneous cross-platform support on Windows NT, MacOS, and UNIX

8.1.5 Performance

Tivoli SANergy FS uses lightweight protocol with low latency which enables:

- Single-node data access rates at full media speeds
- Utilization of total network throughput is virtually unlimited with fabric and switch technologies
- Tivoli SANergy FS supports cross-platform software for basic and dynamic volumes to achieve the highest data rates possible.

8.1.6 Transparency

Tivoli SANergy provides a GUI that allows administrators to manage buses, assign MDCs, run performance tester, and change configuration options. Once configured, there is no user interaction required unless the user chooses to monitor system statistics.

Since Tivoli SANergy FS requires no user interaction once it is installed and configured, access to standard network shares and mounts is accelerated.

Tivoli SANergy FS also delivers and leverages full file-level and byte-level locking capabilities provided by the MDC host (using CIFS or NTFS).

8.1.7 Installation and setup

Tivoli SANergy FS uses standard, platform-optimized automated installation. It installs as a transparent extension to the O/S, network, and file system. Tivoli SANergy integrates with Windows NT system administration utilities.

8.1.8 Administration

Administration of the Tivoli SANergy environment requires no additional software (for example, Java). With the Tivoli SANergy FS management information base (MIB), the configuration, operation, and monitoring of a physically distributed Tivoli SANergy environment can be centralized using standard management consoles. This allows for simple addition or removal of machines and volumes.

8.1.9 Intended customers

Enterprise customers with a SAN seeking to simplify the administration and management of the storage on the SAN behind their servers

Workgroups of high-bandwidth, high-performance workstations connected to a SAN who want to simplify the administration and management of the SAN storage and provide the same data on that storage to multiple workstations simultaneously.

Capabilities made possible with a SAN and Tivoli SANergy:

- LAN-free and server-free backup/archive and restore
- LAN-free and server-free data copies and moves
- LAN traffic reduction
- Centralized, high-availability storage
- Easier expansion/growth of computers and storage to meet future demands
- Reduced administration and management of storage through the elimination of all but one file system

Tivoli SANergy's unique patented technology leverages industry standard file system and network security implementations to ensure maximum compatibility with current and future operating systems, applications, and management software. Tivoli SANergy's open architecture allows the entire industry to leverage and extend Tivoli SANergy's capabilities to meet specific market, application and data/network management demands.

Part 2. SAN construction zone

Amid a lot of the hype that is related to SANs, it is obvious that there has to be a product or solution somewhere. Accepting the realization that there are few companies that can provide a total SAN solution, it is not unreasonable to introduce where IBM is today with its SAN solutions, and how these can be utilized to provide a base for the future, while protecting any prior investment. We show some common problems that face the storage world today and how they can be solved by implementing a SAN.

In Part 2 we show the SAN solutions that can be implemented today, along with some of the basic infrastructure requirements that must be considered.

Chapter 9. SAN planning and design considerations

OK, so you have looked at Fibre Channel architecture, and concluded that Storage Area Networks will be beneficial to your organization. Where do you go from here? How do you plan to go about implementing a SAN? Who should be involved? What do you need to do before you call your vendor and order new equipment? This chapter discusses some of the things you need to consider when you are at the planning and design stage. It does not purport to be a detailed methodology. It is intended only to cover some basic ideas and suggestions. IBM's International Global Services division offers detailed planning, design, and consultant services, which give a structured approach to SAN design and implementation.

9.1 Establishing the goals

There is an old maxim which states, "If it ain't broken, don't fix it". This could easily be applied to discussions about implementing SANs. When you look at your current storage infrastructure, if you find that it meets all your expectations for data availability, performance and connectivity, then implementing a SAN will be difficult to cost justify. Most IT executives will be reluctant to make investments in a new IT infrastructure unless they can be shown that real benefits will accrue.

9.1.1 Business goals

As we have seen in section 1.5, "What the business benefits of a Fibre Channel SAN are" on page 19, there are numerous ways in which a SAN can benefit an organization. Each company will have a unique set of circumstances and needs. If you can identify specific applications which today suffer from lack of connectivity; inability to share information or storage resources with others; which cannot be backed up in a timely manner due to bandwidth constraints on your LAN; or otherwise are limited in the way in which they provide service to the organization, then a SAN could be the solution. If users are always asking for more storage, and your storage costs are growing rapidly, and management of resources is becoming increasingly difficult, then a SAN is a likely answer. If your company is moving into e-business, supporting application operations 24 hours, 7 days a week, implementing Enterprise Resource Planning and Business Intelligence, and cannot tolerate outages of such mission critical applications, then a SAN can solve your problems.

In other words, you need to identify the "pain levels" associated with data movement, data sharing, data growth, and so on, in your own organization.

Then, you can quantify how a SAN will contribute to your ability to achieve the levels of service demanded by your business managers. This might be quantified in terms of improved communications within the business, and externally with customers. It could be a matter of improving the ability of managers and employees to make good business decisions due to better information availability. You might be measuring security and reliability of mission critical applications, or reducing costs of storage hardware and skilled human management resources. The need may be to establish flexible, adaptable IT services, to stay in the race with competitors who are not constrained by legacy applications or inflexible IT infrastructures. The focus could be on the ability to increase revenue and profit with effective growth of new e-business services.

Whatever the level of "the pain", you need to understand your existing IT infrastructure, which are the mission critical applications, and what are the business goals and directions.

9.1.2 Technical goals

When you understand the business goals, these will lead you to evaluate the technical requirements placed on the supporting IT infrastructure; and what a SAN must provide to meet these requirements. These could be measured in terms of reliability, availability and serviceability (RAS); performance; scalability; security; manageability; and affordability.

9.1.2.1 RAS

Assess the nature of the applications to be supported on the SAN. Do they need to be available on a 24 hour, 7 days a week basis? If they are not mission critical, how much downtime, if any, is acceptable? What are the costs of downtime? Non-availability of some applications may be measured in hundreds of thousands or even millions of dollars per hour; for others there may be very limited financial impact. The answer may lead you to focus on hardware aspects, such as mean time between failure (MTBF), mean time to repair; and serviceability characteristics, such as fault tolerance, hot swappable components, failover facilities, error reporting, and call home capabilities.

9.1.2.2 Performance

What are the performance characteristics required to support the various applications on the SAN? How do you measure this? With throughput (MB/second) or I/Os per second, or response time? What is the maximum capacity or bandwidth required for peak loads? What percentage of the SAN capacity will be used on average, and at what level of utilization would it become saturated? What happens to performance in the event of failure of

SAN components? Can sufficient spare bandwidth be provided to continue to deliver acceptable performance?

9.1.2.3 Scalability

How much growth is expected? Will the SAN you design be required to support additional applications? If so, in what time scale, for instance within the next year or two years? How fast is data growing, and will you need to expand storage resources, or add more servers? Do you need to support legacy SCSI hardware? What are the distances between server and storage resources, and will this need to expand to include other departments and locations?

9.1.2.4 Security

How will you protect application data on the SAN from loss or corruption, without losing access to the information? Can you provide backup and recovery and disaster protection capabilities to meet your organizations policies for the data? What failover facilities within the SAN design will be required to ensure continued accessibility in the event of errors or disasters?

If multiple servers are attached to the SAN, can you ensure that each may only access the data or storage devices it is authorized to access? This is particularly critical in a heterogeneous platform environment, especially if Windows NT hosts are participating. For instance, NT expects to see a SCSI bus attachment, and it seeks to attach all the devices which are attached to the bus. It does the same on a SAN, so it is essential to provide security against this occurrence by means of zoning and/or LUN masking (see 4.3.9, "Zoning" on page 91 and 4.3.11, "LUN masking" on page 94). Decide which level of zoning (hardware and/or software) and LUN masking is appropriate, remembering that LUN masking at the storage device level (including SAN Data Gateway) provides the highest level of security because it logically binds storage volumes to specific servers. This ensures that each server can only access its own data, just as though the storage was directly attached to the server.

9.1.2.5 Manageability

Consider how the SAN will be managed in your environment. You will need to have tools to handle a number of critical aspects. A variety of software vendors offer tools to address some of these requirements. Tivoli Systems has a set of software tools which provide complete SAN management (See 7.2, "IBM SAN management solutions" on page 154).

These management tools include:

- **Configuration:** Facilities to identify, operate, collect data from and control the devices in the SAN.

- **Access:** Tools to allow configuration, maintenance, zoning and LUN masking to protect data, and ensure only authorized access to information.

- **Performance:** Managing performance to meet service levels; analyze the traffic on the SAN, and understand the behavior of applications in order to be able to optimize the network, and plan for future requirements.

- **Faults:** The ability to detect, isolate, correct and report on events within the SAN.

9.1.2.6 Affordability

When you are considering a SAN configuration, you have already established the expected benefits. But costs are always one of the most significant aspects of any investment decision. What are the decision criteria which are most important in the solution you are contemplating? For a mission critical enterprise application it may be that high availability is the overriding requirement. In a campus-wide application, the dominating theme may be connectivity. At an individual departmental level, low cost may be the main objective. As with most other choices you can make design trade-offs (Table 9), but each compromise usually involves giving up on something, whether it be performance, availability, security, scalability, manageability, or some other characteristic.

Table 9. Design trade-offs

Design Goal	Trade-off
High availability	Redundant components and higher costs
High performance	Higher cost circuits and more equipment
High level of security	More costly monitoring and reduced ease of use
High scalability	Higher costs with possible availability impacts
High throughput for one application	Lower throughput for another application
Low cost	Reduced availability and performance

9.2 Defining the infrastructure requirements

If you are starting from scratch with a totally new network in a green field site then you can go straight ahead with selection of the optimum SAN topology to meet your needs. But in most situations it is likely that you are replacing an existing infrastructure for storage. You may even be planning to change or upgrade an existing SAN implementation. So, before selecting a design for the new SAN, it makes good sense to fully understand what it is that is being replaced. The current storage configuration, LAN or SAN network structure, application uses, traffic loads, peak periods and performance, as well as current constraints, are all relevant information in determining realistic goals for the SAN. This information will also help you to determine what, if any, of the existing components can be used in a new topology; and what will be involved in migrating from today's environment to the new one.

9.2.1 Use of existing fiber

In many cases you may already have fiber-optic cables laid in your organization. IT budget holders will want to know if you can use the existing cabling. This is discussed in 6.2.4, "Current infrastructures and other protocol link budgets" on page 132. If the existing cabling has been laid for some time the answer may well be that the high speeds and accuracy required of Fibre Channel requires new cable investments. It is possible to test if installed fiber meets the necessary quality, but this can also be a costly exercise. If recent fiber cable has been laid you may need to decide what extensions need to be added to the configuration.

9.2.2 Application traffic characteristics

Before selecting a SAN topology you will need to understand the nature of the estimated traffic. Which servers and storage devices will generate data movements. Which are the sources, and which are the targets? Will data flow between servers as well as from servers to storage? If you plan to implement LAN-free or server-free data movement, what are the implications? How much data will flow directly from storage device to storage device, such as disk to tape, and tape to disk? What is the protocol? For instance, is this standard SCSI, or are you including digital video or audio?

What are the sizes of data objects sent by differing applications? Are there any overheads which are incurred by differing Fibre Channel frames? What Fibre Channel class of service needs to be applied to the various applications (see 3.10, "Framing classes of service" on page 60)? Which departments or user groups generate the traffic? Where are they located, what applications do each community use, and how many in the user group? This information may point to opportunities for physical storage consolidation. It will also help you to calculate the number of Fibre Channel nodes required, the sum of all the data traffic which could be in transit at any time, and potential peaks and bottlenecks.

Can you identify any latent demand for applications, which are not carried out today because of constraints of the existing infrastructure? If you introduce high speed backup and recovery capabilities across a SAN, could this lead to an increase in the frequency of backup activity by user groups? Perhaps today they are deterred by the slow speed of backups across the LAN? Could the current weekly backup cycle move to a daily cycle as a result of the improved service? If so, what would this do to SAN bandwidth requirements?

9.2.3 Platforms and storage

How many servers and what are the operating platforms which will be attached to the SAN? The majority of early SAN adopters have tended to implement homogeneous installations (that is, supporting a single operating platform type, such as all Netfinity, all HP, or all Sun servers). As SANs are maturing, the trend is towards larger scale networks, supporting multiple heterogeneous operating platforms (combining AIX, UNIX, Windows NT and so on). This has implications for security, (as we have already shown in 9.1.2.4, "Security" on page 179).

Fibre Channel capable servers require Fibre Channel HBAs to attach to the SAN fabric. The choice of HBA is probably already decided by the server vendor. Before you decide how many HBAs you require in your host to achieve optimal performance, you need to evaluate the performance of the server. Fibre Channel HBAs today transfer data at 100 MB/s. Can the system bus provide data at the same or higher speed? If not, the HBA will not be fully utilized. The most common system bus in use today is the Peripheral Component Interconnect bus (PCI), which operates at either 132 MB/s or 264 MB/s. Sun SBus operates at 50 MB/s, and HP HSC at only 40 MB/s. If the system bus delivers 132 MB/s or less, you will only need to attach one Fibre Channel HBA to the bus to achieve the required performance, since two would over run the bus speed. If you attach a second HBA it should only be for redundancy purposes. Our recommendation is to install one adapter per system bus.

Another major component of your current assets are the storage systems. You may have a variety of internally attached disk devices, which will not be relevant in a SAN operation. Also you may have externally attached JBODs or RAID disk subsystems, and tape drives or libraries, which can be utilized within the SAN. These current assets have implications for the selection of interconnections to the SAN. You may wish to support existing hardware which are SCSI or SSA compatible, and which will need to be provided with router or gateway connections for protocol conversion to Fibre Channel.

9.3 Selecting the topology

The most fundamental choice in the design of your SAN is the selection of the most appropriate topology. This selection may be colored by the overall approach to SAN planning that your organization wishes to adopt.

The question is — top down, or bottom up design? In other words, should you try to design a corporate strategy, with a view to implement an enterprise wide SAN, or should you address the problem from the perspective of individual departments or user groups, and implement multiple SANlets? Maybe these small SANs will later merge into an enterprise-wide solution.

This is a difficult question to answer. Probably it will be answered differently depending on the size of the organization, the IT management philosophy, the politics of the organization, and the business objectives. It is also colored by the degree of risk which you associate with the implementation of an enterprise wide SAN today. The technologies are still relatively new. Industry standards in some key areas are still to be agreed upon. Not all server platforms can easily participate in Fibre Channel configurations, and the rate of change is extremely rapid. It is probable that in a years time things will look very different than they do today.

The fact is that the majority of SANs which have been implemented today are relatively small, point solutions. By this we mean that they were designed to address a specific "pain" or problem. Many users have implemented simple point to point Fibre Channel solutions to solve distance or performance issues. Many others have installed small clustered server solutions, or shared storage capacity by means of FC-arbitrated loops because this provides improved connectivity and better utilization of storage resources. Others have designed switched fabric solutions for departments, or have used FC directors to facilitate large scale storage consolidation in campus locations.

In practice then, the bottom up approach seems to be the most pragmatic. Solve specific application needs now, to deliver value to your organization. This does not mean that you should not establish some common guidelines or standards regarding the purchase of equipment within the enterprise. This will facilitate interoperability in the future, and avoid dead end investments which cannot be integrated in a larger SAN environment as you expand the topology in the future. You may decide that there are a number of discrete and independent operating environments within your organization, and these will not need to be inter linked in the future. If so, you may choose to establish SAN islands which are configured with different topologies and components in which cross island interoperability is not required.

A strong trend is towards switched fabric environments. This is because fabric offers greatest flexibility and scope for the future. You may choose to instal small FC-AL topologies now, for reasons of cost, or because the application being addressed is small scale today. If so, there is good logic in selecting hardware such as the IBM 3534 Managed Hub. This gives you flexibility for the future, such as more sophisticated function, manageability, and upgrade-ability, and with compatibility within a family of fabric devices.

Remember that FC-AL is not designed for high performance. It does not scale. As you add more devices on a loop performance will tend to reduce because of the shared bandwidth, and arbitration overheads. A maximum of two servers is advisable on an FC-AL. If one server fails and has to reboot, causing a new LIP, it will bring down the whole loop. Availability is, therefore, also a serious consideration.

FC-SW, on the other hand, scales performance as you add nodes. This does not apply to Inter Switch Links (ISLs) which do not add bandwidth between end nodes because ISLs reduce the number of end to end connections. Secure zones and masked LUNs can be created so that only authorized servers can access specific information. FC-SW provides comprehensive, flexible growth options, but is more expensive at the outset.

9.3.1 Assessing the components

IBM provides a hierarchy of interconnect options with which to build Fibre Channel SANs to suit differing application characteristics. These can range from FC-AL topologies for work groups, to departmental switched fabrics, and to highly available topologies based on cascaded switches or fault tolerant directors. In addition, bridge solutions allow for attachment of legacy SCSI and SSA devices. This hierarchy is illustrated in Figure 86.

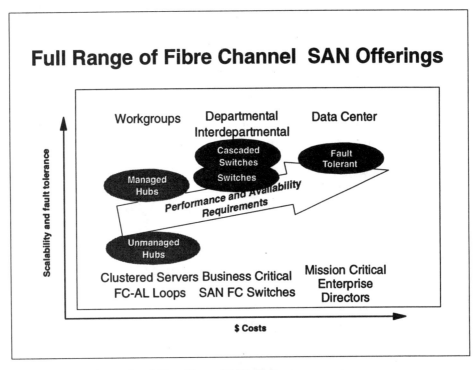

Figure 86. IBM's hierarchy of Fibre Channel SAN offerings

It is worth bearing in mind that new products, features and functions are regularly announced. For the latest information on the products described in this book, and for details of new solutions, refer to IBM's SAN web site:

`www.storage.ibm.com/ibmsan`

Current products are described in outline in Chapter 5, "Fibre Channel products" on page 97. The following section summarizes the major reasons for selecting a device type.

9.3.1.1 When will you use a Router or a Data Gateway?

Routers and Gateways act as "bridges" between different protocols. You would select them to allow you to provide investment protection for IBM or non-IBM storage devices which use SCSI or SSA protocols, and provide attachment to the Fibre Channel SAN.

The IBM SAN Data Gateway Router (IBM 2108-R03) is a low-cost solution supporting attachment between a Fibre Channel attached host and a SCSI tape library, such as a 3575 Magstar MP.

The Vicom Fibre Channel SLIC Router Model FC-SL (7139 model 111) enables all IBM 7133, 7131, and 3527 SSA Disk Systems to attach to host systems using fibre channel host adapters and drivers.

The IBM SAN Data Gateway (2108-G07) provides protocol conversion for connection of SCSI and Ultra SCSI storage devices to Fibre Channel environments using an industry standard Fibre Channel Arbitrated Loop (FC-AL) interface. The SAN Data Gateway enables SCSI devices to benefit from distance extension to 500 meters, increased bandwidth of Fibre Channel, and increased addressability.

A wide range of IBM and non-IBM SCSI based servers are supported (including UNIX and Windows based), plus many IBM and non-IBM SCSI storage devices, including IBM Magstar tape and the Enterprise Storage Server. Because of its comprehensive zoning access control capabilities, including persistent binding of hosts to LUNs (LUN masking), the SAN Data Gateway is an ideal solution to support attachment of a SCSI based ESS to multiple hosts in a Fibre Channel SAN for storage consolidation.

9.3.1.2 When will you use a hub?
Use a hub to implement a Fibre Channel-arbitrated loop. Hubs can also be used as distance extenders, in connection with the IBM SAN Data Gateway.

Usually they are used for entry level homogeneous server implementations. Some of the possible uses of these hubs are clustering, LAN-free backup, storage consolidation and remote disk mirroring.

The IBM products available are the IBM Fibre Channel Storage Hub (2103-H07) and IBM Fibre Channel Managed Hub (3534-1RU). The IBM 3534-1RU offers superior function due to its manageability, with superior fault isolation, planning and controlling. It also has a non-blocking architecture. This means that any two pairs of ports can be active and transferring data, without blocking transfer of data from another pair of ports, therefore, guaranteeing full-speed data delivery irrespective of traffic conditions. This product, technically, is based on the IBM 2109 SAN Fibre Channel Switch. Therefore, it has the potential to be made upgradable in the future, so possibly protecting your investment. For these reasons, we recommend that you normally select the IBM 3534-1RU in preference to the unmanaged hub.

9.3.1.3 When will you use a switch?
You will use a switch as the basis for development of a full switched fabric SAN. IBM's products today are the IBM SAN Fibre Channel Switch, with two models, an 8-port and a 16-port model (IBM 2109 S08 and S16). Multiple switches can be interlinked (cascaded) to build a large SAN comprising many

ports. The ultimate limitation in the fabric design is 239 physical switches (imposed by the maximum number of unique domain IDs that can be defined). Today the practical tested limit is about 15% of this number, and with no more than seven hops allowed from the source port to the destination port. There are fabric designs in production today with between 10 and 20 switches in a single fabric. This number will certainly grow significantly over time.

The IBM 2109 also supports attachment of FL-Ports, so it can interlink to Fibre Channel Arbitrated Loops. In addition, hosts which are not fabric aware, and only operate on a Private Loop, such as HP servers, can be supported on the IBM 2109 using a feature known as QuickLoop (QL), which was introduced in 4.3.5, "QuickLoop" on page 87.

The switch can be set up to create a logical private loop with the storage assigned to that server. The whole switch can operate in QL mode, or individual ports can be configured as QL. In this way the IBM 2109 can be used instead of a hub to support such servers. The IBM 2109 can also be cascaded with the IBM 3534-1RU Fibre Channel Managed Hub. Thus the switch can be used in a number of ways for cost, availability and performance, to satisfy differing SAN application and user group needs within the enterprise.

9.3.1.4 When will you use a director?
You would select the McDATA ED-5000 Fibre Channel Director for high availability applications requiring extensive fault tolerance within the switch, and high port count to support multiple node attachments and high switch bandwidth. These applications might typically be found in large data centers, supporting large numbers of heterogeneous open systems servers.

The McDATA ED-5000 is based on the design of the IBM ESCON Director, which is widely used in S/390 Data Centers for core mission critical applications. The McDATA ED-5000 Director will support cascading of directors using E-Ports, but it does not provide FL-Port connectivity to Arbitrated Loops. Also, due to differences in implementation of name server and zoning techniques, the director is incompatible with the IBM 2109 Fibre Channel Switch and IBM 3534 Managed Hub, so they cannot yet be used together in a cascaded fabric. This may be resolved in the future as standards are agreed and implemented. The McDATA ED-5000 Director does support servers and devices attached using the IBM SAN Data Gateway and the IBM SAN Data Gateway Router.

9.3.2 Building a multi-switch fabric

A single switch or director is limited in the number of ports it can directly interconnect. To increase connectivity in the fabric it is necessary to connect multiple switches or directors. This is known as a cascaded fabric.

9.3.2.1 Cascading

Cascaded fabric is a cost effective, reliable way to achieve very large port counts in the SAN. It is also used as a means of delivering fault tolerant fabrics by eliminating single points of failure, and to service applications requiring high availability. Cascading also increases the maximum distance between interconnected devices. Examples used in this chapter will be based on Inter Switch Links (ISLs) between multiple IBM 2109 Fibre Channel Switches, (the first cascadable Fibre Channel switch available on the market).

9.3.2.2 Inter switch links

When cascading IBM 2109 switches the ports used for ISL will automatically be designated as E-Ports by the switch software. E-Ports reduce the number of ports available for device connection. More switches can be added to the fabric non-disruptively. Multiple links can operate concurrently between any two switches in the fabric, allowing multiple redundant paths to be defined. All ISLs carry traffic. In the event of a link failure, traffic it was carrying will be automatically and immediately transferred to other links. Adding ISLs will automatically cause routing and zoning information to be updated across all ISLs. Changing ISL configurations causes re-calculation of routes within the fabric. This task is a load on all switches in the fabric, so numerous changes should be avoided. The maximum number of ISLs from one switch to a single adjacent switch is 8, but more than 8 ISLs can be configured from a single switch if they attach to several other switches. This is shown in Figure 87.

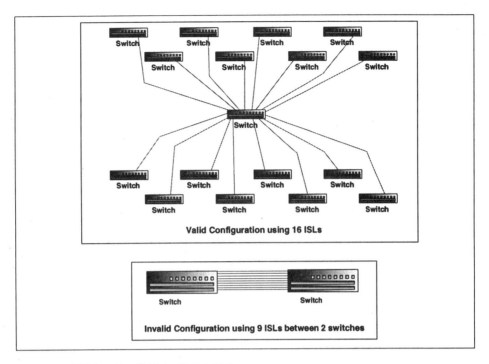

Figure 87. Valid and invalid Inter Switch Links

9.3.2.3 Distributed name server

If a switch fails, the other switches in the fabric, and the nodes attached to them, are unaffected. Nodes attached to the failed switch are of course unable to talk to each other, or to nodes on other switches. However, this problem can be overcome, since any node can have several Fibre Channel interfaces, each one attached to nodes on different switches in the fabric. This is illustrated in Figure 88. If any link fails every switch can still communicate with all the other switches. IBM 2109 switches use a distributed fabric-wide name server. This means that the name server is fully distributed to each switch, thus ensuring no single point of failure. When end nodes attached to servers and devices wish to communicate to other nodes across the fabric, any switch provides information about the devices connected to the fabric by means of the distributed name server, even in the event of a failed switch.

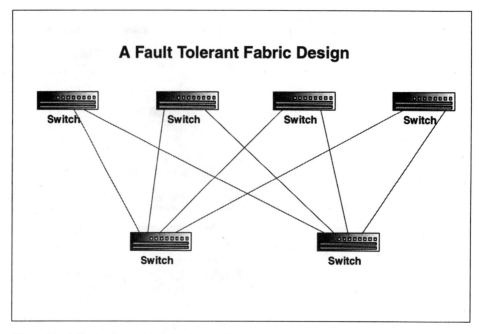

Figure 88. A Fault tolerant fabric design

9.3.2.4 Fabric Shortest Path First (FSPF)

FSPF is the path selection protocol used by the IBM 2109 switch. It automatically calculates the best path between any two switches in the fabric when switches are powered up. It establishes all the routes across the fabric, and these change only in the event of a failure, or if a new ISL is created which offers an equal or better path to a given target. FSPF is very resilient to failures of hardware and software, automatically computing an alternate path around a failed link, typically in less than one second. If several equivalent paths are available between two nodes FSPF will automatically share traffic between these paths. This feature provides high bandwidth as well as fault tolerance, because no paths are held idle as stand-by redundant links. This is quite different to LAN path redundancy, which maintains idle paths for redundancy. FSPF can guarantee in-sequence delivery of frames, even if the routing topology has changed during a failure, by enforcing a "hold down" period before a new path is activated. This allows all frames in transit to a specific destination to be delivered or discarded.

An example of shared traffic routing is shown in Figure 89. Four switches have two ISLs between any two of them. Traffic between Switches 1 and 3, for example, will be shared on two paths, but traffic between Switches 1 and 4 can be shared on four paths.

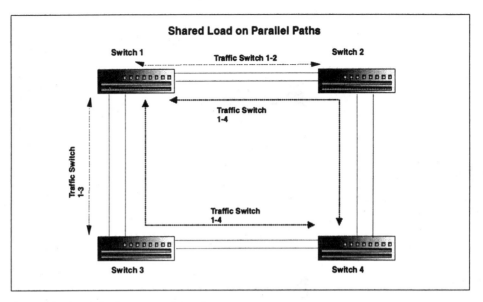

Figure 89. Load sharing on parallel paths

A maximum of seven hops is recommended between any two switches in the fabric to avoid time-outs. We say recommended, because the actual hops are not monitored and restricted to seven. More hops are possible and test beds up to 20 switches have been installed and tested, but every extra hop adds about 1.2 microseconds latency to the transmission. The length of the fiber is another consideration, since each kilometer between nodes adds a further five microseconds delay. Traffic patterns need to be understood, to avoid long paths and bottlenecks. Ideally devices should be attached to the same switch if they exchange large amounts of data, as this minimizes communication delays. If this is not possible then more ISLs should be configured to increase the available bandwidth between switches. Of course this also adds to the resiliency of the fabric.

The fabric design in Figure 90 illustrates a fully meshed fabric in which a switch is only one hop from any other switch. This minimizes latency across the fabric. Also, if any link fails (even with two link failures) all switches can still communicate with each other.

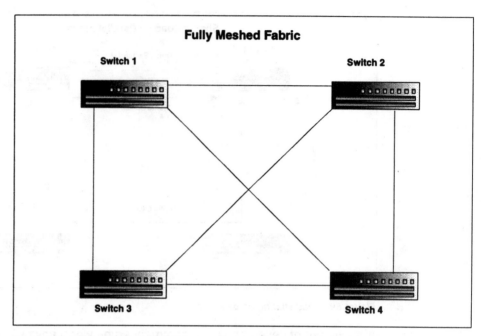

Figure 90. A fully meshed topology

9.3.2.5 Redundant fabrics

We have been discussing redundant elements, like paths and switches, within a single fabric. Another approach, and one which gives many advantages, is to use redundant fabrics. The simplest version of this is two switches which are not inter-connected. If one switch fails data is automatically routed via the second switch. This is initiated by host/device driver software, like IBM's Subsystem Device Driver (formerly Data Path Optimizer), which recognizes the failure of the path and fails over to the alternate path on the redundant switch. This configuration, illustrated in Figure 91, also allows for maintenance or repair actions to be made on one SAN, while the other stays in operation. More detailed examples of redundant fabric designs are described in Chapter 10, "SAN clustering solution" on page 203, and Chapter 11, "Storage consolidation with SAN" on page 221.

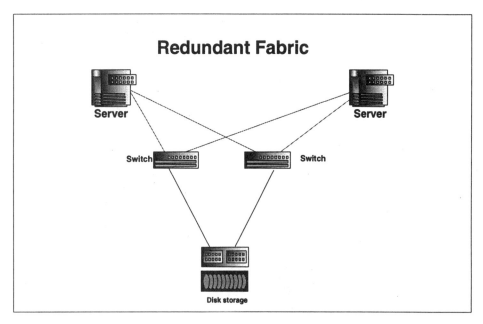

Figure 91. Redundant fabrics

9.3.2.6 Fabric backbone

Building on the concept of departmental SAN islands, each designed with fault tolerant fabrics, it is possible to link such islands together into an enterprise SAN (SAN continent perhaps), by providing a fault tolerant backbone of inter linked switches. This concept is shown in Figure 92. The fabric design shown here provides a total of 186 nodes in total, with up to 150 nodes at the department level, and 36 nodes in the backbone fabric. The backbone SAN can be used for shared devices such as a tape library, which can be accessed from any node in the enterprise fabric.

In this manner you can begin to use building block SANlets, and grow these to larger, resilient cascaded fabrics with multiple alternate paths through the network. Such designs can be easily expanded using tiers of switches for redundancy and increased bandwidth. In such an environment you will need to use zoning and LUN masking to provide appropriate security to application data.

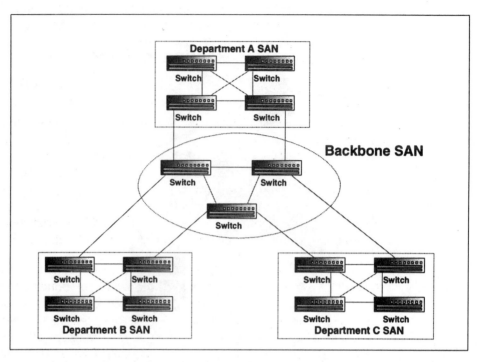

Figure 92. Fabric backbone interconnects SAN islands

9.3.3 Quality of service requirements

An important criterion for selection of SAN components relates to the level of service required from the SAN. This includes all aspects of the technology (hub, switch or director), the topology (loop or fabric), and the degree of redundancy, including fault tolerance. This is particularly relevant for organizations serving the global marketplace 24 hours per day, seven days per week over the internet. In the e-business economy of today, continuous availability is not optional. If you are not online, you are not open for business, and widely reported incidents of system outages in well known e-business companies show that loss of revenue can be immense.

Strategic Research Corporation (SRC) has described the principle of Quality of Service (QoS). This is a framework used to establish appropriate performance and availability characteristics of a complex service, such as a network. Specifically SRC defines service levels for SANs which they call Quality of Connection (QoC). This is built on the concept of system availability commonly used when defining service levels. These are normally described in terms of percentage systems availability.

A 99.999% (five 9s) up time refers to achievement of less than five minutes systems downtime in one year. A one 9 measure refers to a 90% availability (less than 36.5 days systems downtime), and a three 9s level is 99.9% uptime (less than 8 hours 45 minutes systems downtime annually). Downtime can be defined as any complete interruption of service for any reason, whether planned or unplanned.

To meet the very high levels of uptime required by planners and administrators it is essential to design the correct network architecture. It needs built in fault tolerance, failover capabilities, and available bandwidth to handle unplanned outages in a transparent manner. SAN QoC measurements are determined by the network topology, and the interconnect technologies used (hubs, switches). These define how well the SAN can sustain operations in the event of an outage within the network, from the perspective both of connection availability and maintaining performance.

High availability can be built in to the fabric by eliminating single points of failure. This is achieved by deploying hardware components in redundant pairs, and configuring redundant paths. Redundant paths will be routed through different switches to provide availability of connection. In the event of a path failure (for instance due to HBA, port card, fiber-optic cable, or storage adapter) software running in the host servers initiates failover to a secondary path. If the path failover malfunctions the application will fail. Then the only choice is to repair the failed path, or replace the failed device. Both these actions potentially lead to outages of other applications on multiple heterogeneous servers if the device affected is the switch.

Switches, like the IBM 2109, have redundant, hot pluggable components (including fans, power supplies, ASICs and GBICs), which can be replaced during normal operation. These hardware failures cause little or no noticeable loss of service. However, in the case of some failed components (such as the mother board) the switch itself will be treated as the field replaceable unit (FRU). Then all the ports and data paths are taken down. Automatic path failover will occur to another switch, so the network continues to operate, but in degraded mode.

Here there is a distinction between a switch and a director. Using the analogy of disk arrays, an individual switch could be likened to a JBOD in that it is just a bunch of ports. That is to say, although it has redundant components, in the event of certain component failures the total switch can fail, or must be replaced as the FRU. Cascading of multiple switches can achieve a higher level of fault tolerance. A single director could be viewed more like a RAID subsystem, in that it is designed to be highly fault tolerant. Only the failure of the mother board would result in total failure of the director. All other components are redundant, with automatic failover. Redundant field replaceable units are hot swappable, and microcode updates can be made non-disruptively. Maintenance capabilities, such as *call home* are supported.

According to tests run by CLAM Associates, it can take more than an hour to replace and reconfigure a new switch and bring it back into operation. For a 16-port switch this equates to 960 path minutes of degraded performance, as defined by the SRC QoC methodology. A path minute describes one user port being unavailable for one minute. Using path minutes as a way of describing the impact of an outage SRC defines 5 levels of QoC as shown in Figure 93.

SAN Quality of Connection

QoC Class	Fault Tolerance	Availability Annual uptime	Performance Degradation Path minutes/ year	Bandwidth Scaleability	Device Topology
1	Failure sensitive No redundancy	90%	Not applicable	Single Point to Point or Loop	Single Hub
2	Failure resilient Partially redundant paths and interconnects	99%	50,000	Loops and/or Switched Fabric	Single or Dual Hubs or Fabric Switches with single or dual paths
3	Failure resilient Fully redundant paths Fully redundant or fault tolerant interconnects	99.9%	5000	Switched Fabric	Dual Fabric Switches or Single Director
4	Failure tolerant Fully redundant paths and interconnects Fault tolerant backbone interconnects	99.99%	500	100% Switched Fabric + Max # of Ports per backplane	Dual Directors
5	Fault tolerant Fully redundant paths and interconnects All interconnects fault tolerant	99.999%	50	100% Switched Fabric + Max # of Ports per backplane	Dual Directors

Source: Strategic Research Corp.

Figure 93. SAN Quality of Connection

For instance, a single point to point topology has no redundancy and is classified as Class 1 QoC. If a failure occurs there is no access, so there is also 100% performance degradation. Class 2 has some redundancy with multiple paths and interconnects, but an outage can still occur for an extended period. Dual switches, or a single director provide full path and interconnect redundancy in Class 3, but a failure would imply degraded performance delivering variable service levels.

SRC defines Class 4 QoC as Failure Tolerant and Class 5 as Fault Tolerant. The Class 4 network must be able to recover from an outage and not incur more than 500 Path-Minutes of degraded operation per year; and Class 5 must meet the five 9s measure of availability with only 5 minutes down time and 50 Path Minutes degradation. This requires multiple fabric connections between all devices, requiring director level hardware, or multiple inter switch links (ISLs) in a meshed fabric. A consideration with ISLs, using E-port connections, is that they do not add bandwidth to the total configuration, only bandwidth and connectivity between switches. For this reason, SRC concludes that to meet Class 4 and Class 5 QoC requirements today, for fault tolerance with scalable performance, the maximum number of ports per backplane are required; hence directors are favored for these mission critical applications. This is due to their larger number of ports (32), and n+1 fault tolerant design. Future switches with larger port counts would also address this effectively if configured in redundant meshed fabrics.

9.3.4 Hierarchical design

What we have seen is that a SAN can take numerous shapes. When you start thinking about SAN design for your own organization you can learn from the experience gained in the design of other, mature networks such as LANs, and the Internet. In these a hierarchical network structure has generally been adopted, to facilitate change, allow easy replication as the structure grows, and minimize costs. This hierarchy comprises three layers (as shown in Figure 94).

The core
At the centre is a high speed, fault tolerant backbone, which is designed to provide very high reliability (QoC Class 4 or 5 as defined by SRC). This is designed to minimize latency within the fabric, and to optimize performance. This core would normally be built around fault tolerant Fibre Channel directors, like the McDATA ED-5000, or a fully redundant, meshed topology of switches, like the IBM 2109.

The distribution layer
The distribution layer of the hierarchy would comprise fault resistant fabric components, designed to deliver QoC Class 3 or Class 4, depending on the applications. Good connectivity and performance would be prime considerations.

The access layer
Here are the entry point nodes to the fabric, comprising host bus adapters, routers, gateways, hubs, and switches appropriate to service the number of servers and storage devices supported on the fabric.

Figure 94. SAN hierarchical design

This hierarchy is analogous to the telephone switching system. Each user has access to the network using an individual node (the telephone); these link to local area switches, which in turn link to central core switches which serve a large national and international network with very high bandwidth. A similar hierarchy has been built to serve the Internet, with end users linked to local web servers, which in turn communicate with large scale, high performance. core servers.

9.4 The next steps

Now that you are ready to design your SAN, there are many things to do.

9.4.1 The planning team

You will need to bring together the people with the appropriate skills to plan and implement the SAN. Who should be in the team depends on the scale of the project. This might range from installing a simple point to point connection to solve a distance issue in one location, to a large scale SAN comprising multiple meshed fabrics, inter-connected across a large campus, or linking between several locations in order to serve a large organization. In the first case the "team" may just be one or two storage administrators.

In the enterprise wide case you will probably need to include a number of skills. Since you are planning a network, it makes only common sense to include staff who have knowledge of complex networks. You will want to have representatives who know about the various platforms, (UNIX, Windows NT, Novell Netware, AS/400, Numa-Q, and so on), since there are differing system requirements and quirks which must be understood. Also consider the databases and applications you will be supporting, and include advisors for these. Knowledge of fiber cabling and data center planning may be necessary. You will certainly, of course, need strong storage planning and management skills appropriate to the platforms and subsystems and software tools being included in the design. And you will need project management skills to coordinate the whole exercise.

9.4.2 Equipment selection

The detailed list of logical and physical connections required in the SAN should act as the basis for defining your fabric hardware requirements, and arriving at an estimated implementation cost. Now you are ready to make the final selection with your vendor.

9.4.3 Interoperability testing

No doubt you will want to ensure that the SAN solution you are designing will operate correctly in practice. As industry standards are still under development this is particularly pertinent. You may select a pre-tested and certified solution, in which case there is little or no risk. Vendors throughout the industry are testing their hardware and software in many differing environments. IBM IGS has made major investments in laboratories in the USA and Europe to help you with such testing. Details of tested and certified solutions are constantly being up-dated, and are posted on the IBM SAN web site.

9.4.4 Documentation

As with any project, you will need to fully document the SAN plan. This should include details about most of the topics already discussed in this chapter;

- Business goals
- Technical requirements
- Infrastructure — current and planned
- Cabling
- Traffic characteristics today and expected
- Platforms and storage devices — current and planned
- SAN applications
- Logical and physical design

- Hardware and software plan
- Training plan
- Project implementation plan

9.5 Future developments

We can all speculate on what the future will bring for SAN's. Fibre Channel version 2 will bring 2Gb speeds, double what we have today. SAN fabric vendors will most likely develop new, more intelligent and faster gateways, hubs, switches, with more scaleability in port count, bandwidth, and with greater fault tolerance. Server and storage vendors will introduce more native Fibre Channel solutions; faster processors, more scalable and intelligent storage subsystems. Fibre Channel industry standards will continue to be delivered through cooperation between the vendors, creating greater ease of inter operability, and rapid growth in the SAN marketplace. S/390 FICON and FCP protocols will be enabled to operate on the same fabric. Sophisticated software management tools will finally deliver full end-to-end SAN management. The true Enterprise SAN will arrive, as we show in Figure 95.

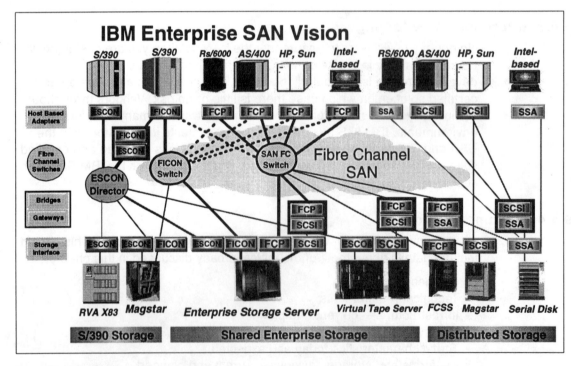

Figure 95. The IBM Enterprise SAN vision

In a fast moving world there is often a tendency to hold back and wait for something better which may be just around the corner. But those who wait are sometimes left behind in the race for competitive advantage. The race is on. Now is the time to join in.

Chapter 10. SAN clustering solution

This chapter presents various implementations and uses for SAN in clustering environments. A SAN is a natural choice for a cluster implementation for the following reasons:

- Practically unlimited distance
- Bandwidth scalability

Today there are three main cluster implementations:

- Operating system clustering with shared storage
- Operating system clustering with mirrored storage
- Application clustering

It is a feature of today's applications that they use increasing amounts of storage space. Especially with SCSI attached storage the capacity and distance of the storage enclosures is limited.

For this reason it is clustering that may make a SAN attractive to an IT enterprise. In the topics that follow, we concentrate on some of the solutions that can be implemented today with products that are available.

10.1 Two-node clustering with IBM Netfinity servers

In this example, we show how to implement a two-node cluster using SAN components.

The basic components of a two-node cluster are:

- Two servers running the same operating system
- Shared storage accessible from both servers
- Cluster software for managing the cluster process

Perhaps the most important item the cluster software deals with is how to handle two servers accessing the same storage. The cluster software has to ensure that data written to shared storage is not corrupted.

Also, because SCSI connected devices have distance limitations, and sharing SCSI storage between two servers is not a recommended solution, Fibre Channel is the architecture of choice. Fibre Channel attached storage devices offer native capability of sharing the storage among different host systems.

Our proposed solution to overcome these problems would be to build a simple SAN. The participants in this SAN will be:

- Two servers
- One storage device

In a SAN we have three available topologies to consider:

- Point to point
- Arbitrated loop
- Switched fabric

Point to Point
Point to point topology can be only used if the storage device supports more than one Fibre Channel port. The disadvantage of this topology is that you are limited to accessing only one storage device. And accessibility to this device is limited by the number of ports. For these reasons the use of Point to Point topology is not recommended.

Arbitrated loop
In our example, arbitrated loop could be the topology of choice. Arbitrated loop does not generate a large IT investment, and could service almost all of the demands that we place upon the environment we are building.

Switched fabric
However, if performance is an issue, and future expansions are planned (as shown in following sections), and cost is not an inhibiting factor, then a switched fabric is the recommended choice.

10.1.1 Clustering solution

The proposed solution for our problem will be to create an arbitrated loop SAN with two servers and the storage device attached to the servers. As we are using Fibre Channel, all participants in the SAN must have Fibre Channel capable connections.

If we wanted to reuse the SCSI storage subsystem, we would need to introduce a gateway to Fibre Channel. From IBM's range of products, you can select from:

- Netfinity Fibre Channel RAID controller

    - See 5.6.2, "Netfinity Fibre Channel RAID Controller" on page 118

- SAN Data Gateway,

    - See 5.5.1, "IBM SAN Data Gateway" on page 110

In our example, we use the Netfinity Fibre Channel RAID controller. We show the proposed solution in Figure 96.

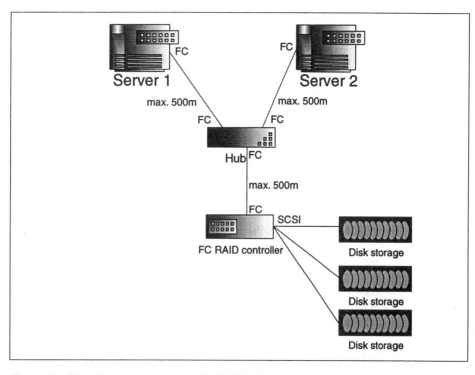

Figure 96. Shared storage clustering with IBM Netfinity servers

We used the following hardware for this configuration:

- Two IBM Netfinity Servers (5000,5500,5600,7000,7000M10,8500R)
- Netfinity Fibre Channel RAID Controller — 35261RU
- Three Netfinity EXP200 Storage Expansion Units — 35301RU
- Netfinity Hot Swap Disks for EXP200 (9.1GB,18.1GB,36.1GB)
- Two Netfinity PCI Fibre Channel Adapters — 01K7297, one adapter for each server
- Netfinity Fibre Channel Hub — 35231RU
- Netfinity SCSI cables
- Fibre Channel cables

It is important to consider that the Netfinity PCI Fibre Channel Adapter and the Netfinity Fibre Channel RAID Controller have only short-wave laser connections. The Netfinity Fibre Channel Hub supports short-wave and long-wave connections. In its standard shipping configuration the Netfinity Fibre Channel Hub comes with four short-wave GBICs. The maximum distance for short-wave laser implementations is 500m using 50 micron cables.

In our configuration we used three Netfinity EXP200 Storage Expansion Units, but this can be expanded because the Netfinity Fibre Channel RAID Controller supports up to six Netfinity EXP200 Storage Expansion units.

The supported software for this configuration is Microsoft Windows NT/2000 Enterprise Edition. The following software also needs to be installed:

- Latest Microsoft Service Pack for Windows NT (current version is 6)
- Latest drivers for Netfinity Fibre Channel PCI Adapter
- Storage Manager 7 for managing and configuring the Netfinity Fibre Channel RAID Controller

All the latest firmware updates for the Netfinity Fibre Channel PCI Adapter and the Netfinity Fibre Channel RAID Controller must also be applied.

Storage Manager 7 is used to manage the Netfinity Fibre Channel RAID Controller. Storage Manager 7 allows you to define your storage partitions (LUNs) and assign them to the servers so that they can access them.

This configuration can also be modified to serve even larger distances than 500m. With an additional hub, using long-wave GBICs, you can extend the distance between servers and storage up to 10km.

We show this configuration in Figure 97.

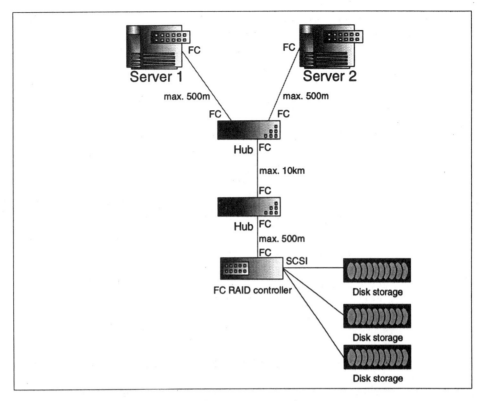

Figure 97. Shared storage clustering with distance extension

In the following sections we will show how to expand this basic SAN configuration to utilize more resources, and also to enable other features of the SAN environment, for example, longer distances between the host and devices in the SAN.

10.2 Two-node clustering with IBM Netfinity servers

The configuration from 10.1, "Two-node clustering with IBM Netfinity servers" on page 203, can be expanded to provide fully redundant data paths. To provide this, you need to add these components to the existing configuration:

- Netfinity Fibre Channel Hub — 35231RU
- Netfinity Fibre Channel Failsafe RAID Controller — 01K7296
- Additional Fibre Channel cables

We show how to configure the fully redundant configuration in Figure 98.

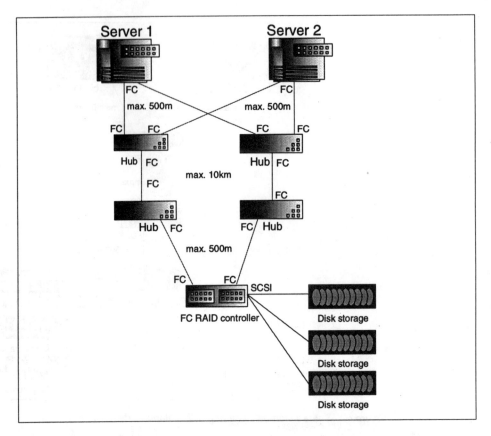

Figure 98. Cluster with redundant paths

To support this installation from the software side, you need to install the Redundant Dual Active Controller (RDAC) driver which is shipped with Storage Manager 7. The RDAC driver takes care of re-routing the I/O flow if one data path becomes unavailable.

We show how RDAC drivers work in Figure 99.

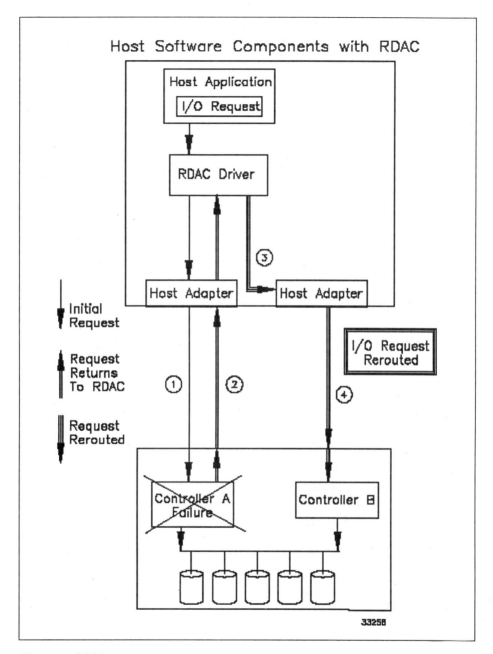

Figure 99. RDAC driver

This redundant configuration can also be expanded to support longer distances.

We show an example of this configuration in Figure 100.

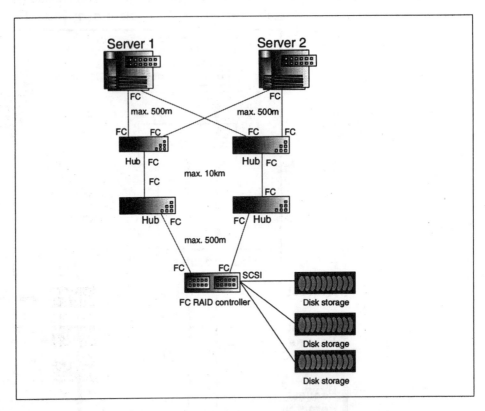

Figure 100. Cluster with redundant paths and distance extension

10.3 Multi-node clustering with IBM Netfinity

Now that we have created our first SANlet, we want to utilize the resources that are available. For example, we want to add more servers to this SAN. We can create more Microsoft Clusters with two servers in each cluster, or we can implement Netfinity Availability Extensions for Microsoft Cluster Server which allows up to eight servers in the cluster. In any of these solutions we are adding more hosts (servers) to the arbitrated loop.

We don't recommend having more than two initiators (hosts) on the same arbitrated loop. To resolve this problem we introduce the IBM Fibre Channel Managed Hub — 35341RU.

The IBM Fibre Channel Managed Hub also has built in **switching capability**. This means that you have non-blocked, 100 MB/s communication **between** ports.

We show the modified configuration in Figure 101.

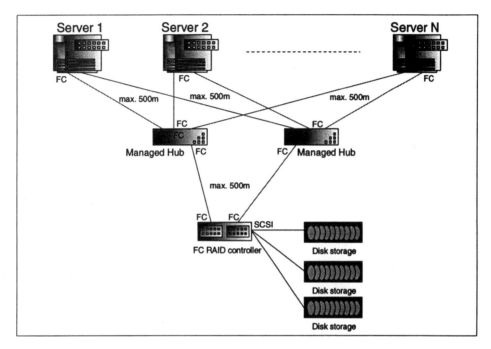

Figure 101. Cluster configuration with Managed Hubs

This configuration can be further modified to serve larger distances **by adding** two more IBM Fibre Channel Managed Hubs.

We show this in Figure 102.

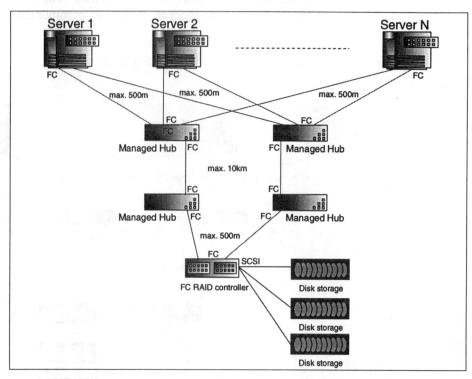

Figure 102. Cluster configuration with Managed Hubs with distance extension

With this configuration you can connect up to seven servers. This is because the IBM Fibre Channel Managed Hub has eight ports available and one port is used to connect the IBM Netfinity Fibre Channel RAID controller.

To implement up to the eight servers which are supported in Netfinity Availability Extensions for Microsoft Cluster Server, we would consider using the IBM Fibre Channel Switch — 2109-S16, which features 16 ports. The configurations from Figure 101 and Figure 102 can be simply modified by replacing all IBM Fibre Channel Managed Hubs with IBM Fibre Channel Switches.

When using the IBM Fibre Channel Switches we need to configure the zoning configuration so that each server can access the ports where the storage is attached to the fabric.

When using this type of configuration for more Microsoft Clusters with two servers per node, we must make sure that we correctly configure the IBM Netfinity Fibre Channel RAID controller, so that only the servers in the same cluster will have access to their shared storage.

All the configurations described so far with IBM Netfinity Fibre Channel RAID Controller and EXP200 external enclosure, can also be achieved using the new IBM Fibre Channel RAID Controller (3552-1RU) with IBM Netfinity EXP500 FC external enclosure (3560-1RU) which supports IBM Fibre Channel Hard Disk Drives.

10.4 Multi-node clustering using the Enterprise Storage Server

When the cluster you implement requires higher performance and more storage space you should consider using the Enterprise Storage Server — ESS. The ESS features Fibre Channel connections so it can easily participate in the SAN.

We show a sample cluster configuration with redundant paths in Figure 103.

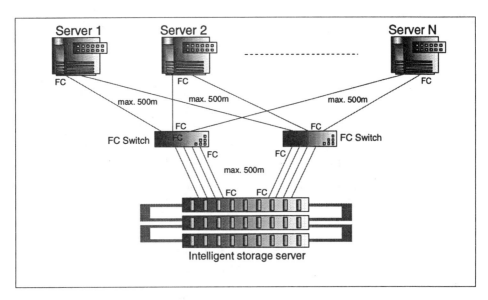

Figure 103. Multi node cluster with ESS

In this configuration we used the following components:

- IBM Netfinity servers
- Two IBM Fibre Channel Switches — 2109-S16 (the eight port IBM Fibre Channel Switches — 2109-S08 can also be used if it provides enough ports)
- One IBM Enterprise Storage Server — 2105
- Two Netfinity PCI Fibre Channel Adapters — 01K7297 for each server

- Fibre Channel cables

The software used for implementing the cluster could be Microsoft Windows Enterprise Edition with Microsoft Cluster, or Netfinity Availability Extensions for Microsoft Cluster can be added which supports up to eight nodes.

Before any installation and configuration of the cluster software, it is vital to update the firmware and microcode on all components.

Because of the ESS fibre channel implementation of the Fibre Channel attachment where all LUNs are seen on all Fibre Channel ports, the IBM Subsystem Device Driver must be installed before you install cluster software.

Note

It is important that you configure ESS with correct LUN masking security. The ESS has to be configured with restricted access in case you use several cluster groups using the same ESS.

LUN masking security means that you define which LUNs are accessible by each host (server). The ESS will then take care of preventing any unauthorized host from accessing the wrong LUNs. If all hosts attached to the ESS are members of the same cluster, you can use unrestricted access.

Note

It is important that you correctly configure zoning in the IBM Fibre Channel Switch.

This configuration can be further expanded to serve larger distances with the addition of two more IBM Fibre Channel Switches.

This is similar to that shown in Figure 104.

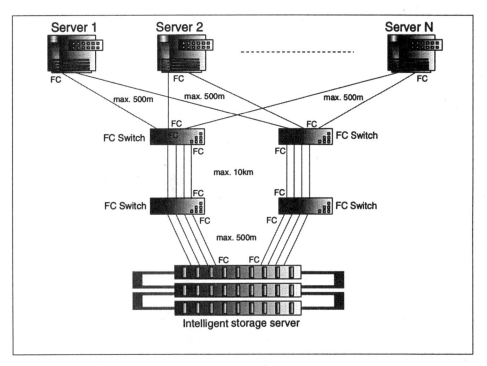

Figure 104. Multi-node cluster with ESS with extended distance

In our example it is possible to use two 16-port IBM Fibre Channel Switches for connecting servers to the fabric, and two 8-port IBM Fibre Channel Switches to extend the distance of the fabric. You need long-wave GBICs and 9 micron cables to achieve distances larger than 500m.

This type of SAN configuration can also be designed using the McDATA Fibre Channel Director. The McDATA Fibre Channel Director features 32 ports connectivity which allows the option of connecting up to 31 server connections, assuming that you use only one connection to the storage device.

The optimal configuration for the ESS will be using four Fibre Channel connections for ESS. In this case you can connect up to 14 servers with two connections.

We show the configuration using a McDATA Fibre Channel Director in Figure 105.

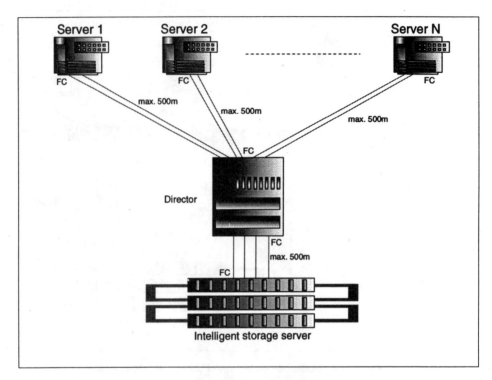

Figure 105. Multi node cluster using McDATA Fibre Channel Director

When using the McDATA Fibre Channel Director, consideration must be given as to how the servers and storage are connected to the director. The McDATA ED-5000 has eight, 4-port cards which provides up to a maximum of 32 ports. Connections from a host should be in pairs. Each connection must be to a different port card, to ensure redundancy and failover capability. If the pair of connections are to the same port card, a card failure would result in loss of both paths.

Note

Always connect the connections from a source (server or storage) to different port cards in the McDATA Fibre Channel Director.

The McDATA Fibre Channel Director also features fully redundant components.

This configuration can also be expanded to increase the distance by adding another McDATA Fibre Channel Director. This is similar to adding more IBM Fibre Channel Switches as shown in Figure 104 on page 215.

10.5 Two-node clustering with RS/6000 servers

The SAN environment can also be used to implement clustering in a RS/6000 environment. In our example we will show how to implement two way, HACMP configurations in a RS/6000 environment.

The solution is shown in Figure 106:

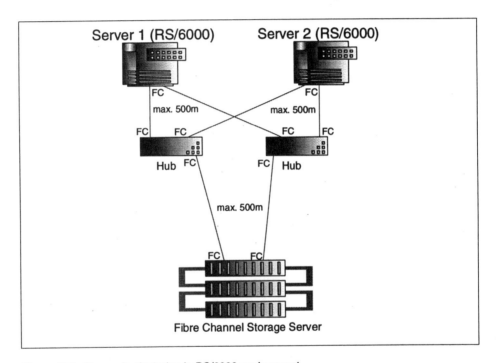

Figure 106. Two-node clustering in RS/6000 environment

For this configuration we used the following components:

- Supported RS/6000 server — S80,S70,S7A,F50,H50 or H70
- Two Gigabit Fibre Channel Adapters — FC 6227 for each server
- Fibre Channel Storage Server — FCSS
- Two IBM Fibre Channel Storage Hubs — 2103-H07
- Fibre Channel cables

Before configuring the cluster, firmware level 3.01 must be applied to the Fibre Channel Storage Server and firmware level 2.22X1 to all Gigabit Fibre Channel Adapters.

The required level of the AIX operating systems software is 4.3.3 with APAR IY05369 applied and the version of HACMP must be 4.3.1 with APAR IY05196 applied.

More information about the needed prerequisites can be viewed at:

www.storage.ibm.com/hardsoft/products/fcss/download/aix.htm

This configuration can also be extended to support larger distances as shown in Figure 107.

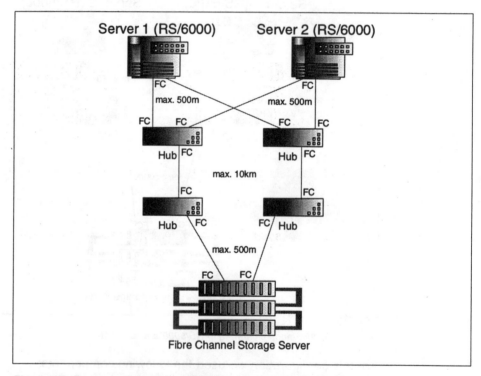

Figure 107. Two node clustering in RS/6000 environment with extended distance

A failover configuration can also be implemented using two Fibre Channel Storage Servers similar to that shown in Figure 108.

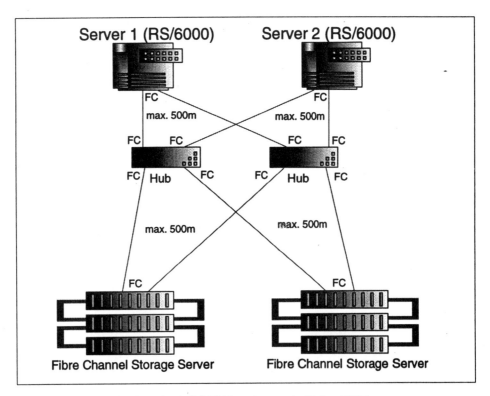

Figure 108. Two-node clustering in RS/6000 environment with two FCSS

This chapter has shown the possibilities that exist and which can be created making use of the infrastructure as it exists today. This can be used as a base for a high-level system design to maximize return on investment.

Chapter 11. Storage consolidation with SAN

Storage consolidation involves combining data from different sources, the same source, or in disparate types. Consolidation brings with it the promise of attaching storage to multiple servers concurrently, and leveraging any IT investment.

However, this is not an easy task. Data is treated differently at many levels within the operating systems and applications, and within the system architecture.

The challenges that present themselves whenever storage consolidation is considered include:

- Different attachment protocols, such as SCSI, ESCON, and FICON.
- Different Data formats, such as Extended Count Key Data (ECKD), blocks, clusters, and sectors.
- Different file systems, such as Virtual Storage Access Method (VSAM), Journal File System (JFS), Andrew File System (AFS), and Windows NT File System (NTFS).
- OS/400, with the concept of single-level storage.
- Different file system structures, such as catalogs and directories.
- Different file naming conventions, such as AAA.BBB.CCC and DIR/Xxx/Yyy.
- Different data encoding techniques, such as EBCDIC, ASCII, floating point, and little or big endian.

In Figure 109, we show a summary of these differences.

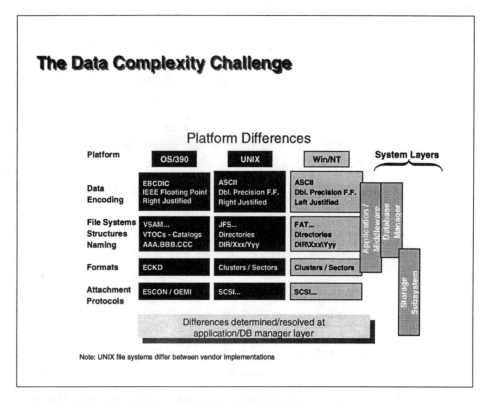

Figure 109. Hardware and operating systems' differences

This chapter describes various basic environments where storage is consolidated in a number of different ways, starting from a non-consolidated solution and migrating to fully consolidated within a storage area network.

11.1 Non-consolidated storage solution

Data plays an increasingly critical role in the IT industry today, and organizations have begun to understand that it must be managed and stored in a way that has never really been considered necessary before. It is a valuable business asset and, therefore, must be treated as such.

11.1.1 The initial configuration

This simple configuration shows an existing non-consolidated storage solution, which is operating system independent (Microsoft Windows NT, Novell Netware, AIX, HP-UX, or Sun Solaris).

Each server needs one host bus adapter (HBA) for each storage expansion unit. The host bus adapter is used to connect server or storage to the fibre channel network. HBAs control the electrical protocol for communications.

For storage consolidation, the limitation, as shown in Figure 110, is the SCSI attached storage, the capacity and distance of the storage enclosures are limited. This will serve as our initial configuration.

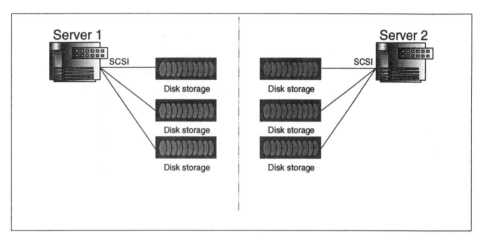

Figure 110. Initial configuration

The hardware used and tested in this configuration is:

- IBM Netfinity Server type (5000, 5500, 5600, 7000 7000M10, 85000R)
- IBM Host Bus Adapters
- IBM Netfinity EXP200 Storage Expansion Units — 35301RU
- IBM Netfinity Hot Swap Disks for EXP200 (9.1Gb, 18.1Gb, 36,1Gb)
- IBM Netfinity SCSI cables

11.1.2 The consolidated storage configuration

In the new configuration, as shown in Figure 111, we have consolidated the storage in a SAN.

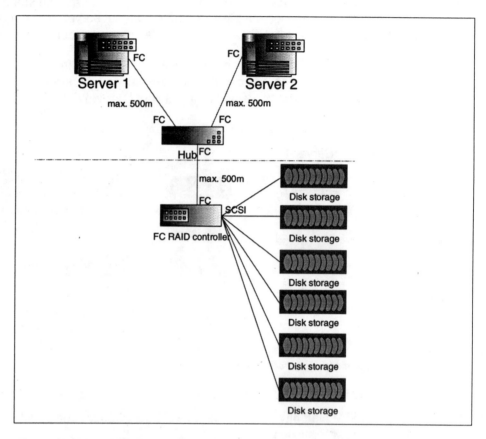

Figure 111. SAN Configuration with an FC Hub

With the introduction of the Fibre Channel hub to this configuration, we have created an arbitrated loop storage area network and added greater distances via the FC-AL topology.

The IBM Fibre Channel Storage Hub is a seven port central interconnection for Fibre Channel arbitrated loop (FC-AL). The FC Hub provides four short wave optical Gigabit Interface Converter (GBIC) ports, and the option to add up to three additional long wave or short wave optical GBIC ports. The short wave GBIC ports allow fiber cable connection of up to 500m to the host based FC-AL initiator adapter, to the FC port on the SAN Data Gateway or Router.

Either short-wave or long-wave GBIC ports can be used to connect two FC Storage Hubs, extending the distance up to an additional 500m with the short wave GBIC, or up to an additional 10km with the long wave GBIC. The maximum distance for shortwave laser implementations is 500m using 50 micron cables.

11.1.3 A consolidated, extended distance configuration

With the Fibre Channel RAID Controller Unit, we can reuse the storage from Figure 110 on page 223, where the data storage can be located, for data protection, in a separate location from the server. The IBM Fibre Channel RAID Controller Unit supports IBM's high performance, reliable Ultrastar disk drives in capacities of 9.1, 18.2, and 36.4 GB.

The management software for the Fibre Channel RAID controller, and for defining and assigning the storage partitions of the storage enclosures, to the servers is IBM Netfinity Fibre Channel Storage Manager Version 7.0.

The hardware used and tested in this configuration is:

- BM Netfinity Server type (5000, 5500, 5600, 7000 7000M10, 85000R)
- IBM Host Bus Adapters
- IBM Netfinity Fibre Channel Hub — 35231RU
- IBM Netfinity Fibre Channel RAID Controller — 45261RU)
- IBM Netfinity EXP200 Storage Expansion Units — 35301RU
- IBM Netfinity Hot Swap Disks for EXP200 (9.1Gb, 18.1Gb, 36,1Gb)
- IBM Fibre Channel cables
- IBM Netfinity SCSI cables

We put all these together as shown in Figure 112.

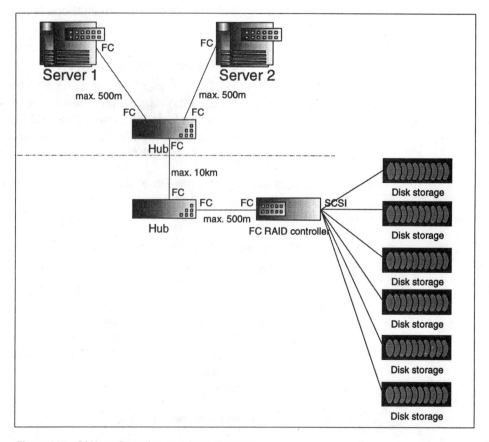

Figure 112. SAN configuration over long distance

In the last example of this section, we extended the configuration shown in Figure 111 on page 224, with a second Fibre Channel Hub. The hub will be used to extend the distance between the servers, controller units and storage expansion units by using long-wave GBICs, which support distances up to 10km with the use of longwave cables.

11.2 Managed Hub

This section changes our last configuration and makes it suitable for more servers with the same operating system. With one hub we are limited to seven servers.

11.2.1 Managed Hub function

The managed hub offers eight hot pluggable FC-AL ports and is similar to non-managed hubs in their function, but they have built-in software to manage them. Because of their manageability they offer better fault isolation, planning and control. Usually they are used for entry level homogeneous server implementations.

We show our configuration in Figure 113.

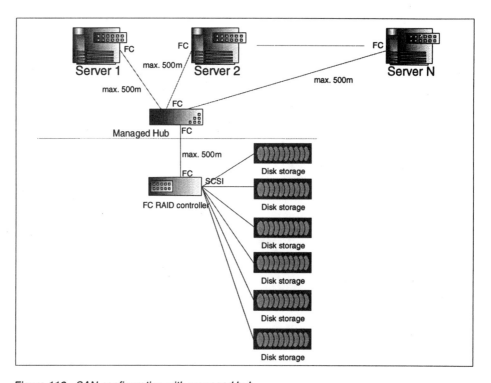

Figure 113. SAN configuration with managed hub

Configuration management is performed using a command-line interface or the graphical administrative capability offered by the StorWatch Fibre Channel Managed Hub Specialist.

The hardware used and tested in this configuration is:

- IBM Netfinity Server type (5000, 5500, 5600, 7000 7000M10, 85000R)
- IBM Host Bus Adapters
- IBM Netfinity Fibre Channel Managed Hub — 35341RU
- IBM Netfinity Fibre Channel RAID Controller — 45261RU
- IBM Netfinity EXP200 Storage Expansion Units — 35301RU

- IBM Netfinity Hot Swap Disks for EXP200 (9.1Gb, 18.1Gb, 36,1Gb)
- IBM Fibre Channel cables
- IBM Netfinity SCSI cables

11.2.2 Redundant paths

With more than two servers, it is better for load balancing and reliability to use a second hub.

Figure 114 shows a configuration summary of redundant data paths. To support this new configuration, with two managed hubs and an extra FC RAID controller adapter, we need to install a RDAC driver. This driver comes with Storage Manager version 7. The responsibility of the RDAC driver is rerouting of the I/O flow if one of the data paths is unavailable. You can see how the RDAC driver works in Figure 99 on page 209.

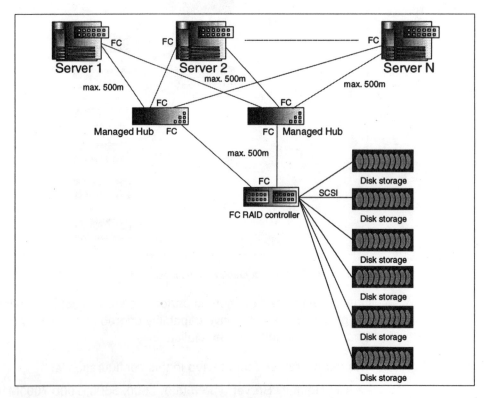

Figure 114. Redundant data paths in a SAN configuration

The hardware used and tested in this configuration is:

- IBM Netfinity Server type (5000, 5500, 5600, 7000, 7000M10, 85000R)
- IBM Host Bus Adapters
- IBM Netfinity Fibre Channel Managed Hub — 35341RU
- IBM Netfinity Fibre Channel RAID Controller — 45261RU
- IBM Netfinity EXP200 Storage Expansion Units — 35301RU
- IBM Netfinity Hot Swap Disks for EXP200 (9.1Gb, 18.1Gb, 36.1Gb)
- IBM Fibre Channel cables
- IBM Netfinity SCSI cables

11.2.3 Redundancy and distance extension

In the last example of this section, we expanded it to support longer distances. We show this in the configuration shown in Figure 115. We used long-wave GBICs, which support distances up to 10km with the use of long-wave cables to extend the distance between the servers, controller units and storage expansion units.

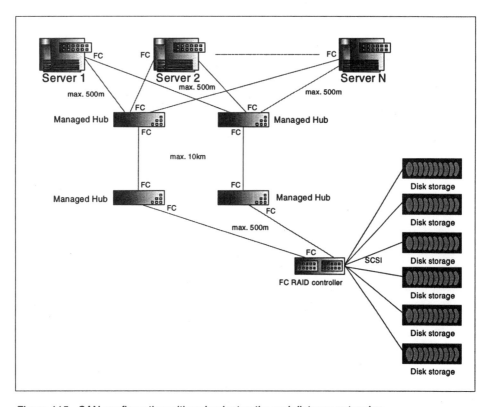

Figure 115. SAN configuration with redundant paths and distance extension

The hardware used and tested in this configuration is:

- IBM Netfinity Server type (5000, 5500, 5600, 7000, 7000M10, 85000R)
- IBM Host Bus Adapters
- IBM Netfinity Fibre Channel Managed Hub — 35341RU
- IBM Netfinity Fibre Channel RAID Controller — 45261RU
- IBM Netfinity EXP200 Storage Expansion Units — 35301RU
- IBM Netfinity Hot Swap Disks for EXP200 (9.1Gb, 18.1Gb, 36.1Gb)
- IBM Fibre Channel cables
- IBM Netfinity SCSI cables

11.3 Switches

Fibre Channel switches are used to implement a Fibre Channel fabric. Fibre Channel switches can be used in entry level enterprise heterogeneous implementations and also in large enterprise environments. You can connect any kind of Fibre Channel enabled devices to a Fibre Channel switch.

11.3.1 Replacing a hub with a switch

If we want to implement up to eight servers, we can select, for example, the IBM 2109-S16. This model has a 16-port Fibre Channel switch and 4 short-wave Gigabit Interface Convertors (GBICs)

Here we can simply modify our configuration of Figure 115 by replacing the managed hub with the Fibre Channel switch and this is shown in Figure 116.

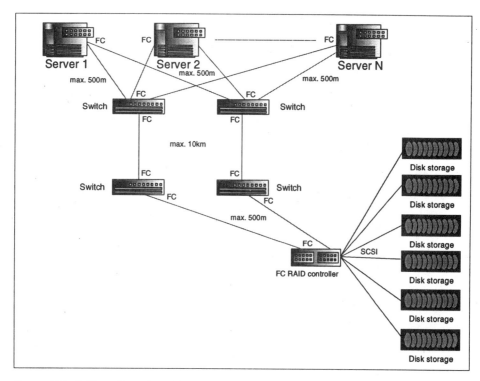

Figure 116. SAN configuration with switches and distance extension

When we have changed the configuration we need to configure the zoning configuration. After this each server can access the ports where the storage is attached to the fabric.

When we use this configuration for more Microsoft clusters with two servers per node, we must connect the FC RAID controller. It is important that only servers on the same cluster have access to their shared storage.

The IBM Fibre Channel Switch supports attachments to multiple host subsystems:

- Intel-based servers running Microsoft Windows NT or Novell Netware
- IBM RS/6000 running AIX
- SUN servers running Solaris

As switches allow any-to-any connection, the switch and management software can restrict which other ports a specific port can connect to. This is called port zoning.

The hardware used and tested in this configuration is:

- IBM Netfinity Server type (5000, 5500, 5600, 7000, 7000M10, 85000R)
- IBM Host Bus Adapters
- IBM Fibre Channel Switches — 2109-S16
- IBM Netfinity Fibre Channel RAID Controller — 45261RU
- IBM Netfinity EXP200 Storage Expansion Units — 35301RU
- IBM Netfinity Hot Swap Disks for EXP200 (9.1Gb, 18.1Gb, 36.1Gb)
- IBM Fibre Channel cables
- IBM Netfinity SCSI cables

11.3.2 Enterprise Storage Server and switches

New in this configuration is the Enterprise Storage server (ESS), or more familiarly referred to as Shark, which is a member of the Seascape family. The ESS can be configured in a variety of ways to provide scalability in capacity and performance. For more information see 5.6.3, "Enterprise Storage Server" on page 119.

We show this configuration in Figure 117.

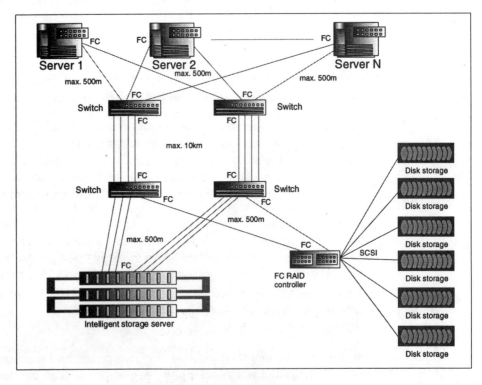

Figure 117. SAN configuration with switches and ESS

To supporting the ESS we need to use the Subsystem Device Driver (previously the Data Path Optimizer), as the RDAC driver is not supported for the ESS.

The hardware used and tested in this configuration is:

- IBM Netfinity Server type (5000, 5500, 5600, 7000, 7000M10, 85000R)
- IBM Host Bus Adapters
- IBM Fibre Channel Switches — 2109S16
- IBM Enterprise Storage Server — 2105
- IBM Netfinity Fibre Channel RAID Controller — 45261RU
- IBM Netfinity EXP200 Storage Expansion Units — 35301RU
- IBM Netfinity Hot Swap Disks for EXP200 (9.1Gb, 18.1Gb, 36,1Gb)
- IBM Fibre Channel cables
- IBM Netfinity SCSI cables

11.4 Director

In the next configuration, we show the McDATA Enterprise Fibre Channel Director. Similar to the switch, IBM offers the Director for high end e-business and other mission-critical business applications.

Director implementation
The Fibre Channel Director (ED5000 or 2032-001) offers 32 port switching capability. Each port delivers 100 MB/s, full-duplex data transfer. Industry-leading 3,200 MB/s transmission bandwidth supports full non-blocking 32-port switch performance.

The Fibre Channel Director is based upon the IBM ESCON Director which, over a number of years has provided industry leading data availability, performance, and the data integrity required by the most demanding data centers.

The Fibre Channel Director offers multiple configuration options for Fibre Channel connectivity. There can be up to eight 4-port cards in each Fibre Channel Director combining together to total 32 ports. The port cards can have these configurations:

- All four ports with short-wave laser
- All four ports with long-wave laser
- Combo card with three short-wave and one long-wave laser

We show this configuration in Figure 118.

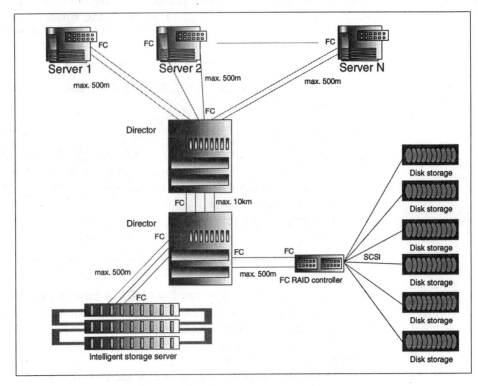

Figure 118. SAN configuration with Directors

The hardware used and tested in this configuration is:

- IBM Netfinity Server type (5000, 5500, 5600, 7000, 7000M10, 85000R)
- IBM Host Bus Adapters
- IBM Netfinity Fibre Channel RAID Controller — 45261RU
- IBM Netfinity EXP200 Storage Expansion Units — 35301RU
- IBM Netfinity Hot Swap Disks for EXP200 (9.1Gb, 18.1Gb, 36,1Gb)
- IBM Netfinity PCI Fibre Channel Adapters — 01K7297
- IBM Netfinity SCSI cables
- IBM Fibre Channel cables
- IBM Enterprise Storage Server — 2105

11.5 Serial Storage Architecture

This section shows how an SSA SAN configuration can be built. For our examples we are using IBM's AIX operating system. RS/6000 solutions offer the flexibility and reliability to handle your most mission-critical and data-intensive applications.

11.5.1 SSA non-consolidated configuration

This simple SSA configuration in Figure 119 shows a non-consolidated storage solution with each RS/6000 server needed for each storage expansion.

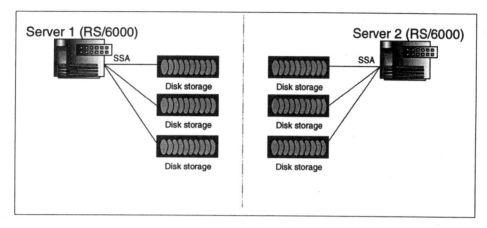

Figure 119. Initial configuration

The hardware used and tested in this configuration is:

- IBM RS/6000
- IBM Host Bus Adapters
- IBM 7133 Serial Disk System Advanced Models D40 and T40
- IBM Hot Swap Disks (4.5 Gb, 9.1Gb, 18.1Gb, 36.1Gb)
- IBM SCSI cables

11.5.2 SSA and Vicom SLIC Router

For our next configuration, we introduce the SSA Gateway. The SSA Gateway will be used to extend the distance between the hub and the connection to the disk storage. The SSA Gateway is the Vicom Fibre Channel SLIC Router. The Vicom Fibre Channel SLIC Router enables all IBM 7133, 7131 and 3527 Serial Disk Systems to attach to the RS/6000 using Fiber Channel host adapters and drivers. In this example the IBM 7133 Serial Disk system Advanced models D40 and T40 are used. This is shown in Figure 120.

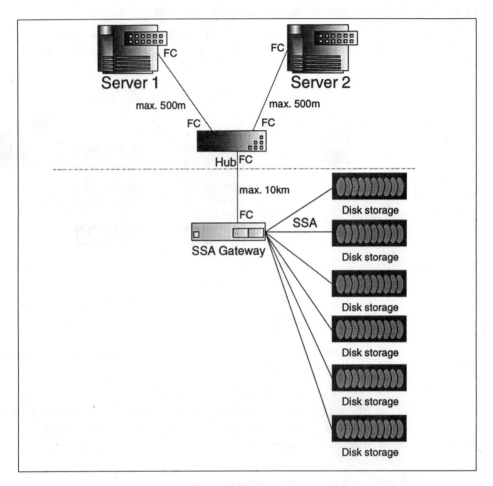

Figure 120. SSA SAN Configuration for long distance

The hardware used and tested in this configuration is:

- IBM RS/6000
- IBM Host Bus Adapters
- IBM Netfinity Fibre Channel Hub — 35231RU
- SSA Gateway, Vicom Fibre Channel SLIC Router
- IBM 7133 Serial Disk System Advanced Models D40 and T40
- IBM Hot Swap Disks (4.5 Gb, 9.1Gb, 18.1Gb, 36.1Gb)
- IBM RS/6000 Fibre Channel cables

11.5.3 ESS, SSA and switches

Fibre Channel switches are used to implement a Fibre Channel fabric. Fibre Channel switches can be used in entry level enterprise heterogeneous implementations and also in larger enterprise environments. You can connect any kind of Fibre Channel enabled devices to a Fibre Channel switch.

If we want to implement up to eight servers we can select, for example, the IBM 2109-S16. This model has a 16-port Fibre Channel switch and four short-wave GBICs. We show this configuration in Figure 121.

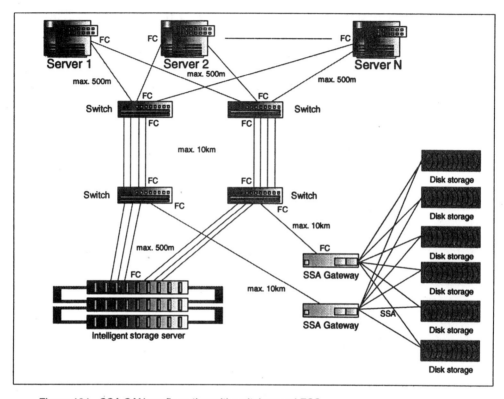

Figure 121. SSA SAN configuration with switches and ESS

As switches allow any-to-any connection, the switch and management software can restrict which port can connect to any other port. We call this port zoning. When we have changed the configuration, we need to configure the zoning. After this, each server can access the ports where the storage is attached to the fabric.

The ESS is a member of the Seascape family. The ESS can be configured in a variety of ways to provide scalability in capacity and performance. For more information see 5.6.3, "Enterprise Storage Server" on page 119.

For supporting the ESS we would need to use the Subsystem Device Driver (SDD).

The hardware used and tested for this configuration is:

- IBM RS/6000
- IBM Host Bus Adapters
- IBM Fibre Channel Switches — 2109S16
- IBM Netfinity Enterprise Storage Server
- SSA Gateway, Vicom Fibre Channel SLIC Router
- IBM 7133 Serial Disk System Advanced Models D40 and T40
- IBM Hot Swap Disks — (4.5 Gb, 9.1Gb, 18.1Gb, 36,1Gb)
- IBM RS/6000 Fibre Channel cables

These examples are meant to show how a SAN can be configured to utilize resources.

Chapter 12. IBM Enterprise Storage Server configurations

This chapter shows sample configurations of how to implement the IBM Enterprise Storage Server (ESS) in a SAN environment.

The ESS is the preferred choice for the SAN environments because it offers up to 11 TB of storage space. This storage space can be split across 4096 LUNs. The ESS also features three different types of connections:

- SCSI
- ESCON
- Fibre Channel

12.1 Connecting the ESS to a SAN using the SAN Data Gateway

Before a native Fibre Channel connection is available, the ESS can be connected to the SAN using the SAN Data Gateway. The SAN Data Gateway features four SCSI ports and a maximum of six Fibre Channel ports. Each SAN Data Gateway can see up to 255 LUNs on the SCSI interfaces. The SAN Data Gateway also has built in security features:

- Port based zoning
- LUN masking

Port based zoning
In port based zoning, the administrator of the SAN Data Gateway can limit the Fibre Channel ports access to the SCSI attached LUNs. This can be done by defining which SCSI port can be seen by each Fibre Channel port. You can see a sample zoning configuration in Figure 122.

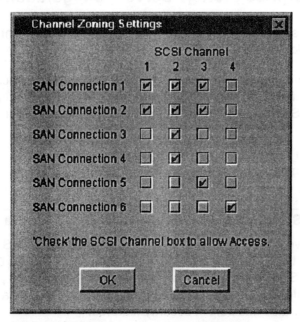

Figure 122. SAN Data Gateway port based zoning

LUN masking

In LUN masking security mode, the SAN Data Gateway administrator defines which LUN can be seen by which Fibre Channel initiator (host). The host is identified by its World Wide Name. The SAN Data Gateway allows up to eight initiators (hosts) on each Fibre Channel port. This means that you can define up to 48 hosts.

The LUN masking feature is a feature for today's SAN Data Gateways. To enable this feature, a Virtual Private SAN (VP SAN) license has to be obtained (RPQ 8S0511 - Virtual Private SAN). After obtaining the license, the LUN masking feature is enabled with the StorWatch Specialist for SAN Data Gateway.

Because the SAN Data Gateway supports only four SCSI attachments, while ESS supports up to 32, it is likely that more than one SAN Data Gateway will be used to utilize the full performance of the ESS. An example of such a configuration is shown in Figure 123.

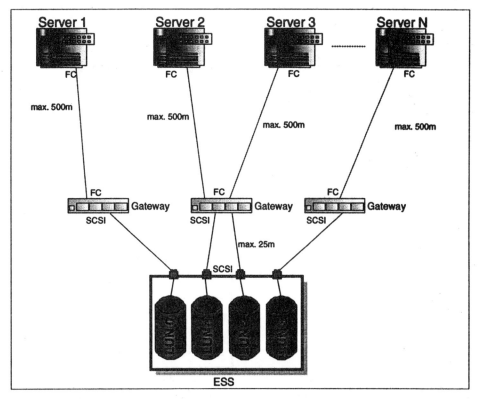

Figure 123. ESS with SAN Data Gateway

In such a configuration, each Fibre Channel enabled server can access the ESS storage. In this configuration we used three SAN Data Gateways — 2108-G07.

Note

When connecting the ESS over the SAN Data Gateway ensure that each LUN is assigned to just one SCSI interface in the ESS. Otherwise the information in the SAN Data Gateway will be reported twice as the same LUN will appear on two SCSI interfaces.

You can also connect the SAN Data Gateway to the SAN fabric as shown in Figure 124.

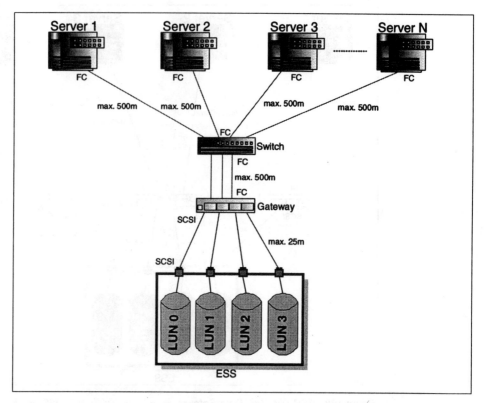

Figure 124. ESS connected to the SAN fabric

In this configuration and in addition to the SAN Data Gateway, we used a Fibre Channel Switch. This configuration can be further expanded to satisfy larger distance requirements. We show an example of this configuration in Figure 125.

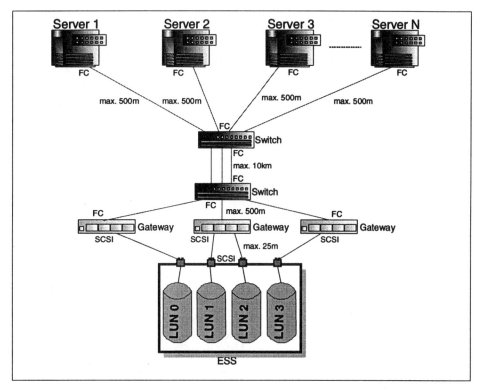

Figure 125. ESS connected to the SAN fabric with extended distance

Today, the only supported platform in configurations with the SAN Data
Gateway and Fibre Channel Switches is Windows NT. If you want to use other
platforms and you need extended distance, you should use an IBM Fibre
Channel Hub.

12.2 Connecting ESS to SAN with native Fibre Channel

With native Fibre Channel connections, the ESS can be connected directly to
the SAN fabric. Before using native Fibre Channel connections the following
must be considered:

- Each LUN defined for Open Systems storage can be seen by all Fibre
  Channel interfaces

- ESS supports LUN masking for restricted access

We show an example of a high availability SAN environment in Figure 126.

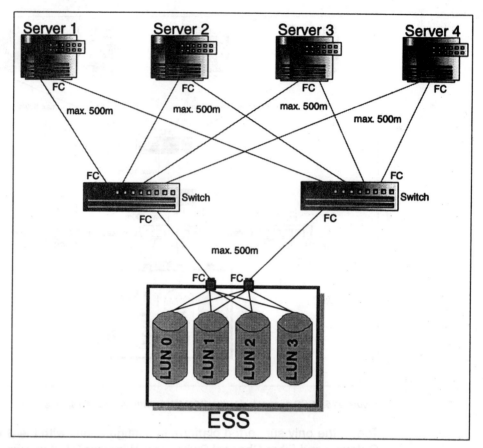

Figure 126. High availability SAN configuration using ESS

In this example, each server can reach the storage (LUNs) in the ESS through two different paths. When you install the IBM Subsystem Device Driver (SDD) on each host, the device driver will register all available paths from the host to the storage. If all paths are available, SDD will load balance the traffic. In cases of failure of any one component, the SDD will failover all traffic to working paths.

Note

IBM Subsystem Device Driver is available at no additional cost with each ESS. It is available on all major platforms: AIX, Windows NT, SUN, HP with more to follow.

With the ESS support for LUN masking, you can restrict access to each LUN. This can be done with the ESS StorWatch Specialist. The LUN masking is done on the basis of World Wide Name (WWN) of host bus adapters (HBA) in the server. To restrict access in the configuration, you define which LUNs can be seen by each servers HBAs (WWN).

> **Note**
>
> When you are using more than one HBA adapter in the host ensure that you assign the same LUNs to all HBAs in the host.

Using LUN masking security, you ensure that a non-authorized server will be denied access to non-assigned LUNs. This prevents data corruption. You can still share LUNs amongst different servers, for example, for clustering solutions, but in this case the clustering software must take care of ensuring data consistency.

> **Note**
>
> LUN masking in the storage device is the most secure way of protecting the storage (LUNs).

Each Fibre Channel interface can see all LUNs, and the ESS supports hot-adding of the interface adapters (in our example, Fibre Channel interface adapters). More Fibre Channel interface adapters to increase availability and performance easily can be added. In our example, we added two more Fibre Channel interface adapters, as shown in the configuration in Figure 127.

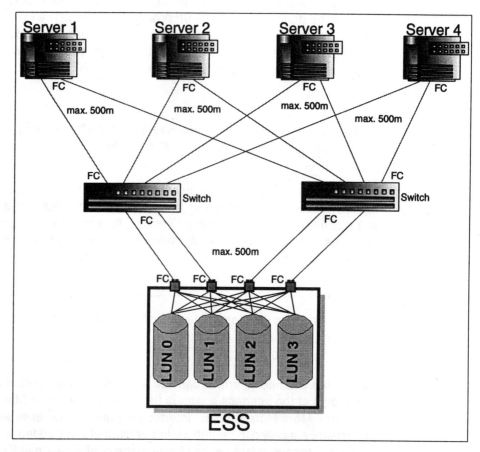

Figure 127. High availability SAN configuration using ESS - II

As all LUNs are automatically seen by all Fibre Channel interfaces in the ESS, there is no need for additional configuration changes. You can enjoy using your new bandwidth immediately.

After adding two more Fibre Channel adapters into the ESS, each server can now reach the storage (LUNs) through four paths. The SDD will automatically discover these new paths and add them to the available paths.

Each Fibre Channel interface can see all LUNs, which means that the same LUN is reported to the host system several times as different storage. If we assume that we have a configuration similar to that shown in Figure 124.

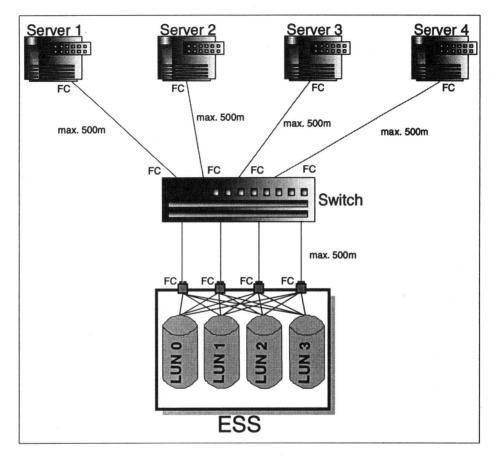

Figure 128. ESS with native Fibre Channel attachment

All four ports can see all four LUNs. All four ESS Fibre Channel interfaces are registered in the Simple Name Server (SNS) of the fabric (switch in our example) as storage capable devices. When the host logs into the fabric and requests the storage devices from the SNS, it will see that there are four storage devices (Fibre Channel interfaces) available.

After obtaining this information, the host will perform direct Port login to each device and query the available storage (LUNs). In our example, Server 1 will actually see 16 LUNs instead of four, because each Fibre Channel interface will report all LUNs. This situation can be solved by using the IBM Subsystem Device Driver (SDD) which acts as an interface between the operating system and the storage device. The SDD will see that each LUN is reported four times, and will present just one image of each LUN to the host.

> **Note**
>
> Use the IBM Subsystem Device Driver when you are using more than one Fibre Channel connection to the ESS.

If the operating system does not support the SDD, or you do not want to use it, the situation can be solved by using zoning in the fabric. We show a zoning solution for our configuration in Figure 129.

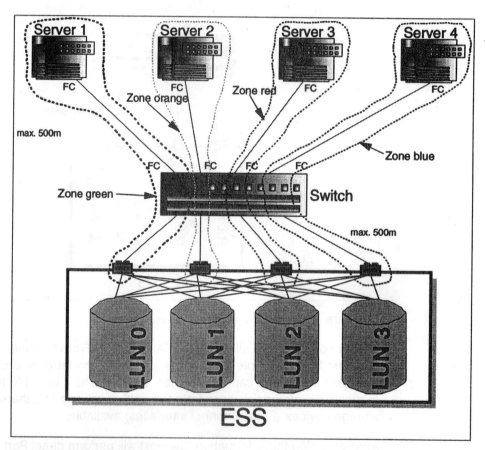

Figure 129. ESS with zoning

In this example, we created a zone in the fabric for each host. In this configuration all LUNs are seen by the host only once, because each host is accessing the ESS through only one Fibre Channel interface.

Chapter 13. Tape consolidation

This chapter describes basic tape environments, where tape is consolidated in different ways.

13.1 Using the SAN Data Gateway

For tape consolidation, the limitation, as shown in Figure 130, is the SCSI cable length. With the SAN Data Gateway we have solved the SCSI cable length restriction. With the SAN Data Gateway we can also accommodate distances between the SAN Data Gateway and the host bus adapter (HBA), of up to 500 meters with multi-mode fiber cables.

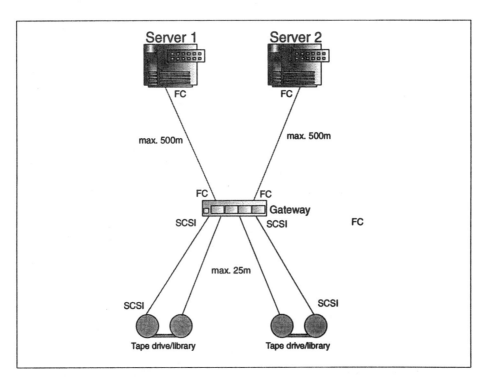

Figure 130. SAN Configuration with Data Gateway

The hardware used and tested in this configuration is:

- IBM Netfinity Server, type 5000, 5500, 5600, 7000, 7000M10, 8500R
- IBM Host Bus Adapters
- IBM SAN Data Gateway Router
- IBM Magstar MP 3570 tape library

- IBM Fibre Channel cables
- IBM SCSI cables

13.2 Using managed hubs

The two managed hubs, shown in Figure 131, are used to extend the distance between the servers and the SAN Data Gateway, by using long-wave GBICs, which support distances of up to 10 km with the use of long-wave cables.

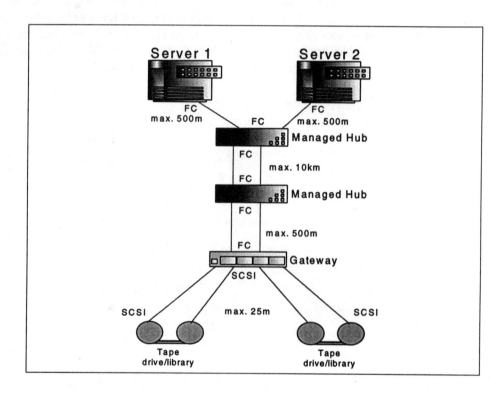

Figure 131. SAN configuration with Managed HUB for long distance

The hardware used and tested in this configuration is:

- IBM Netfinity Server (5000, 5500, 5600, 7000, 7000M10, 8500R)
- IBM Host Bus Adapters
- IBM Netfinity Managed Hub — 35341RU
- IBM Fibre Channel Switch — 2109-S08 or 2109S16
- IBM SAN Data Gateway Router — 2108-R03
- IBM Magstar MP 3570 tape library
- IBM Fibre Channel cables

- IBM SCSI cables

13.3 Using a switch

For large enterprise environments and also in entry level enterprise heterogeneous implementations, we can implement a Fibre Channel fabric using switches. It is possible to connect any Fibre Channel enabled devices to Fibre Channel switches.

If we want to implement up to eight servers we can select, for example, the IBM 2109 model S16. This model has a 16-port Fibre Channel switch and four short-wave Gigabit Interface Convertors (GBICs). The IBM Fibre Channel switch supports attachments to multiple host subsystems:

- Intel-based servers running Microsoft Windows NT or Novell Netware
- IBM RS/6000 running AIX
- SUN servers running Solaris

As switches allow any-to-any connection, the switch and management software can restrict which other ports a specific port can connect to. We call this port zoning. When we have changed the configuration we need to configure the zoning configuration. After this is done, each server can access the ports where the storage is attached to the fabric.

The IBM Fibre Channel Switch, together with the IBM SAN Data Gateway Router, makes it possible to avoid the 25m cable restriction for SCSI attached devices. The IBM Fibre Channel Switch supports both shortwave as well as longwave connections. We show this in Figure 132.

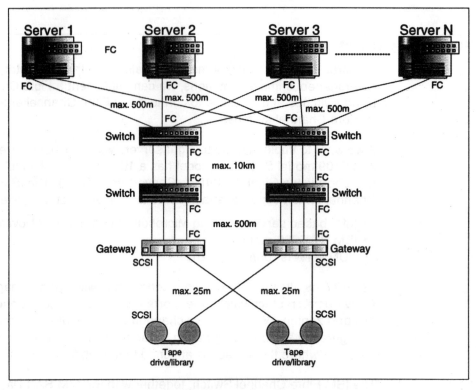

Figure 132. Stretching the 25m SCSI restriction

The hardware used and tested in this configuration is:

- IBM Netfinity Server (5000, 5500, 5600, 7000, 7000M10, 8500R)
- IBM Fibre Channel Switch — 2109-S08 or 2109-S16)
- IBM SAN Data Gateway Router — 2108-R03
- IBM Magstar MP 3570 tape library
- IBM Fibre Channel cables
- IBM SCSI cables

These simple tape configurations show the ease with which the transition to a SAN tape environment can be made.

Appendix A. Special notices

This publication is intended to help professionals design a Storage Area Network. The information in this publication is not intended as the specification of any programming interfaces that are provided by the solutions or products mentioned. See the PUBLICATIONS section of the IBM Programming Announcement for each described product for more information about what publications are considered to be product documentation.

References in this publication to IBM products, programs or services do not imply that IBM intends to make these available in all countries in which IBM operates. Any reference to an IBM product, program, or service is not intended to state or imply that only IBM's product, program, or service may be used. Any functionally equivalent program that does not infringe any of IBM's intellectual property rights may be used instead of the IBM product, program or service.

Information in this book was developed in conjunction with use of the equipment specified, and is limited in application to those specific hardware and software products and levels.

IBM may have patents or pending patent applications covering subject matter in this document. The furnishing of this document does not give you any license to these patents. You can send license inquiries, in writing, to the IBM Director of Licensing, IBM Corporation, North Castle Drive, Armonk, NY 10504-1785.

Licensees of this program who wish to have information about it for the purpose of enabling: (i) the exchange of information between independently created programs and other programs (including this one) and (ii) the mutual use of the information which has been exchanged, should contact IBM Corporation, Dept. 600A, Mail Drop 1329, Somers, NY 10589 USA.

Such information may be available, subject to appropriate terms and conditions, including in some cases, payment of a fee.

The information contained in this document has not been submitted to any formal IBM test and is distributed AS IS. The information about non-IBM ("vendor") products in this manual has been supplied by the vendor and IBM assumes no responsibility for its accuracy or completeness. The use of this information or the implementation of any of these techniques is a customer responsibility and depends on the customer's ability to evaluate and integrate them into the customer's operational environment. While each item may have been reviewed by IBM for accuracy in a specific situation, there is no guarantee that the same or similar results will be obtained elsewhere. Customers attempting to adapt these techniques to their own environments do so at their own risk.

Any pointers in this publication to external Web sites are provided for convenience only and do not in any manner serve as an endorsement of these Web sites.

Any performance data contained in this document was determined in a controlled environment, and therefore, the results that may be obtained in other operating environments may vary significantly. Users of this document should verify the applicable data for their specific environment.

This document contains examples of data and reports used in daily business operations. To illustrate them as completely as possible, the examples contain the names of individuals, companies, brands, and products. All of these names are fictitious and any similarity to the names and addresses used by an actual business enterprise is entirely coincidental.

Reference to PTF numbers that have not been released through the normal distribution process does not imply general availability. The purpose of including these reference numbers is to alert IBM customers to specific information relative to the implementation of the PTF when it becomes available to each customer according to the normal IBM PTF distribution process.

The following terms are trademarks of the International Business Machines Corporation in the United States and/or other countries:

AIX	AS/400
AT	DB2
DFSMSrmm	ECKD
Enterprise Storage Server	ESCON
FICON	IBM ®
Magstar	Netfinity
OS/390	OS/400
RS/6000	S/390
Seascape	SP
StorWatch	Ultrastar
Versatile Storage Server	400

The following terms are trademarks of other companies:

Tivoli, Manage. Anything. Anywhere.,The Power To Manage., Anything. Anywhere.,TME, NetView, Cross-Site, Tivoli Ready, Tivoli Certified, Planet Tivoli, and Tivoli Enterprise are trademarks or registered trademarks of Tivoli

Systems Inc., an IBM company, in the United States, other countries, or both. In Denmark, Tivoli is a trademark licensed from Kjøbenhavns Sommer - Tivoli A/S

C-bus is a trademark of Corollary, Inc. in the United States and/or other countries.

Java and all Java-based trademarks and logos are trademarks or registered trademarks of Sun Microsystems, Inc. in the United States and/or other countries.

Microsoft, Windows, Windows NT, and the Windows logo are trademarks of Microsoft Corporation in the United States and/or other countries.

PC Direct is a trademark of Ziff Communications Company in the United States and/or other countries and is used by IBM Corporation under license.

ActionMedia, LANDesk, MMX, Pentium and ProShare are trademarks of Intel Corporation in the United States and/or other countries.

UNIX is a registered trademark of The Open Group in the United States and other countries.

SET and the SET logo are trademarks owned by SET Secure Electronic Transaction LLC.

Other company, product, and service names may be trademarks or service marks of others.

Appendix B. Related publications

The publications listed in this section are considered particularly suitable for a more detailed discussion of the topics covered in this redbook.

B.1 IBM Redbooks publications

For information on ordering these publications see "How to get IBM Redbooks" on page 261.

- *Introduction to Storage Area Network, SAN,* SG24-5470
- *IBM Storage Solutions for Server Consolidation*, SG24-5355
- *Implementing the Enterprise Storage Server in Your Environment,* SG24-5420
- *Storage Area Networks: Tape Future In Fabrics*, SG24-5474
- *Introduction to IBM S/390 FICON*, SG24-5176
- *IBM Enterprise Storage Server*, SG24-5465

B.2 IBM Redbooks collections

Redbooks are also available on the following CD-ROMs. Click the CD-ROMs button at `http://www.redbooks.ibm.com/` for information about all the CD-ROMs offered, updates and formats.

CD-ROM Title	Collection Kit Number
System/390 Redbooks Collection	SK2T-2177
Networking and Systems Management Redbooks Collection	SK2T-6022
Transaction Processing and Data Management Redbooks Collection	SK2T-8038
Lotus Redbooks Collection	SK2T-8039
Tivoli Redbooks Collection	SK2T-8044
AS/400 Redbooks Collection	SK2T-2849
Netfinity Hardware and Software Redbooks Collection	SK2T-8046
RS/6000 Redbooks Collection (BkMgr)	SK2T-8040
RS/6000 Redbooks Collection (PDF Format)	SK2T-8043
Application Development Redbooks Collection	SK2T-8037
IBM Enterprise Storage and Systems Management Solutions	SK3T-3694

B.3 Other resources

These publications are also relevant as further information sources:

- *Designing Storage Area Networks: A Practical Reference for Implementing Fibre Channel SANs (The Addison-Wesley Networking Basics Series)*, ISBN 0201615843

B.4 Referenced Web sites

These Web sites are also relevant as further information sources:

- www.storage.ibm.com/ibmsan/index.htm   IBM Enterprise SAN
- www.storage.ibm.com/hardsoft/products/fchub/fchub.htm   IBM Fibre Channel Storage HUB
- www.pc.ibm.com/ww/netfinity/san   IBM Storage Area Networks: Nefinity Servers
- www.storage.ibm.com/hardsoft/products/fcswitch/fcswitch.htm   IBM SAN Fibre Channel Switch
- www.storage.ibm.com/hardsoft/products/sangateway/supserver.htm   IBM SAN Data Gateway
- www.storage.ibm.com/hardsoft/products/tape/ro3superserver.htm   IBM SAN Data Gateway Router
- www.storage.ibm.com/hardsoft/products/fcss/fcss.htm   IBM Fibre Channel RAID Storage Server
- www.storage.ibm.com/hardsoft/products/ess/ess.htm   Enterprise Storage Server
- www.brocade.com   Brocade Communications Systems, Inc.
- www.fibrechannel.com   Fibre Channel Industry Association
- www.mcdata.com   McData Corporation
- www.pathlight.com   Pathlight
- www.sanergy.com   Tivoli SANergy
- www.snia.org   Storage Networking Industry Association
- www.tivoli.com   Tivoli
- www.t11.org   Technical Committee T11
- www.vicom.com   Vicom Systems
- www.vixel.com   Vixel

- `www.scsita.org` SCSI Trade Association
- `www.futureio.org` InfiniBand (SM) Trade Association
- `www.nsic.org` National Storage Industry Consortium
- `www.ietf.org` Internet Engineering Task Force
- `www.ansi.org` American National Standards Institute
- `www.standards.ieee.org` Institute of Electrical and Electronics Engineers
- `www.qlc.com` Qlogic
- `www.emulex.com` Emulex
- `www.pc.ibm.com/us` US Personal Systems Group

How to get IBM Redbooks

This section explains how both customers and IBM employees can find out about IBM Redbooks, redpieces, and CD-ROMs. A form for ordering books and CD-ROMs by fax or e-mail is also provided.

- **Redbooks Web Site** `http://www.redbooks.ibm.com/`

  Search for, view, download, or order hardcopy/CD-ROM Redbooks from the Redbooks Web site. Also read redpieces and download additional materials (code samples or diskette/CD-ROM images) from this Redbooks site.

  Redpieces are Redbooks in progress; not all Redbooks become redpieces and sometimes just a few chapters will be published this way. The intent is to get the information out much quicker than the formal publishing process allows.

- **E-mail Orders**

  Send orders by e-mail including information from the IBM Redbooks fax order form to:

	e-mail address
In United States	usib6fpl@ibmmail.com
Outside North America	Contact information is in the "How to Order" section at this site: `http://www.elink.ibmlink.ibm.com/pbl/pbl`

- **Telephone Orders**

United States (toll free)	1-800-879-2755
Canada (toll free)	1-800-IBM-4YOU
Outside North America	Country coordinator phone number is in the "How to Order" section at this site: `http://www.elink.ibmlink.ibm.com/pbl/pbl`

- **Fax Orders**

United States (toll free)	1-800-445-9269
Canada	1-403-267-4455
Outside North America	Fax phone number is in the "How to Order" section at this site: `http://www.elink.ibmlink.ibm.com/pbl/pbl`

This information was current at the time of publication, but is continually subject to change. The latest information may be found at the Redbooks Web site.

IBM Intranet for Employees

IBM employees may register for information on workshops, residencies, and Redbooks by accessing the IBM Intranet Web site at `http://w3.itso.ibm.com/` and clicking the ITSO Mailing List button. Look in the Materials repository for workshops, presentations, papers, and Web pages developed and written by the ITSO technical professionals; click the Additional Materials button. Employees may access MyNews at `http://w3.ibm.com/` for redbook, residency, and workshop announcements.

IBM Redbooks fax order form

Please send me the following:

Title	Order Number	Quantity

First name _____ Last name _____

Company _____

Address _____

City _____ Postal code _____ Country _____

Telephone number _____ Telefax number _____ VAT number _____

☐ Invoice to customer number _____

☐ Credit card number _____

Credit card expiration date _____ Card issued to _____ Signature _____

We accept American Express, Diners, Eurocard, Master Card, and Visa. Payment by credit card not available in all countries. Signature mandatory for credit card payment.

Glossary

8B/10B A data encoding scheme developed by IBM, translating byte-wide data to an encoded 10-bit format. Fibre Channel's FC-1 level defines this as the method to be used to encode and decode data transmissions over the Fibre channel.

Adapter A hardware unit that aggregates other I/O units, devices or communications links to a system bus.

ADSM Adstar Distributed Storage Manager

Agent (1) In the client-server model, the part of the system that performs information preparation and exchange on behalf of a client or server application. (2) In SNMP, the word agent refers to the managed system. See also: Management Agent

AIT Advanced Intelligent Tape - A magnetic tape format by Sony that uses 8mm cassettes, but is only used in specific drives.

AL See Arbitrated Loop

ANSI American National Standards Institute - The primary organization for fostering the development of technology standards in the United States. The ANSI family of Fibre Channel documents provide the standards basis for the Fibre Channel architecture and technology. See FC-PH

Arbitration The process of selecting one respondent from a collection of several candidates that request service concurrently.

Arbitrated Loop A Fibre Channel interconnection technology that allows up to 126 participating node ports and one participating fabric port to communicate.

ATL Automated Tape Library - Large scale tape storage system, which uses multiple tape drives and mechanisms to address 50 or more cassettes.

ATM Asynchronous Transfer Mode - A type of packet switching that transmits fixed-length units of data.

Backup A copy of computer data that is used to recreate data that has been lost, mislaid, corrupted, or erased. The act of creating a copy of computer data that can be used to recreate data that has been lost, mislaid, corrupted or erased.

Bandwidth Measure of the information capacity of a transmission channel.

Bridge (1) A component used to attach more than one I/O unit to a port. (2) A data communications device that connects two or more networks and forwards packets between them. The bridge may use similar or dissimilar media and signaling systems. It operates at the data link level of the OSI model. Bridges read and filter data packets and frames.

Bridge/Router A device that can provide the functions of a bridge, router or both concurrently. A bridge/router can route one or more protocols, such as TCP/IP, and bridge all other traffic. See also: Bridge, Router

Broadcast Sending a transmission to all N_Ports on a fabric.

Channel A point-to-point link, the main task of which is to transport data from one point to another.

Channel I/O A form of I/O where request and response correlation is maintained through some form of source, destination and request identification.

CIFS Common Internet File System

Class of Service A Fibre Channel frame delivery scheme exhibiting a specified set of delivery characteristics and attributes.

Class-1 A class of service providing dedicated connection between two ports with confirmed delivery or notification of non-deliverability.

Class-2 A class of service providing a frame switching service between two ports with confirmed delivery or notification of non-deliverability.

Class-3 A class of service providing frame switching datagram service between two ports or a multicast service between a multicast originator and one or more multicast recipients.

Class-4 A class of service providing a fractional bandwidth virtual circuit between two ports with confirmed delivery or notification of non-deliverability.

Class-6 A class of service providing a multicast connection between a multicast originator and one or more multicast recipients with confirmed delivery or notification of non-deliverability.

Client A software program used to contact and obtain data from a *server* software program on another computer -- often across a great distance. Each *client* program is designed to work specifically with one or more kinds of server programs and each server requires a specific kind of client program.

Client/Server The relationship between machines in a communications network. The client is the requesting machine, the server the supplying machine. Also used to describe the information management relationship between software components in a processing system.

Cluster A type of parallel or distributed system that consists of a collection of interconnected whole computers and is used as a single, unified computing resource.

Coaxial Cable A transmission media (cable) used for high speed transmission. It is called *coaxial* because it includes one physical channel that carries the signal surrounded (after a layer of insulation) by another concentric physical channel, both of which run along the same axis. The inner channel carries the signal and the outer channel serves as a ground.

Controller A component that attaches to the system topology through a channel semantic protocol that includes some form of request/response identification.

CRC Cyclic Redundancy Check - An error-correcting code used in Fibre Channel.

DASD Direct Access Storage Device - any on-line storage device: a disc, drive or CD-ROM.

DAT Digital Audio Tape - A tape media technology designed for very high quality audio recording and data backup. DAT cartridges look like audio cassettes and are often used in mechanical auto-loaders. typically, a DAT cartridge provides 2GB of storage. But new DAT systems have much larger capacities.

Data Sharing A SAN solution in which files on a storage device are shared between multiple hosts.

Datagram Refers to the Class 3 Fibre Channel Service that allows data to be sent rapidly to multiple devices attached to the fabric, with no confirmation of delivery.

dB Decibel - a ratio measurement distinguishing the percentage of signal attenuation between the input and output power. Attenuation (loss) is expressed as dB/km

Disk Mirroring A fault-tolerant technique that writes data simultaneously to two hard disks using the same hard disk controller.

Disk Pooling A SAN solution in which disk storage resources are pooled across multiple hosts rather than be dedicated to a specific host.

DLT Digital Linear Tape - A magnetic tape technology originally developed by Digital Equipment Corporation (DEC) and now sold by Quantum. DLT cartridges provide storage capacities from 10 to 35GB.

E_Port Expansion Port - a port on a switch used to link multiple switches together into a Fibre Channel switch fabric.

ECL Emitter Coupled Logic - The type of transmitter used to drive copper media such as Twinax, Shielded Twisted Pair, or Coax.

Enterprise Network A geographically dispersed network under the auspices of one organization.

Entity In general, a real or existing thing from the Latin ens, or being, which makes the distinction between a thing's existence and it qualities. In programming, engineering and probably many other contexts, the word is used to identify units, whether concrete things or abstract ideas, that have no ready name or label.

ESCON Enterprise System Connection

Exchange A group of sequences which share a unique identifier. All sequences within a given exchange use the same protocol. Frames from multiple sequences can be multiplexed to prevent a single exchange from consuming all the bandwidth. See also: Sequence

F_Node Fabric Node - a fabric attached node.

F_Port Fabric Port - a port used to attach a Node Port (N_Port) to a switch fabric.

Fabric Fibre Channel employs a fabric to connect devices. A fabric can be as simple as a single cable connecting two devices. The term is most often used to describe a more complex network utilizing hubs, switches and gateways.

Fabric Login Fabric Login (FLOGI) is used by an N_Port to determine if a fabric is present and, if so, to initiate a session with the fabric by exchanging service parameters with the fabric. Fabric Login is performed by an N_Port following link initialization and before communication with other N_Ports is attempted.

FC Fibre Channel

FC-0 Lowest level of the Fibre Channel Physical standard, covering the physical characteristics of the interface and media

FC-1 Middle level of the Fibre Channel Physical standard, defining the 8B/10B encoding/decoding and transmission protocol.

FC-2 Highest level of the Fibre Channel Physical standard, defining the rules for signaling protocol and describing transfer of frame, sequence and exchanges.

FC-3 The hierarchical level in the Fibre Channel standard that provides common services such as striping definition.

FC-4 The hierarchical level in the Fibre Channel standard that specifies the mapping of upper-layer protocols to levels below.

FCA Fiber Channel Association.

FC-AL Fibre Channel Arbitrated Loop - A reference to the Fibre Channel Arbitrated Loop standard, a shared gigabit media for up to 127 nodes, one of which may be attached to a switch fabric. See also: Arbitrated Loop.

FC-CT Fibre Channel common transport protocol

FC-FG Fibre Channel Fabric Generic - A reference to the document (ANSI X3.289-1996) which defines the concepts, behavior and characteristics of the Fibre Channel Fabric along with suggested partitioning of the 24-bit address space to facilitate the routing of frames.

FC-FP Fibre Channel HIPPI Framing Protocol - A reference to the document (ANSI X3.254-1994) defining how the HIPPI framing protocol is transported via the fibre channel

FC-GS Fibre Channel Generic Services -A reference to the document (ANSI X3.289-1996) describing a common transport protocol used to communicate with the server functions, a full X500 based directory service, mapping of the Simple Network Management Protocol (SNMP) directly to the Fibre Channel, a time server and an alias server.

FC-LE Fibre Channel Link Encapsulation - A reference to the document (ANSI X3.287-1996) which defines how IEEE 802.2 Logical Link Control (LLC) information is transported via the Fibre Channel.

FC-PH A reference to the Fibre Channel Physical and Signaling standard ANSI X3.230, containing the definition of the three lower levels (FC-0, FC-1, and FC-2) of the Fibre Channel.

FC-PLDA Fibre Channel Private Loop Direct Attach - See PLDA.

FC-SB Fibre Channel Single Byte Command Code Set - A reference to the document (ANSI X.271-1996) which defines how the ESCON command set protocol is transported using the fibre channel.

FC-SW Fibre Channel Switch Fabric - A reference to the ANSI standard under development that further defines the fabric behavior described in FC-FG and defines the communications between different fabric elements required for those elements to coordinate their operations and management address assignment.

FC Storage Director See SAN Storage Director

FCA Fibre Channel Association - a Fibre Channel industry association that works to promote awareness and understanding of the Fibre Channel technology and its application and provides a means for implementers to support the standards committee activities.

FCLC Fibre Channel Loop Association - an independent working group of the Fibre Channel Association focused on the marketing aspects of the Fibre Channel Loop technology.

FCP Fibre Channel Protocol - the mapping of SCSI-3 operations to Fibre Channel.

Fiber Optic Refers to the medium and the technology associated with the transmission of information along a glass or plastic wire or fiber.

Fibre Channel A technology for transmitting data between computer devices at a data rate of up to 4 Gb/s. It is especially suited for connecting computer servers to shared storage devices and for interconnecting storage controllers and drives.

FICON Fibre Connection - A next-generation I/O solution for IBM S/390 parallel enterprise server.

FL_Port Fabric Loop Port - the access point of the fabric for physically connecting the user's Node Loop Port (NL_Port).

FLOGI See Fabric Log In

Frame A linear set of transmitted bits that define the basic transport unit. The frame is the most basic element of a message in Fibre Channel communications, consisting of a 24-byte header and zero to 2112 bytes of data. See also: Sequence

FSP Fibre Channel Service Protocol - The common FC-4 level protocol for all services, transparent to the fabric type or topology.

Full-Duplex A mode of communications allowing simultaneous transmission and reception of frames.

G_Port Generic Port - a generic switch port that is either a Fabric Port (F_Port) or an Expansion Port (E_Port). The function is automatically determined during login.

Gateway A node on a network that interconnects two otherwise incompatible networks.

GBIC GigaBit Interface Converter - Industry standard transceivers for connection of Fibre Channel nodes to arbitrated loop hubs and fabric switches.

Gigabit One billion bits, or one thousand megabits.

GLM Gigabit Link Module - a generic Fibre Channel transceiver unit that integrates the key functions necessary for installation of a Fibre channel media interface on most systems.

Half-Duplex A mode of communications allowing either transmission or reception of frames at any point in time, but not both (other than link control frames which are always permitted).

Hardware The mechanical, magnetic and electronic components of a system, e.g., computers, telephone switches, terminals and the like.

HBA Host Bus Adapter

HIPPI High Performance Parallel Interface - An ANSI standard defining a channel that transfers data between CPUs and from a CPU to disk arrays and other peripherals.

HMMP HyperMedia Management Protocol

HMMS HyperMedia Management Schema - the definition of an implementation-independent, extensible, common data description/schema allowing data from a variety of sources to be described and accessed in real time regardless of the source of the data. See also: WEBM, HMMP

HSM Hierarchical Storage Management - A software and hardware system that moves files from disk to slower, less expensive storage media based on rules and observation of file activity. Modern HSM systems move files from magnetic disk to optical disk to magnetic tape.

HUB A Fibre Channel device that connects nodes into a logical loop by using a physical star topology. Hubs will automatically recognize an active node and insert the node into the loop. A node that fails or is powered off is automatically removed from the loop.

HUB Topology see Loop Topology

Hunt Group A set of associated Node Ports (N_Ports) attached to a single node, assigned a special identifier that allows any frames containing this identifier to be routed to any available Node Port (N_Port) in the set.

In-Band Signaling Signaling that is carried in the same channel as the information.

Information Unit A unit of information defined by an FC-4 mapping. Information Units are transferred as a Fibre Channel Sequence.

Intermix A mode of service defined by Fibre Channel that reserves the full Fibre Channel bandwidth for a dedicated Class 1 connection, but also allows connection-less Class 2 traffic to share the link if the bandwidth is available.

I/O Input/output

IP Internet Protocol

IPI Intelligent Peripheral Interface

Isochronous Transmission Data transmission which supports network-wide timing requirements. A typical application for isochronous transmission is a broadcast environment which needs information to be delivered at a predictable time.

JBOD Just a bunch of disks.

Jukebox A device that holds multiple optical disks and one or more disk drives, and can swap disks in and out of the drive as needed.

L_Port Loop Port - A node or fabric port capable of performing Arbitrated Loop functions and protocols. NL-Ports and FL_Ports are loop-capable ports.

LAN See Local Area Network - A network covering a relatively small geographic area (usually not larger than a floor or small building). Transmissions within a Local Area Network are mostly digital, carrying data among stations at rates usually above one megabit/s.

Latency A measurement of the time it takes to send a frame between two locations.

Link A connection between two Fibre Channel ports consisting of a transmit fibre and a receive fibre.

Link_Control_Facility A termination card that handles the logical and physical control of the Fibre Channel link for each mode of use.

Local Area Network (LAN) A network covering a relatively small geographic area (usually not larger than a floor or small building). Transmissions within a Local Area Network are mostly digital, carrying data among stations at rates usually above one megabit/s.

Login Server Entity within the Fibre Channel fabric that receives and responds to login requests.

Loop Circuit A temporary point-to-point like path that allows bi-directional communications between loop-capable ports.

Loop Topology An interconnection structure in which each point has physical links to two neighbors resulting in a closed circuit. In a loop topology, the available bandwidth is shared.

LVD Low Voltage Differential

Management Agent A process that exchanges a managed node's information with a management station.

Managed Node A managed node is a computer, a storage system, a gateway, a media device such as a switch or hub, a control instrument, a software product such as an operating system or an accounting package, or a machine on a factory floor, such as a robot.

Managed Object A variable of a managed node. This variable contains one piece of information about the node. Each node can have several objects.

Management Station A host system that runs the management software.

Meter 39.37 inches, or just slightly larger than a yard (36 inches)

Media Plural of medium. The physical environment through which transmission signals pass. Common media include copper and fiber optic cable.

Media Access Rules (MAR).

MIA Media Interface Adapter - MIAs enable optic-based adapters to interface to copper-based devices, including adapters, hubs, and switches.

MIB Management Information Block - A formal description of a set of network objects that can be managed using the Simple Network Management Protocol (SNMP). The format of the MIB is defined as part of SNMP and is a hierarchical structure of information relevant to a specific device, defined in object oriented terminology as a collection of objects, relations, and operations among objects.

Mirroring The process of writing data to two separate physical devices simultaneously.

MM Multi-Mode - See Multi-Mode Fiber

MMF See Multi-Mode Fiber - - In optical fiber technology, an optical fiber that is designed to carry multiple light rays or modes concurrently, each at a slightly different reflection angle within the optical core. Multi-Mode fiber transmission is used for relatively short distances because the modes tend to disperse over longer distances. See also: Single-Mode Fiber, SMF

Multicast Sending a copy of the same transmission from a single source device to multiple destination devices on a fabric. This includes sending to all N_Ports on a fabric (broadcast) or to only a subset of the N_Ports on a fabric (multicast).

Multi-Mode Fiber (MMF) In optical fiber technology, an optical fiber that is designed to carry multiple light rays or modes concurrently, each at a slightly different reflection angle within the optical core. Multi-Mode fiber transmission is used for relatively short distances because the modes tend to disperse over longer distances. See also: Single-Mode Fiber

Multiplex The ability to intersperse data from multiple sources and destinations onto a single transmission medium. Refers to delivering a

single transmission to multiple destination Node Ports (N_Ports).

N_Port Node Port - A Fibre Channel-defined hardware entity at the end of a link which provides the mechanisms necessary to transport information units to or from another node.

N_Port Login N_Port Login (PLOGI) allows two N_Ports to establish a session and exchange identities and service parameters. It is performed following completion of the fabric login process and prior to the FC-4 level operations with the destination port. N_Port Login may be either explicit or implicit.

Name Server Provides translation from a given node name to one or more associated N_Port identifiers.

NAS Network Attached Storage - a term used to describe a technology where an integrated storage system is attached to a messaging network that uses common communications protocols, such as TCP/IP.

NDMP Network Data Management Protocol

Network An aggregation of interconnected nodes, workstations, file servers, and/or peripherals, with its own protocol that supports interaction.

Network Topology Physical arrangement of nodes and interconnecting communications links in networks based on application requirements and geographical distribution of users.

NFS Network File System - A distributed file system in UNIX developed by Sun Microsystems which allows a set of computers to cooperatively access each other's files in a transparent manner.

NL_Port Node Loop Port - a node port that supports Arbitrated Loop devices.

NMS Network Management System - A system responsible for managing at least part of a network. NMSs communicate with agents to help keep track of network statistics and resources.

Node An entity with one or more N_Ports or NL_Ports.

Non-Blocking A term used to indicate that the capabilities of a switch are such that the total number of available transmission paths is equal to the number of ports. Therefore, all ports can have simultaneous access through the switch.

Non-L_Port A Node or Fabric port that is not capable of performing the Arbitrated Loop functions and protocols. N_Ports and F_Ports are not loop-capable ports.

Operation A term defined in FC-2 that refers to one of the Fibre Channel *building blocks* composed of one or more, possibly concurrent, exchanges.

Optical Disk A storage device that is written and read by laser light.

Optical Fiber A medium and the technology associated with the transmission of information as light pulses along a glass or plastic wire or fiber.

Ordered Set A Fibre Channel term referring to four 10 -bit characters (a combination of data and special characters) providing low-level link functions, such as frame demarcation and signaling between two ends of a link.

Originator A Fibre Channel term referring to the initiating device.

Out of Band Signaling Signaling that is separated from the channel carrying the information.

Peripheral Any computer device that is not part of the essential computer (the processor, memory and data paths) but is situated relatively close by. A near synonym is input/output (I/O) device.

PLDA Private Loop Direct Attach - A technical report which defines a subset of the relevant standards suitable for the operation of peripheral devices such as disks and tapes on a private loop.

PLOGI See N_Port Login

Point-to-Point Topology An interconnection structure in which each point has physical links to only one neighbor resulting in a closed circuit. In point-to-point topology, the available bandwidth the is dedicated

Port The hardware entity within a node that performs data communications over the Fibre Channel.

Port Bypass Circuit A circuit used in hubs and disk enclosures to automatically open or close the loop to add or remove nodes on the loop.

Private NL_Port An NL_Port which does not attempt login with the fabric and only communicates with other NL Ports on the same loop.

Protocol A data transmission convention encompassing timing, control, formatting and data representation.

Public NL_Port An NL_Port that attempts login with the fabric and can observe the rules of either public or private loop behavior. A public NL_Port may communicate with both private and public NL_Ports.

Quality of Service (QoS) A set of communications characteristics required by an application. Each QoS defines a specific transmission priority, level of route reliability, and security level.

RAID Redundant Array of Inexpensive or Independent Disks. A method of configuring multiple disk drives in a storage subsystem for high availability and high performance.

Raid 0 Level 0 RAID support - Striping, no redundancy

Raid 1 Level 1 RAID support - mirroring, complete redundancy

Raid 5 Level 5 RAID support, Striping with parity

Repeater A device that receives a signal on an electromagnetic or optical transmission medium, amplifies the signal, and then retransmits it along the next leg of the medium.

Responder A Fibre Channel term referring to the answering device.

Router (1) A device that can decide which of several paths network traffic will follow based on some optimal metric. Routers forward packets from one network to another based on network-layer information. (2) A dedicated computer hardware and/or software package which manages the connection between two or more networks. See also: Bridge, Bridge/Router

SAF-TE SCSI Accessed Fault-Tolerant Enclosures

SAN A Storage Area Network (SAN) is a dedicated, centrally managed, secure information infrastructure, which enables any-to-any interconnection of servers and storage systems.

SAN System Area Network - term originally used to describe a particular symmetric multiprocessing (SMP) architecture in which a switched interconnect is used in place of a shared bus. Server Area Network - refers to a switched interconnect between multiple SMPs.

SC Connector A fiber optic connector standardized by ANSI TIA/EIA-568A for use in structured wiring installations.

Scalability The ability of a computer application or product (hardware or software) to continue to function well as it (or its context) is changed in size or volume. For example, the ability to retain performance levels when adding additional processors, memory and/or storage.

SCSI Small Computer System Interface - A set of evolving ANSI standard electronic interfaces that allow personal computers to communicate with peripheral hardware such as disk drives, tape drives, CD_ROM drives, printers and scanners faster and more flexibly than previous interfaces. The table below identifies the major characteristics of the different SCSI version.

SCSI Version	Signal Rate MHz	Bus-Width (bits)	Max. DTR (MB/s)	Max. Num. Devices	Max. Cable Length (m)
SCSI-1	5	8	5	7	6
SCSI-2	5	8	5	7	6
Wide SCSI-2	5	16	10	15	6
Fast SCSI-2	10	8	10	7	6
Fast Wide SCSI-2	10	16	20	15	6
Ultra SCSI	20	8	20	7	1.5
Ultra SCSI-2	20	16	40	7	12
Ultra2 LVD SCSI	40	16	80	15	12

SCSI-3 SCSI-3 consists of a set of primary commands and additional specialized command sets to meet the needs of specific device types. The SCSI-3 command sets are used not only for the SCSI-3 parallel interface but for additional parallel and serial protocols, including Fibre Channel, Serial Bus Protocol (used with IEEE 1394 Firewire physical protocol) and the Serial Storage Protocol (SSP).

SCSI-FCP The term used to refer to the ANSI Fibre Channel Protocol for SCSI document (X3.269-199x) that describes the FC-4 protocol mappings and the definition of how the SCSI protocol and command set are transported using a Fibre Channel interface.

Sequence A series of frames strung together in numbered order which can be transmitted over a Fibre Channel connection as a single operation. See also: Exchange

SERDES Serializer Deserializer

Server A computer which is dedicated to one task.

SES SCSI Enclosure Services - ANSI SCSI-3 proposal that defines a command set for soliciting basic device status (temperature, fan speed, power supply status, etc.) from a storage enclosures.

Single-Mode Fiber In optical fiber technology, an optical fiber that is designed for the transmission of a single ray or mode of light as a carrier. It is a single light path used for long-distance signal transmission. See also: Multi-Mode Fiber

SMART Self Monitoring and Reporting Technology

SM Single Mode - See Single-Mode Fiber

SMF Single-Mode Fiber - In optical fiber technology, an optical fiber that is designed for the transmission of a single ray or mode of light as a carrier. It is a single light path used for long-distance signal transmission. See also: MMF

SNIA Storage Networking Industry Association. A non-profit organization comprised of more than 77 companies and individuals in the storage industry.

SN Storage Network. See also: SAN

SNMP Simple Network Management Protocol - The Internet network management protocol which provides a means to monitor and set network configuration and run-time parameters.

SNMWG Storage Network Management Working Group is chartered to identify, define and support open standards needed to address the increased management requirements imposed by storage area network environments.

SSA Serial Storage Architecture - A high speed serial loop-based interface developed as a high speed point-to-point connection for peripherals, particularly high speed storage arrays, RAID and CD-ROM storage by IBM.

Star The physical configuration used with hubs in which each user is connected by communications links radiating out of a central hub that handles all communications.

StorWatch Expert These are StorWatch applications that employ a 3 tiered architecture that includes a management interface, a StorWatch manager and agents that run on the storage resource(s) being managed. Expert products employ a StorWatch data base that can be used for saving key management data (e.g. capacity or performance metrics). Expert products use the agents as well as analysis of storage data saved in the data base to perform higher value functions including -- reporting of capacity, performance, etc. over time (trends), configuration of multiple devices based on

policies, monitoring of capacity and performance, automated responses to events or conditions, and storage related data mining.

StorWatch Specialist A StorWatch interface for managing an individual fibre Channel device or a limited number of like devices (that can be viewed as a single group). StorWatch specialists typically provide simple, point-in-time management functions such as configuration, reporting on asset and status information, simple device and event monitoring, and perhaps some service utilities.

Striping A method for achieving higher bandwidth using multiple N_Ports in parallel to transmit a single information unit across multiple levels.

STP Shielded Twisted Pair

Storage Media The physical device itself, onto which data is recorded. Magnetic tape, optical disks, floppy disks are all storage media.

Switch A component with multiple entry/exit points (ports) that provides dynamic connection between any two of these points.

Switch Topology An interconnection structure in which any entry point can be dynamically connected to any exit point. In a switch topology, the available bandwidth is scalable.

T11 A technical committee of the National Committee for Information Technology Standards, titled T11 I/O Interfaces. It is tasked with developing standards for moving data in and out of computers.

Tape Backup Making magnetic tape copies of hard disk and optical disc files for disaster recovery.

Tape Pooling A SAN solution in which tape resources are pooled and shared across multiple hosts rather than being dedicated to a specific host.

TCP Transmission Control Protocol - a reliable, full duplex, connection-oriented end-to-end transport protocol running on top of IP.

TCP/IP Transmission Control Protocol/ Internet Protocol - a set of communications protocols that support peer-to-peer connectivity functions for both local and wide area networks.

Time Server A Fibre Channel-defined service function that allows for the management of all timers used within a Fibre Channel system.

Topology An interconnection scheme that allows multiple Fibre Channel ports to communicate. For example, point-to-point, Arbitrated Loop, and switched fabric are all Fibre Channel topologies.

Twinax A transmission media (cable) consisting of two insulated central conducting leads of coaxial cable.

Twisted Pair A transmission media (cable) consisting of two insulated copper wires twisted around each other to reduce the induction (thus interference) from one wire to another. The twists, or lays, are varied in length to reduce the potential for signal interference between pairs. Several sets of twisted pair wires may be enclosed in a single cable. This is the most common type of transmission media.

ULP Upper Level Protocols

UTC Under-The-Covers, a term used to characterize a subsystem in which a small number of hard drives are mounted inside a higher function unit. The power and cooling are obtained from the system unit. Connection is by parallel copper ribbon cable or pluggable backplane, using IDE or SCSI protocols.

UTP Unshielded Twisted Pair

Virtual Circuit A unidirectional path between two communicating N_Ports that permits fractional bandwidth.

WAN Wide Area Network - A network which encompasses inter-connectivity between devices over a wide geographic area. A wide area network may be privately owned or rented, but the term usually connotes the inclusion of public (shared) networks.

WDM Wave Division Multiplexing - A technology that puts data from different sources together on an optical fiber, with each signal carried on its own separate light wavelength. Using WDM, up to 80 (and theoretically more) separate

wavelengths or channels of data can be multiplexed into a stream of light transmitted on a single optical fiber.

WEBM Web-Based Enterprise Management - A consortium working on the development of a series of standards to enable active management and monitoring of network-based elements.

Zoning In Fibre Channel environments, the grouping together of multiple ports to form a virtual private storage network. Ports that are members of a group or zone can communicate with each other but are isolated from ports in other zones.

Index

Numerics

1000BASE-LX   132
1000BASE-SX   132
12-fiber MTP connector   142
16 port   215
16 ports   212
2 Gbit speeds   200
2032-001   107, 233
2102-F10   117
2103-H07   103
2105-F10   119
2105-F20   119
2108   186
2108-G07   110
2108-R03   114
2109-S08   106
2109-S16   106, 212
24 bit addressing   81
32 ports   215
32064
   H__h3
      4.3.5 Quick Loop   87
3534   186
3534-1RU   104
50 micron   50
62.5 micron   50
7133 Serial Disk System   235, 236, 238
7139-111   115
8 port   215
8B/10B   54
8b/10b   56
9 micron   50
9 pin   49
9032   138
9672   138

A

ACC   84
access fairness mechanism   73
Affordability   180
AFS   221
air conditioning   140
air movement   140
AL_PA   76, 84
   priority   77

alert   156
American National Standards Institute   16, 45, 125
ANCOR   48
Ancor   48
ANSI   16, 33, 45, 125
   T11   126
any-to-any connection   231
API   31
Application Programming Interfaces   31
Arbitrated Loop   127
arbitrated loop   16
Arbitrated Loop Physical Address   76
Arbitrated Loop SAN   204
arbitration   72, 76
Area   82
area   83
ASCII   221
Asynchronous Transfer Mode   126, 130
ATM   126, 130
ATTO   48
automated system management   159
Automation for Disk Allocation   163
availability   178

B

backbone   197
backbone fabric   193
bandwidths   131
benchmark   31
BER   56, 126
BI   5
Bit Error Rate   126
bit error rate   56
bottlenecks   13
bridge solutions   184
Brocade   48
bus   7
Business Intelligence   177
byte-encoding scheme   56

C

cable   48
Camp On   61
campus   128, 183
campus SAN   18
campus topology   51

reuse
    SCSI devices 204
RFI 49
RNID 162
Router 185
routers 12
RS/6000 234, 236, 238
RS/6000 server 217
RSM 161
RTIN 162
running disparity 77

S

SAN 10
SAN Data Gateway 138, 239
SAN Data Gateway Router 185, 249, 250, 251
SAN design objectives 151
SAN Disk Manager 162
SAN enabled hardware 151
SAN Fibre Channel Switch 138, 186
SAN islands 184
SAN Manager 164
SANergy 21, 169
SANergy FS 169
SANergyXA 169
SANlet 210
SANlets 183
SC connectors 51
SC Duplex 128
Scalability 179
scalability 178
scanner 162
SC-DC Connectivity Solutions 141
SCSI 6, 130, 221
    arbitration protocol 10
    commands 10
    protocol 10
    unused ports 10
SCSI commands 10
SCSI distance limitations 8
SCSI Trade Association 32
SCSI-3 18
SCSITA 32
SDD 247
security 91, 94, 169, 178
segmentation 91
self-updating agent 165
Sequent 48

SERDES 52
Serial Storage Architecture 130
Serial transfer 17
server clustering 24
server free data movement 23
Server-free data movement 160
Server-free Data Transfer 158
serviceability 178
SG 128
shared bus 10, 72
short jumper 139
Short Wave Laser 50
signal interference 10
signaling layers 54
signaling protocol 54
Signalling layer 54
Simple Name Server 82, 247
single mode distances 131
single-level storage 221
Single-Mode Fiber 50
skew 7, 17
Slotted Loop 17
Small Computer Systems Interface 6, 130
Small Form Factor 141
Small Form Factor SC-DC 145
SMF 50
SMS 159
SNIA 32, 33
SNMP 162
SNS 82, 84, 85, 86, 247
SOF 58
software management tools 152
software zoning 93
SONET 126
SRC 194
SSA 18, 130, 234
SSA Gateway 235, 236, 238
stable monitoring mode 73
Stacked Connect 62
star wiring scheme 127
Start-of-Frame 58
STK 48
Storage Area Networks 3
storage consolidation 183
Storage Manager 7 206
Storage Manager backup/archive client 156
Storage Network Industry Association 32
Storage Networking Industry Association 33
StorWatch 26

IBM Redbooks review

Your feedback is valued by the Redbook authors. In particular we are interested in situations where a Redbook "made the difference" in a task or problem you encountered. Using one of the following methods, **please review the Redbook, addressing value, subject matter, structure, depth and quality as appropriate.**

- Use the online **Contact us** review redbook form found at ibm.com/redbooks
- Fax this form to: USA International Access Code + 1 914 432 8264
- Send your comments in an Internet note to redbook@us.ibm.com

Document Number **Redbook Title**	SG24-5758-00 Designing an IBM Storage Area Network
Review	
What other subjects would you like to see IBM Redbooks address?	
Please rate your overall satisfaction:	O Very Good O Good O Average O Poor
Please identify yourself as belonging to one of the following groups:	O Customer O Business Partner O Solution Developer O IBM, Lotus or Tivoli Employee O None of the above
Your email address: The data you provide here may be used to provide you with information from IBM or our business partners about our products, services or activities.	O Please do not use the information collected here for future marketing or promotional contacts or other communications beyond the scope of this transaction.
Questions about IBM's privacy policy?	The following link explains how we protect your personal information. ibm.com/privacy/yourprivacy/